The Good Society
and the Inner World

The Good Society and the Inner World

Psychoanalysis, Politics and Culture

MICHAEL RUSTIN

VERSO

London · New York

First published by Verso 1991
© Michael Rustin 1991

Verso
UK: 6 Meard Street, London W1V 3HR
USA: 20 Jay Street, Suite 1010, Brooklyn, NY 11201

Verso is the imprint of New Left Books

British Library Cataloguing in Publication Data

Rustin, Michael
The good society and the inner world : psychoanalysis,
politics and culture.
1. Psychoanalysis, related to society
I. Title
150.195

ISBN 0-86091-328-7
ISBN 0-86091-344-1 pbk

US Library of Congress Cataloging-in-Publication Data

Rustin, Michael.
The good society and the inner world : psychoanalysis, politics,
and culture / Michael Rustin.
p.   cm.
Includes bibliographical references and index.
ISBN 0-86091-328-7. – ISBN 0-86091-544-1 (pbk.)
1. Psychoanalysis.   2. Psychoanalysis and culture.   3. Klein,
Melanie.   I. Title.
RC506.R87   1991
306–dc20   91-11764
                                                      CIP

Typeset by Leaper and Gard Ltd, Bristol
Printed in the United States Of America

To Margaret

Contents

Acknowledgements

Earlier versions of various chapters have been previously published as follows: chapters 2 and 7 in *New Left Review* 121 (1982), and 173 (1989), respectively; chapter 5 in *The International Review of Psychoanalysis*, 12 (1985); chapters 3 and 6 in *Free Associations* Pilot Issue (1984), and *Free Associations* 9 (1987), respectively; chapter 8 in Francis Barker (ed.) *The Politics of Theory* (University of Essex, 1983). I am grateful to the editors of these various journals and publications for allowing the republication of this work.

I have had much encouragement in undertaking this writing over many years, given in the form of friendly cooperation and written comments, and in invitations to give papers and seminars in various places. It is invidious to mention some and not others in this respect, but I would like in particular to thank Perry Anderson, Roy Bhaskar, Robin Blackburn, Karl Figlio, John Forrester, Donald Meltzer, Diomira Petrelli, Barry Richards, Carole Satyamurti, Gabriella Spano, Margot Waddell, Gianna Williams, Isca Wittenberg and Bob Young.

A number of institutions should be mentioned for the support they have given — the Department of Sociology at the Polytechnic of East London, where I work; the Tavistock Clinic and its associated courses in Italy, which have given me an indispensable access to clinical and observational work in psychoanalysis and psychoanalytic psychotherapy; and the Institute for Advanced Study, Princeton, which generously provided time and a stimulating setting in which a part of this work could be done.

My publishers, Verso, and its capable staff, in particular Lucy Morton, Gillian Beaumont, Anna Del Nevo, and Jenny Boyce, have made the production of this book a pleasure, once again. Gillian Elinor very kindly provided her skills in picture research.

Finally, I am indebted to Margaret Rustin for the contact with psychoanalytic thinking and practice which she has made possible for me, in many years of conversation and shared work. She will not be surprised by many of the ideas developed in this book, but is not to be held responsible for any of its failings. I owe to Dr Yolanda Glaser another quite indispensable qualification for writing about psychoanalytic topics, and express my warm thanks to her.

Introduction

This book brings together a number of essays on psychoanalysis and its applications, written over the last ten years. It is concerned largely with the Kleinian analytic tradition as this has evolved in Britain, following in particular the work of Melanie Klein and Wilfred Bion, which it defends as clinically and theoretically the most important of the various psychoanalytic developments of Freud's own discoveries.

These essays examine aspects of this psychoanalytic tradition from a point outside rather than from within the professional analytic world, since its author is neither a psychoanalyst nor a psychotherapist. Their main concerns are with the implications of analytic thinking for neighbouring fields of social scientific, political and cultural interest, not primarily with the clinical or theoretical issues central to psychoanalytic practice. The justification for all this is the view that the Kleinian psychoanalytic tradition has much of relevance to contribute to the broader concerns of the human sciences, and constitutes one of the most important resources for such understanding developed in Britain over the last sixty years. Despite this, psychoanalysis has remained for the most part on the margins of British intellectual life, kept there by the prevailing spirit of empiricism and the hostility to theoretical imagination which have pervaded the fields of psychology and, for the most part, psychiatry. In reaction to this tradition, from the late 1960s onwards, advocates of psychoanalysis in the cultural sphere have looked for a mode of thinking as far away from empiricism as possible — that is, to Lacan and his field of influence in Paris. Thus what is in fact the distinctive strength of British psychoanalysis — its basis in clinical or 'empirical' work, and its concern for the perceived realities of emotional experience as these are observed in analytic practice — was for a time, paradoxically, neglected in the rediscovery of Freud in Britain.[1]

The first group of essays in this collection is concerned with politics. 'A Socialist Consideration of Kleinian Psychoanalysis', the first of these essays to be written and published, explores the contribution which Kleinian ideas can make to a 'social' and thus socialist conception of human nature, in contrast to the more individualist presuppositions on which Freud's own work was based, which have affected the political inferences predominantly drawn from his work. 'Psychoanalysis and Social Justice' goes on to suggest that the ideas of emotional and psychological well-being to which psychoanalytic practice is directed can be understood as giving rise to legitimate social claims and goals. This argument seeks to give the definition of social rights central to the social-democratic political agenda in Britain a psychosocial dimension. The third essay, 'Psychoanalysis, Racism and Anti-Racism', examines the contribution which psychoanalytic ideas might make to the understanding of racism, which are seen from this perspective as rooted in predominantly psychotic kinds of mental process.

The essays in the second part of the book approach psychoanalysis with sociological rather than political questions in mind. 'The Social Organization of Secrets' attempts to characterize the institutional practices of psychoanalysis and its forms of training in sociological terms, connecting the organizational strategies followed by the psychoanalytic profession with the particularly difficult and potentially 'explosive' nature of its task in investigating and attempting to transform unconscious mental structures. 'Psychoanalysis, Philosophical Realism, and the New Sociology of Science', on the other hand, is concerned with issues of scientific method rather than with institutional practices. This essay defends the clinically based methods of psychoanalysis as it is mainly taught and practised in Britain as being based on its own rigorous kind of empirical discipline, whose essence lies in consensually grounded observational procedures. It draws both on the ideas of 'realism' as these have recently been developed in the philosophy of science by Roy Bhaskar and others, and on the more phenomenological and less prescriptive approach to scientific methods developed by sociologists of science such as Barry Barnes, in opposition to the empiricist philosophy of science of Popper and others. The final essay in this part, 'Post-Kleinian Psychoanalysis and the Post-Modern', continues these reflections on the later Kleinian tradition, exemplified by the work of Wilfred Bion, Herbert Rosenfeld and Donald Meltzer. Noted in particular here is a shift of psychoanalytic attention towards the understanding of processes of thought and their disturbance by unconscious forces. Whereas the classical Kleinian tradition visualized the mind as something of a struggle between the unconscious forces of love and hate, Bion and his contemporaries recognized that the processes by which the mind contained — or failed to contain — these emotions had a distinct importance of its own, and that it was especially vital to understanding these containing mental functions if progress was to be made in treating psychotic patients or those suffering from 'narcissistic' or 'borderline' character disorders. This essay identifies parallels between these late Kleinian developments, which questioned some Kleinian orthodoxies, and wider 'post-modern' rejections of ethical and teleological theories of human nature, but argues that they are opposed in their fundamental spirit.

The third and final part of the book is concerned with the application of Kleinian psychoanalysis to the understanding of cultural and aesthetic issues. These issues were always important in the Kleinian tradition, as they were to Freud. They gave rise to important work such as Hanna Segal's writing on symbol formation and its preconditions in emotional development and, closely linked to this, on the reparative functions and meanings of art. The main application of Hanna Segal's aesthetic writings has been to literature, but important contributions informed by Kleinian ideas were also made in the sphere of criticism of the visual arts — by Adrian Stokes, and later by Peter Fuller and Richard Wollheim. Later Kleinian analysis, with its particular interest in thought processes and their development or non-development, has also had a particular concern with aesthetic issues — even, in Meltzer's work, leading to the assertion that aesthetic experience is a primary one in the development of the human infant, and remains throughout life central to the capacity for emotional understanding and change.

The first of these essays, 'Kleinian Psychoanalysis and Cultural Theory', was one of the first in this collection to be written. It is an attempt to understand what was at issue in the choices then being posed between Lacanian psychoanalytic approaches to culture and those of the British object-relations school, including Klein and Winnicott. 'Psychoanalysis and Aesthetic Experience', the last of these essays to be completed, develops the arguments of 'Post-Kleinian Psychoanalysis and the Post-Modern', in their application to aesthetic issues. This essay identifies the aesthetic experience with the process of understanding itself, starting from the earliest manifestations of this in infant mental life. It argues that the main contribution of the later Kleinian tradition to the understanding of art lies in its attention to how symbolic forms contain and find order and harmony in sensations and experiences, not with the particular set of unconscious objects of symbolism previously emphasized in psychoanalytic literary and art criticism. It connects this analysis with the arguments of Kant's *Critique of Judgement* and argues, following Kant and Habermas, that the aesthetic is a primary and essential aspect of human experience, not one which can be subordinated to ethical or instrumental values. This essay identifies the domain of the aesthetic, in the democratic sense given to it here, as an emergent value of an information-based, 'post-industrial', but — so far — by no means post-capitalist society, and identifies it as a ground of critique of the conditions of life which it provides.

The final essay in this collection, 'Thinking in *Romeo and Juliet*', reflects on how psychoanalytic understanding of a Shakespeare play might be shaped by late Kleinian psychoanalytic insights, especially as these have been influenced by Bion. This reading emphasizes the representation in the play of the inability to reflect on overwhelming emotions, and its tragic consequences. The source of this situation as it is dramatized lies not merely in the adolescent passions of Romeo and Juliet, but in the authoritarian social relationships which surround and attempt to control them. Even in the context of a specific literary application, the ideas of Kleinian tradition are shown here to have their critical implications for social forms and their relationship to choice and emotional well-being.

Each of these essays was originally written to stand on its own, and attempted to explore a particular aspect of Kleinian psychoanalytic thinking and its applications. Some development of ideas will be evident between the earlier and later texts, notably in an increased interest over time in the contributions of 'late' or 'post-Kleinian' analysts and their distinctive concern with mental processes. No attempt has been made here to construct a didactic Kleinian theory of culture and society. So important are the roots of psychoanalytic thinking in specific clinical experiences, and in their cognates of emotionally concrete responses to other kinds of cultural or social experience, that such a theoretical codification might in any case be a mistake, inevitably reducing what above all needs to remain a method of understanding to what could so easily become a lifeless system of ideas.

Nevertheless, I hope it will be evident that this field of psychoanalytic thinking and practice can illuminate many areas of social and cultural life, from its particular focus or 'vertex' of attention on unconscious emotions and their pervasive role. I hope also that the range of these essays will stimulate others to explore applications to other topics and fields of this remarkable but still neglected body of psychoanalytic thinking. At this point, these various essays should probably be left to speak for themselves.

Notes

1. This situation has recently been changing for the better. In the Kleinian tradition there has been a considerable increase in publication and in the availability of key texts, published from many sources including the Institute of Psycho-Analysis, the Tavistock Clinic, and recent entrants to the analytic publishing scene such as Free Association Books. Recent publications — for example, collections of papers by Hanna Segal (1986), Betty Joseph (1989), Herbert Rosenfeld (1987) and Isabel Menzies Lyth (1988-9) and many publications of Bion and Meltzer — now provide a substantial Kleinian literature in book form. The recent collections by Elizabeth Bott Spillius, *Melanie Klein Today, Vols 1-2* (1988), provide a valuable overview of recent work, including non-clinical applications, and Hinshelwood's *Dictionary of Kleinian Thought* (1989) now complements Laplanche and Pontalis's *The Language of Psychoanalysis* (1973) as an indispensable reference work.

This work is also gaining some consideration within a broader field of social scientific discussion — for example in works by Frosh (1987, 1989), Craib (1989) and Richards (1989b) in England, and by Alford (1989), and from a feminist point of view Chodorow (1989) in the United States. As the training and practice of analytic psychotherapy increase and spread beyond their narrow London enclave, this academic interest is likely to intensify further.

PART I

Kleinian Perspectives on Politics

1

A Socialist Consideration of
Kleinian Psychoanalysis*

This chapter may be best introduced autobiographically, since the general project it touches, the relationship between psychoanalytic and political theory, isn't one that I think has often been very fruitfully pursued from the point of view in which I am interested, and may seem unpromising at the outset. The autobiographical point is this: I have regarded myself for many years as a socialist. For a lesser number of years I have also been considerably influenced by psychoanalytic ideas of a largely Kleinian kind, through reading, through a personal analysis, and through a continuing acquaintance with my wife's work as a psychotherapist. The issue is: what, if any, is the relationship between these two powerful perspectives? Are they compatible or not? Do they tend in the same or in inconsistent directions? This issue perhaps has a more than personal interest. It might be relevant to the purposes of Kleinian psychoanalysis to clarify what implications its ideas might have for the wider society in which it is practised. It might also be relevant to the purposes of a socialist view of society to take into account the insights psychoanalysis can provide into the human needs which socialist political ideas purport to meet. For a long time, my feeling and experience was that these two 'systems of ideas', which are also 'structures of feeling' in Raymond Williams's phrase, were in tension with one another. The stress in analytic work on the processes of one's own mind and feelings, and the insistence in Kleinian work on the individual's taking responsibility for

*This chapter originated as a paper presented in January 1981 to a seminar of the New Imago Group, whose members I wish to thank for their encouragement. I am grateful to Perry Anderson, Jerry Cohen and Donald Meltzer for their written comments.

his or her emotions, undermine certain forms of political commitment and action. This tends of its very nature to attribute agency and responsibility in a collective way, and to generate, as its normal response to perceived wrongs, activity that is external in its objectives, if open to other interpretations as to its inner motivation. Such externalization of feelings can become frenetic, and one's experience can be deeply structured by a split between the idealization of the project of change and denunciation of the many evils of the present. Such powerful preconceptions are not infallible guides to realistic understanding and action. This is a frame of mind in which the events described by the morning newspapers can produce almost daily indignation and the impulse to take part in activities — meetings, demonstrations, magazines — that respond to these. The patient work of mastering the detail of a field of understanding, or even the apparently less demanding task of maintaining an organizational form which can achieve specific ends, can be casualties of such an impassioned activism. My immediate experience was that without this ever being a matter of conscious decision, the period of my greatest involvement with psychoanalytic experience was also a period of withdrawal from political activity, partly due simply to time and preoccupation, but also to a rather subtle and gradual change in the direction of one's feelings and in one's definition of problems. There might be various ways of reading such an experience.

From the individual case one might suggest, with accuracy, an instance of a shift from youthful radical politics, in which the solidarities of the generational group have precedence and personal difficulties could be submerged in activities of various kinds, to a more conventional later phase of family relationship and professional work in which their disruptive effects were more threatening, insistent and demanding of attention. There is also a more general psychoanalytic perception of political activity as such, as inevitably representing displacements and projections of inner feelings. Idealistic political commit-ments are seen in this view as irrational, to a greater or lesser degree, and as diverting attention away from the more fundamental problems of individual maturity. Such a concentration on the personal at the expense of the political, a psychoanalytic project of change which has individuals as its exclusive objects, seems to be the dominant perspective in the psychoanalytic culture, in the Kleinian tradition as much as in others. Its privatization of experience and its reluctance to seek connections between personal and wider social issues are major reasons for the distance and latent hostility between the psychoanalytic and socialist modes of thought.

This chapter, however, takes a different and more positive view of the connections between the personal and the political. The exploration of these links by feminists among others has been a positive feature of recent politics on the left, and is in any case clearly consonant with a much wider shift of emphasis in advanced societies from economic to cultural and social forms of deprivation. Socialists need to recover some deep and grounded view of the meaning of human life, and to this an understanding of their own experiences is highly relevant. If socialists are again to be recognized as having some far-sighted grasp of the future direction of their society, it will not come only through their political courage and militancy, important as these qualities will remain in these regressive times. It will depend also on their understanding of a capacity to live by meanings and values clearly more civilized, sociable and altruistic than their antagonists', and more equal to the difficulties of life. It is for this reason that this chapter addresses itself to Kleinian psychoanalytic ideas, as an exploration of areas of experience to which most socialist thought has been closed.

Psychoanalysis and Human Nature

We should perhaps establish first that all political theories in principle need to assume some view of human need and relationship: we might say as 'building blocks' from which models of natural or desirable social arrangements can be made. Conservative political theory of a traditionalist type has characteristically given great importance to the family and to other primary groups (based on locality or common culture, for example) as sources of social stability and continuity. Such theories assert the value of established moral beliefs *per se*, and since the heritage of these has been religious it is natural that the assumptions held by traditionalists about family life, and about the obligations of individuals towards society, tend to be religious in conception and sanction. It is evident today that the strongest ideological and institutional source for those who defend traditional structures of familial and social authority remains religion. Religiously inspired defences of family authority and sexual restriction have been important elements in the development of the New Right in Britain and even more in the United States, and have encouraged a generally repressive moral climate. These movements have given expression to anxieties, however little one may like their definition of them. Conservative traditionalists tend to be somewhat opposed to the application of scientific and rationalistic pro-cedures to established beliefs and patterns of behaviour, as naturally tending to challenge established bases of authority. Furthermore, Freud himself engaged in one of the most influential reinterpretations of the nature and function of religious belief from a scientific and humanist standpoint, and provided a continuing challenge to the legitimacy of religion. For these reasons, the perceived affinity between traditionalist approaches to fundamental questions of human nature and needs, and those of psychoanalysis, is small — even in those spheres where the human needs posited or asserted by psychoanalysts may be unexpectedly congruent with the assertions of some religious traditions.

It should be added that the development of conservative political ideas in sociological theory has shared the traditionalist concern with socialization as a key mechanism in the maintenance of social and individual order, the primary moral concern of these theories. In their most elaborate form, the writings of Talcott Parsons, substantial use is made of the ideas of Freud in order to explain how social roles and conceptions of society become deeply and affectively internalized through familial experience. Parsons's use of Freud's ideas has been criticized for its undue emphasis on a supposed natural integration of the individual into his or her social group, and for his disavowal of tension and conflict as unnatural and unhealthy. Nevertheless, his awareness of the specifically lengthy and elaborate process of intellectual and emotional development which the modern family — especially the middle-class family — is 'designed' to support, and his use of psychodynamic ideas to understand this, are important to our subsequent argument. The functionalist sociologists have in effect transposed a conservative ethic, committed to the values of stability, tradition, differentiation and hierarchy, on to a liberal democratic society, and have in this way been able to make use of modern sociological and psychodynamic theories of socialization to support their view. Later writers such as Daniel Bell, responding to a supposed crisis of excessive personal, economic and political demands in contemporary capitalism, have further posited the imperative need for religious belief as a means of 'containing' excessive and disordered wants. A number of writers, including Rieff and Lasch, have criticized the misuse of psychoanalytic ideas as legitimations of excessive hedonism and individualism, though Christopher Lasch (1981) has taken note of the different orientation of Kleinian approaches.

Conservative and socialist theories have both, in their different ways, stressed humanity's social nature — an absolute dependence on social life and on its moral and cultural traditions, for identity, existence and a sense of meaning. Liberal individualist theories, on the contrary, have adopted an opposite starting point: the idea of the free and independent individual for whom relations with others are undertaken on the basis of mutual advantage. In liberal theory the spheres of politics and economics become defined as instruments for meeting and reconciling the conflicts of individual desires through the mechanisms of the market and the ballot box. Running against the utilitarianism of impersonal interests reflected in the working of markets and bureaucracies, there are cultural definitions of personal fulfilment — Romanticism in its many forms — which become carriers of personal meaning even while being relatively excluded from the dominant political discourse. As Charles Taylor (1979) has recently put it, 'Modern society, we might say, is Romantic in its private and imaginative life, and utilitarian or instrumentalist in its public, effective life' (see also Richards, 1989b).

Liberal political theory's lack of interest in the actual content of human wants, and in any notion of humankind as having fundamentally social rather than hedonistic needs, has made it indifferent or hostile to psychoanalytic ideas, except in so far as Freud could himself be regarded as providing a pessimistic endorsement of the idea that man is a creature of insatiable individual desires. But the attraction of psychoanalysis to liberals from that point of view has been more than counterbalanced by the scientism of liberal theory — for example in the work of such key proponents as Karl Popper — and by a consequent hostility to the hermeneutic and imaginative procedures always central to psychoanalytic work. Furthermore, behavioural psychology and psychiatry, successful professional rivals to psychodynamic ideas, are closely congruent with the instrumentalist assumptions of liberal utilitarian theory, and can indeed be understood as attempting to provide a psychological technology for it, whereby criminals and deviants may be scientifically rewarded and sanctioned into conformity to the needs of the majority. The influence of psychoanalytic work in English liberal culture has been characteristically most strongly felt in the field of aesthetics, where positivist theory has had least to say and where, therefore, Romantic concerns have more easily held their own.[1]

Placing supreme value on individual experience (however attenuated the content which is given to that) does of course have an important connection with the values of psychoanalytic work. While attempts to construct a social morality around the pleasure principle — as in the work of some Freudian Marxists as well as that of some liberals — seem inherently asocial and therefore unsatisfactory, there may be a greater potential in the inverse argument that seeks to establish universal moral claims on the basis of the common human experience of pain. Thus contemporary moral philosophers such as Bernard Williams[2] have based their argument for a concept of human equality upon the common propensity of human beings for suffering. In a different context, the creation of the British National Health Service reflected a similar concept of the primacy of the claims of suffering over all other statuses. Indeed, the widespread moral commitment to the relief of suffering — however commonplace it may seem — remains perhaps the most widely felt egalitarian belief in this society.

The building blocks of socialist theory do of course include an adamantly social and relational view of human nature and also a Romantic idea of creativity, especially evident through the Hegelian influences on the early Marx. But while for these reasons we shall argue for a congruence of socialist and psychoanalytic approaches to human nature, in practice during much of this century these affinities have only partially been realized. On the socialist side, theoretical preoccupations have been mainly with the 'external' structures of economy and state. Despite Engels's work on the family, there has been little attention until recently in Marxist theory to gender relations or to the dependent needs of children and adults. On the psychoanalytic side, the liberal-individualist assumptions of Freud's work, together with his own political pessimism, constitute major barriers to synthesis with socialist ideas. There were important attempts in the work of the Frankfurt School and of Wilhelm Reich to connect a Freudian view of the repression of libidinal and creative energy to a social theory of repression, and to utilize Freud's insights into unconscious psychic forces to understand the ideological power of fascism. These significantly converged with Freud's own pessimism about political authority. In the interwar years there were reasons enough to attend to the forms and consequences of repression, and to overlook differences between social and hedonistic views of human need and desire, which in fact separate socialist and orthodox Freudian theory. This engagement of psychoanalytic theory with Marxism, by Marcuse and Reich in particular, has been limited by its preoccupations with instinctual repression, and the implicitly hedonistic utopia which it tends to presuppose as its inverse. It is difficult to construct a benign view of a potential society from the primary human motives of libidinal self-gratification.

This criticism must be qualified in practice by Reich's actual sensitivity, especially in his earlier work, to the problems of character development and to the difficult connections between the individual unconscious and social experience,[3] as well as by Marcuse's original and important attempt to escape the confines of instinct theory through attention to expressiveness, art and culture as means of transcending the conflict of the pleasure and reality principles. Nevertheless, from the orthodox starting point of these writers, a relational concept of humankind always had to be rescued and reconstructed from their psychoanalytic model rather than being the basis of it. It is only with the development of 'object-relations theory' through the work of Klein, Winnicott, Fairbairn and others, especially in Britain, that psychoanalysis has transcended the crippling antithesis of 'individual' and 'social'.

Structuralist Models

More recently there has been a different absorption of Freud's ideas on the left through the medium of Lacan: first in France by Louis Althusser, and subsequently by followers in Britain. This work has been principally concerned with the forms and methods of thought, rather than with feelings and relationships. That is to say, it has tended to see affective states and relationships through the conscious and unconscious meanings assigned to them, and has been preoccupied with the mechanisms and procedures by which meanings are repressed, distorted and transposed. This rationalistic procedure, making use of advances in the science of language following Saussure, undoubtedly developed one aspect of Freud's method of interpretation. There is nevertheless a singular lack of attention within this Lacanian work to the experience of human feeling and relationship. Neither libidinal nor cognitive readings of Freud yield a view of the human individual as a sentient, social, and moral being.

The switch of emphasis in the reading of Freud from his model of instinct and repression to his account of mental process has been a central element in a widespread movement of social and cultural theory, especially in France[5] but lately with substantial influence in Britain. This influence has been felt through 'structuralist' theory, in which the mechanisms for the coding and decoding of meanings described in Freud's work, especially in his *Interpretation of Dreams*, have been assimilated to the theory of post-Saussurean linguistics, and have become the basis for a systematic and scientific form of cultural analysis. Among structuralist Marxists, such as Althusser, interest in Freud is concentrated on his analytic method, rather than on his theory of feelings. (All ideas of universal human nature, whether of Freud or the early Marx, are in any case heavily criticized on historical materialist grounds by this school. The concept of 'desire' retains its place in this theory only as an infinitely open and plastic force, with no fixed existence apart from its cultural definitions.) This work seeks to transpose Freud's idea of the symptomatic revelation of inner psychic structures, through condensed and displaced symbols, from the individual psyche to the social structure. This method thus becomes a way of establishing very complex interrelationships between different levels of the social system, which it conceptualizes — following Freud's later model of the mind — as symbolic transformations rather than causal mechanisms. Whether this is in fact an explanatory theory or merely a metaphor for social relations is not clear. Meanwhile, the idea of a determinate deep structure, corresponding to the fundamental assertions of Marx regarding the final determination of social systems by their dominant mode of production, is preserved. In Althusser's work, the deep structure posited by Marxism has little or no relation to the deep structures posited by Freud other than the common inscription of all human experiences in the forms of language. There are, however, links of a meta-theoretical kind, if not in substantive formulation, between these perspectives. The idea of a deep structure of theoretical entities (modes of production in the one case, unconscious mental formations in the other) again potentially links Marxism and psychoanalysis, as human sciences positing objects of study which are both theoretical and real against the empiricist and atomistic critiques which have been, since Popper, the common philosophical enemy of both.

One development in this structuralist tradition, however, has brought substantive rather than methodological connections between psychoanalytic and Marxist theory. This is the concern to explain at a deep level the processes of the 'reproduction' of social relations through socialization. The problematic of this work is not dissimilar to the earlier problematic of 'social repression', but whereas writers of the 1930s and 1940s tended to rely on social psychology to provide the mediating terms between social and unconscious forces, contemporary writers in this tradition posit cultural forms of control. The idea of a cultural code, developed from structuralist ideas, has especially been used to explain the perpetuation of gender roles and gender subordination through the mechanism of the family. Psychoanalytic ideas have been introduced, as in Juliet Mitchell's influential *Psychoanalysis and Feminism* (1975), to explain the deep-level acquisition of gender characteristics through the oedipal stage, and thus the unconscious implantation of existing role structures. There are similarities between this account and the conclusions of American sociologists regarding the usefulness for capitalist society of the existing division of roles between the instrumental (corresponding to the demands on the individual of work in market and bureaucratic organizations) and the expressive (corresponding to the role requirements of family care and its social extensions). Unconscious mechanisms of socialization, taken from Freud, were also a key element in Parsons's explanatory model. But whereas the functionalists by and large endorsed this division of role, feminists, while accepting much of the analysis, forcefully contested it and redefined difference as subordination and oppression. Whereas Lacanian-influenced work has principally stressed the 'deficit' aspects of women's socialization (taking up Freud's emphasis on the phallus, penis envy, and so on), there has recently been a more searching exploration, especially by American writers,[6] of the substantive conditions of women's socialization, which has enabled a more positive valuation to be given of what women actually do. This has particularly focused on the demands of relationships with infants and young children, and has identified the qualities required for these — for example, responsiveness to feelings, and empathy with the infant's disregard for time and other 'rational' boundaries. This amounts to a tolerance of exposure to unconscious processes, not merely in dreams or in art but in everyday life, and is clearly shown to be in conflict with the routinized and repressive demands of the workaday world. These arguments can lead to the conclusion that men as well as women lack or are deprived of valued opportunities and attributes, and they thus support feminists' demands for a radical reconstruction of role boundaries and divisions of function to valorize qualities of sensitivity and responsiveness.

Habermas and Timpanaro

Another application of Freud's concept of interpretative method to the societal sphere has been made, from a more phenomenological standpoint, by Jürgen Habermas (1972). He argues that social reality is necessarily constituted through the experience of social actors who are subjects as well as objects of understanding, and that therefore wholly external or positivist methods of social science are both incomplete and improperly manipulative. Freud's model of an interpretative discourse, in which the patient provides phenomenological material for understanding and is himself in part the authority for the truth of proffered conjectures about the meaning of his mental phenomena, is presented as a methodological model for social knowledge. In Habermas's account of a democratic, ideal state, knowledge should be constituted to include and account for men's own conceptions, and should also be knowledge evolved and tested out with its human objects, and then taken by them into their own understandings. This conception has some similarities with the methodology developed in the Tavistock Institute for the use of analytic methods for the self-understanding of group and organizational processes. In

Habermas's theory, obstacles to communication, through educational or linguistic deprivation, or distorted or dominative systems of communication in society, become the principal impediments to a shared and equal rationality. Habermas's ideas have a predominantly cognitive emphasis as well as a characteristic reliance on cognitive theories drawn from phenomenology and generative linguistics. His approach can perhaps be best understood as a radical and egalitarian Kantianism, positing an ideal universe of rational choosing subjects, without too much concern for the material or biological substratum out of which choices are made.

While I think it is important to note the considerable influence of these interpretations of Freud on recent socialist thought, I hope it is also apparent that most of the above developments have done little to elaborate socialist theory in the areas of primary experience and relationship, where it has hitherto been weakest. The most important recent suggestion in this direction has recently been made from a possibly surprising source: Sebastiano Timpanaro, the author of a highly critical work on Freud's interpretative method called *The Freudian Slip* (1976). In his work *On Materialism* (1975), Timpanaro draws attention to the biological foundations of human experience, whose neglect by Marxists is, he argues, quite inconsistent with their supposedly materialist standpoint. The material basis of human life is in part provided by man's biological needs and destiny, and an account which pays regard to these fundamental and irreducible facts of experience should also pay regard to this biological basis. Timpanaro points to the work of a nineteenth-century Italian writer, Leopardi — whom he describes as a hedonistic pessimist — as a model of a proper and necessary regard for the facts of death and suffering. While polemicizing against the idealist misapplications of Romanticism in social thought ('existential vapourings'), Timpanaro is in fact asking Marxists to address themselves to phenomena of feeling (concern with bereavement and loss, for example) which have been much more seriously addressed within Romantic literary work (and within psychoanalysis) than elsewhere in this culture.

Now 'materialism' has many possible interpretations and, in the field of competing psychologies, psychoanalysis is by no means the most obvious candidate for this description. Raymond Williams,[7] for example, has coupled a strong commendation of the importance of Timpanaro's work with the suggestion that perhaps the experimental tradition in psychology has a much greater claim to be considered as a materialist science than psychoanalysis, and is certainly more consistent and continuous in method and approach with the natural sciences than Freud's work. But I think the force of Timpanaro's recommendation is its assertion of the importance of universal human experience and the emotions which its inevitable contingencies evoke. Whatever strengths experimental psychology may have — for example, in the exact measurement of behaviour or in the understanding of cognitive processes — they do not yet appear to extend to the understanding of deep and complex emotions and mental states, the principal subject matter of psychanalysis. In contrast, Timpanaro emphasizes that these contingencies are inevitable, now and always. Deaths can be postponed, not for ever avoided. Some illnesses can be cured or prevented, but there will always be others. Some relationships will always be severed from biological causes, and human beings will have to live with the consequences of this. It is not that we should be indifferent to the social causes of these contingencies, nor abandon the struggle to relieve individuals of the pains inflicted by their biological natures; but socialist theory must take account of these facts and construct a frame of meanings — a theodicy — with which we can face them. And we should attend not only to matters of pain and death, but also to matters of our sexual natures and of the needs of infancy and nurture. There is also the matter of inborn individual differences, in natures and capacities, also disregarded and rejected as epiphenomenal by environmentalists of the left. There is always a biological or natural substratum formed and structured by social arrangements, just as there are the properties of matter with which people must cope through their labour. The relevance of Kleinian 'object-relations' theory to socialists is, I shall argue, the contribution it makes to the understanding of these natural human needs and capacities.

The 'Object-Relations' Approach

Kleinian Moralism

Let me now outline what seem to me the most salient features of Kleinian psychoanalytic practice, considered not so much theoretically or clinically, or from the point of view of the internal development of psychoanalysis,[8] but in relation to a wider field of cultural and ideological meanings. I would summarize this body of work as offering a view of human beings which in an intense and unusual way assumes them to be moral in their fundamental nature. It also — and in close relation to this — assumes them to be constituted as social beings in a primary and continuing interdependency with others. Kleinian theory is impregnated with moral categories, and its developmental concepts — especially those of paranoid-schizoid and depressive 'positions' — incorporate moral capabilities (notably of concern for the well-being of other persons) into their theoretical definition. A stage of development is partially defined in terms of the moral capacities typical of it. There is also an important revision of Freud's view of the moral sense in Klein's account of development, especially in the distinction between persecutory and reparative guilt. Freud's superego is conceived as having a repressive and persecutory function, and Freudian analysis could therefore be understood as aiming to achieve emancipation from guilt, especially sexual guilt. In contrast, guilt in Klein's 'depressive position' arises from the recognition of the pain suffered by or inflicted on others, and as an essential part of relatedness. Capacity for moral feeling, therefore, in its more and less benign forms, is seen as a defining attribute shared by human beings, rather than as an unavoidable external constraint upon them.

This is not to say that these moral concepts need or ought to be applied in therapy in a judgemental spirit, though they often are. I have the sense that a tendency to relapse into judgemental modes is one reason for a certain impatience with these aspects of Kleinian theory even among some of those now working within this tradition. The important issue here is that Kleinian theory uniquely ascribes moral and altruistic capacities to human beings. Kleinian theory is in no way unusual in building evaluations into its theoretical concepts — all social theories concerned with descriptions of human need and nature can be said to do this. What is unusual is its attribution of moral capacity to its subjects as their essential nature. This view appears to derive, scientifically, from the Kleinian view of the infant's early relationship with its mother. Individuality is shown to be not the starting point but rather the emergent result of a prolonged and delicate process of dependency. Innate concern for the well-being of the other, at a very deep level, appears in this conception to arise from the earliest lack of differentiation between self and other, and from the process whereby this differentiation comes about. Pleasure and pain are only slowly located in space and time, and in relation to whole persons. This intense experience of pain, as given and received, and this deep involvement with the caring person as the perceived source of all well- and ill-being, gives rise to the capacity to experience the pains and pleasures of the other with an intensity comparable to the pains and pleasures of the self. While committed to the development of individuality, object-relations theory starts from the assumption that social relationships are always primary. Indeed, some research linked to this tradition — the attachment theory of Bowlby and his colleagues, for example — has tried to provide experimental proof for the assertion that social relationships form the precondition for human cognition *per se*.[9]

Kleinian theory also offers a distinctively uncompromising view of human destructiveness, and the continuing and unavoidable problem in human lives of coping with this. The omnipresence of envy is perhaps the distinguishing doctrine of Kleinian work, as well as one of the main sources of others' reservations towards it.[10] The idea of envy is how Klein came to see destructive feelings, or Freud's death instinct, as these became directed towards the good internal object as a result of the pain of early separation and development. Philip Rieff (1959) suggests that the death instinct arose in Freud's theory as a result of his wish to explain all important psychic phenomena as a result of innate psychic forces, rather than as responses to external or biological threat. On this account, since there is death, there must be a death instinct. If one considers the origin of an instinct to be by definition genetic, and therefore to depend on adaptive advantages for species survival, it seems hard to explain how this very antithesis of life-preservative impulses can have arisen. It seems far more plausible to see this as a transformation of innate aggressiveness, turned on internal or external objects who are experienced as a source of pain. Be this as it may, the very intransigence of Kleinian theory in its emphasis on the destructive has been one of its principal intellectual strengths. Understanding of negative and perverse character-formations has subsequently developed, through Segal's (1983) explorations of Klein's concept of envy, Rosenfeld's (1964, 1971, 1987) concept of 'negative narcissism' as destructiveness directed towards the self, and Meltzer's (1968) idea of an addictive relation to a bad part of the self, or submission to internal tyranny. This work has greatly deepened analytic understanding of destructive aspects of the personality, and their role in resisting change through analysis (Rosenfeld, 1987). (On these and other theoretical issues in Kleinian analysis, Hinshelwood's *Dictionary of Kleinian Thought* [1989] is now indispensable.)

It seems characteristic of the assimilation of Freudian ideas into the culture of the United States that it has on the one hand emphasized the individualist and hedonistic basis of Freudian theory, and on the other hand undermined the weight of the truly structural and unconscious basis of destructiveness. So while individuals are defined as fundamentally self-regarding in their motivation, an optimistic gloss is put on the possibilities of constructing a tolerable social order from that basis. Better that the obstacles to life should be exaggerated than minimized, if they are to be surmounted! The attractions of this rigorous doctrine seem to me to be parallel to the attractions of a similarly intransigent Marxism, which also draws our attention to structural and material obstacles to improvement which cannot be merely wished or idealized away, and must be resolved at their root (in the latter case through the processes of history and political action) before good human lives will be generally possible.

While the overt emphasis on the forces of hate, envy, greed, and so on in Kleinian theory seem to be stronger than in orthodox Freudian work, the implications of these for one's view of humankind seem to me to be para-doxically less pessimistic. Freud's word has been widely received as funda-mentally pessimistic in its implications, part of the break-up of a nineteenth-century consensus about the inevitability of progress. It drew attention to the 'dark forces' of destructiveness and limitless appetites, also reflected, as a 'will to power', in the writings of Schopenhauer and Nietzsche. The absorption in this new scientific psychology of the concerns of Romanticism — especially its darker concerns — is the main theme of a famous essay on Freud's cultural importance by Lionel Trilling (1951). Kleinian work manifests some particularly important differences in this respect. The first is the greater stress on the possibilities and normality of what we might call powerful 'positive' emotions, especially in the concept of reparation. For example, the Kleinian theory of art as concerned with the recovery and restor-ation of 'damaged and lost internal objects', and the resolution of internal conflicts in this way, is more socially positive in its implications than Freud's concept of sublimated libido.[11] Art and creative work in general become not merely acts of symbolic wish-fulfilment arising from hedonistic appetites, but activities symbolically commemorating and preserving the relation to a loved other.

A second important difference lies in the Kleinian attention to the location and explanation of destructive emotion in the early experiences of the infant and its relation to the sensations of pain and anxiety. This seems to be a more fruitful explanatory stress than the positing of 'instincts'. This developmental account identifies not only the occurrence but also the containment, through relationship, care and thought, of rage and hate. Without minimizing or glossing over the ever-presence of these psychic forces, they are nevertheless shown as capable of integration and resolution, essentially if others are available to help the infant to share the burden of its pain and anxiety. There is therefore a hopefulness in the Kleinian account, based on this view of a normal and possible process of maturation. While this does not in any way minimize the subsequent outcropping and hidden vigour of envy in all its forms, there is a primary assumption in this model that these feelings are (depending on the degrees of early damage) capable of integration and modification through a process of understanding. This process of understanding has to have qualities which reflect the containment of feelings during infant care, being the shared experience and bearing of emotions, as well as a mental process. This is one reason for the emphasis on the transference in Kleinian and related work, and also the reason for the emphasis on the experience of mothers and babies, not so much as a theoretical construction for subsequent analytic excavation but as a ground for the learning and reliving by therapists of the mental states which they must be able to tolerate and understand in order to work effectively. This theoretical model of the containment of mental pain (and its various uncon-scious coping strategies — the mechanisms of splitting, projection, projective identification, and so on) has more recently been extended in this tradition to the explanation of more deeply disordered conditions, such as autism and schizophrenia. This exploration of the most acute and terrible forms of psychic suffering (though they are not always socially recognized as such) is a further aspect of the essentially compassionate stance of this body of work towards mental pain, which is very far from any kind of metaphysical complacency about 'dark forces' or from celebration of the allegedly subversive qualities of the schizoid (for example, in Deleuze and Guattari, 1983).

The Politics of Nurture

A third distinguishing feature of the approach of the 'British School' is its emphasis, following on what has been said about the developmental needs of infants, on the family as *the* nurturing unit of human lives. Positive valuation of the functions of the family is most often associated in social theory with conservative beliefs. Liberal approaches place greater emphasis on the desires and rights of individuals (especially adult individuals), and this is reflected in libertarian attitudes to such matters as divorce, abortion, sexual deviance and birth control, where liberal deregulation of behaviour by the state serves to weaken the grip of familial norms of structures over individuals. Marxist theorists have most often regarded the institution of the family in a rather negative light, because of its privatization of social loyalties and its traditional removal of women from the public world into a personal and less rationalistic mode of being. It is seen as an upholder of authority and class domination.

Reformist socialist thinking in Britain — or what can broadly be described as the tradition of British social democracy — has, however, given a central positive weight to the development of the family. The principal links between the therapeutic approaches we are considering and radical politics have occurred in Britain through the theory and practice of social democracy, though in a rather oblique way. I have described elsewhere (Rustin, 1979) the positive importance of the family to social-democratic reforms, and this has been more fully (and critically) characterized by other writers such as Elizabeth Wilson (1977). To some degree, the family stands in this tradition as the exemplar of more altruistic and caring values than obtain in capitalism at large. This emphasis on the moral qualities identified with the family and generalized in the ideal of a caring welfare state is partly Christian in its inspiration. In this respect social-democratic thinking takes over and democratizes values which are originally organicist. Its social and altruistic conception of humankind causes it to find in both Christian and Romantic critiques of the individualism and competitiveness of industrial society a usable critical vocabulary.[12] Nonconformist elements in the development of the British labour movement have now been extensively described by historians. Social-democratic thinking in Britain — for example through such influential writers as Tawney, an avowed Christian socialist, and Titmuss — has long had a strongly ethical cast.

There are some direct connections between social-democratic reforms (I use this term broadly to describe the development of the welfare state in the post-war period) and the psychoanalytic ideas with which we are concerned. One such link can be seen in the early influence of Bowlby's work on official attitudes and policies towards juvenile delinquency, and the subsequent shift towards more 'therapeutic' social work approaches to young offenders in preference to more utilitarian and punitive ones. A particular interest in the quality of family life seems to have arisen in the war partly as a consequence of concern over the effects of evacuation on children — no doubt this was also a matter of working-class children thus becoming more visible to the middle classes. The recurring connections between the Tavistock Clinic[13] and the British army also appear to be important in deciphering the underlying ideological affinities of this school. Notwithstanding the more open and democratic character of the army during mass mobilization, this link seems also to bear out the key significance for this school of the concept of social membership and responsibility. The paternalist traditions of the military are one aspect of this; the absorption of notions of collective social (or indeed state) responsibility by Fabian socialists, often coming from the same upper-middle-class social groups, is another. In the post-war period the state's positive social policies towards the family, both as the hoped-for source of richer lives and as the best preventive against moral disorder, was the main reason for official backing for psychoanalytic work and its derivatives, for example in social work. We can see this in the state's support for the child guidance movement, and in the relatively more generous attitude towards the provision of help for children and parents compared, for example, with that available for the adult mentally ill. Indeed, the development of an identifiable profession or sub-profession of child psychotherapists has depended on this government support. An important institutional division in the organization of psychoanalysis in Britain has depended on support from the state, through its education and national health services, for psychoanalytic therapy provided free to clients in relation to need. Characteristically, this state provision has been relatively more generous in regard to psychotherapeutic services for children and parents than for adults *per se*, though restricted and localized (mainly to the south-east of England) even here. Correspondingly, those professionals concerned with these services have been somewhat more socially orientated than the mainstreams of psychoanalytic practice. The material basis for such activities cannot be neglected in understanding them.

However, this latent link with social-democratic reformism, and especially with positive valuations of the family, has not encouraged interest in Kleinian or Kleinian-influenced ideas by more radical and Marxist socialists. So far as relational and sexual matters are concerned, they have tended rather to be ultra-libertarian in their orientation. The *intentions* of this position have been anarchistic-utopian rather than explicitly individualistic. The idea, powerfully felt in the emotional aftermath of the 1968 May Events and of a comparable euphoria in the student culture of the United States, was that if artificial moral restraints on sexual behaviour could be removed, individuals would be able to create loving and intimate relationships, more generous and less exclusive than the traditional monogamous family, and much less repressive for the young. Radical Freudianism played its part in this ideology of personal liberation, which had both sexual and political dimensions. However, the reality was more individualist than the rhetoric, since gaining freedom from restraints, both internal and external, doesn't and didn't produce spontaneous social harmony. The attempt to work out forms and institutions of personal life less exclusive than the nuclear family, but nevertheless able to provide some comparable continuity and context for dependency both for children and adult members, has become a social problem — though it is probably true that a greater climate of toleration and a stronger culture of mutual help and development have provided much more personal space than was previously available to any except very small artistic and intellectual minorities.

Related to this issue of the family, in an ambiguous way, is the implication of Kleinian theory for the role of women. Its striking valuation of the power and potency of motherhood, markedly displacing the genital emphasis of Freudian theory, is surely among all social theories that which gives the greatest pre-eminence to the role of women. This is effected within Kleinian theory by attention to pre-oedipal phases of development and the potency implied in the capacity to provide food and comfort to the infant. The breast and the nipple are observed through psychoanalysis and in observational studies to be experienced as images of plenitude and potency comparable to — and perhaps, in view of its developmental location, more primary than — the role of the penis. A tempting way of describing this is as a shift of focus from sexual to parental functions, but it would be more accurate to say that sexuality is perceived in this account as essentially related to procreative powers rather than merely as a bearer of individual desires. The role of 'mothering' is not in this framework of ideas necessarily gender-specific, but nevertheless, given the way roles are currently divided in this society, these ideas might be expected to change the evaluation of what women mostly do, and promote respect for the transformations of those functions into other containing and nurturing roles in other voluntary and paid work. The fact that the Kleinian development in psychoanalysis was at first the work of women psychoanalysts and writers — Melanie Klein's early collaborators were women — and that the contribution of women analysts to this school has remained important to the present day, is itself of significance. There are rather few theoretical advances in the social sciences, apart from feminism itself, of which this can be said. It seems extraordinary, given these facts, that these ideas have been until recently scarcely at all taken up, even to be actively disputed, within the feminist movement, whose initial mode of access of Freud's ideas, in Britain anyway, has been through the ultra-cerebral and phallus-centred approaches of Lacan. Even the connection, for example, of that writer's 'Mirror-Stage' paper with object-relations theory, and with Winnicott's ideas in particular, have apparently led to little interest in what one might have thought to have been for feminists a more promising line of thought. (*New Left Review* provided an early translation of Lacan's paper, at the very beginning of the reception of his ideas in England, but did not at the time take note of these more local parallels.)

Of course the reasons for this lack of feminist interest are not hard to understand. Kleinian theory does give enormous emphasis to the mothering role. It doesn't, it is true, do so in a sentimental spirit. There is much emotional violence described as having to be contained in mother–infant relations. Its account of the phantasy life of the infant (and adult) insists on its primitive and violent physicality even more forcefully than Freud. Its therapeutic method is singularly rigorous, prescribing toleration of pain in both therapist and patient as a necessary condition for development to proceed, and insisting on the value of analytic work, rather than comfort, as its main task. (Nevertheless, tough-minded as it is, this analytic relationship still depends on a basis of loving concern for the patient.) But for all these rigorous qualities, Kleinian theory is nevertheless valorizing the caring functions predominantly assigned to women in their normal existing roles in this society. The women's movement, to put the matter rather starkly, has been chiefly seeking means of *escape* from the ideological and practical dominance of the role, into the relative freedom and apparent power which it perceives in assigned masculine functions. It has not been looking for a theoretical endorsement of the role of caring for babies.

The Radicalism of the 'British School'

In a number of respects, therefore, Kleinian work goes against the grain of much contemporary radical thinking. Its emphasis on envy and destructiveness seems to run against the hopefulness, even utopianism, about human nature that seems natural to radicals. Its interest in 'caring relationships' seems rather out of sympathy with a much tougher-minded and more aggressive attitude of mind which has characterized the British New Left since the mid sixties. Its various discreet connections with the social reformism of post-war social democracy have not been exactly a recommendation of Kleinian work to a new generation of socialist theorists, for whom the critique of the practical failures and inherent limitations of social democracy has been a major theme.

More generally, as I have tried to show, this tradition of psychoanalytic work does not plainly locate itself in any one ideological affiliation. It draws attention to the inevitable presence of both powerful positive and negative feelings in human beings. It defines development in terms of a process of differentiation and individuation, providing a rather powerful schooling by analysis in how to separate one context and its appropriate feelings from another. Even the lodging of so intense a relationship as an analysis in the time-frame, and in the contractual conditions in which it often occurs, is to dislocate the idea of an intense affective relationship from anything like its expected social setting. While the family may be the analytic starting point of all this process, it is far from its termination. The insistence in Kleinian training on firm segregation of the different roles of analyst, patient, tutor, colleague and so on, from one another, and the avoidance of 'democratic' and 'egalitarian' looseness in these matters, enforces a similar attention to boundaries. This is very far from the radical idea of a unified, holistic, non-specialized community in which people might find all their needs realized. Its commitments to understanding, choice and responsibility take forward the liberal and rationalistic ethos of Freud's own work, while its stress on containment and dependency points towards a more 'social' and organicist conception of an individual's relation to society. While stressing the biological and phantasy basis of the differentiation of sexual role and identity, it reverses the typical patriarchalism of Freud's work, and in developing his view of normal bisexual aspects to the personality also offers a more potent and creative view of 'female' qualities. I have stressed the applications of Kleinian-orientated work in the context of welfare services to the family. But it should also be recalled that most psychoanalysis is practised by individual private contract, for middle-class patients in search of solutions to their individually defined problems (many of which may, however, lie in the area of family relationships in the present as well as the past). In this respect it is strongly rooted in a liberal cultural and economic setting, even though its underlying view of a personality seems to give little sustenance to hedonism. Patients who go to Kleinian analysts only with self-gratification in mind must be rudely surprised.

I would stress the egalitarian force of an emphasis on human capacities for feeling. These are not distributed in any standard relation to status, income, power or education. This is perhaps the most important single pointer to this school's potential importance for socialist theory: that its values appear to measure individuals in their moral and relational capacities above all. The implicit claims of these values on social arrangements are also potentially subversive of the role of psychoanalysis itself. Whatever may be said about its core values, psychoanalysis as a practice is now inherently privileged, because of the scarce yet considerable human resources analysis takes up. It is possible to conclude conservatively from this that its benefits must therefore be confined to a few, whose responsibility is that of a special calling. While this conception is not necessarily self-seeking — the theory of Kleinian analysis suggests that health consists in creating as well as taking good — it is at best the self-definition of a minority. The sense of the 'specialness' of the analytic experience does in many practitioners take precedence over all other more social claims on it. There is also a more democratic view: that the insights of analysis must, in view of the inevitable scarcity of curative resources, be applied primarily in preventive ways, in the improvement of everyday institutions and practices (for example, in childrearing) so that better possibilities for development are created for all. This approach is also influential in the psychoanalytic world. There is a dilemma for egalitarians in such matters, as in intellectual or aesthetic life, where qualities which it is desired to universalize have depended for their evolution — and if we are honest we have to say do now continue to depend — on their being privileged, on certain scarce resources. The rather subdued stance of Kleinian psychoanalytic work in relation to such wider cultural and political issues as these perhaps reflects these ambiguities.

In attempting to characterize the British School, I am tempted to draw a parallel, especially with the history of the *Scrutiny* group of English literary critics whose central figure was F.R. Leavis. The work of this crucial cultural grouping has been described with insight in a historical study by Francis Mulhern (1981). Mulhern identifies this group as working in opposition to dominant upper-class concepts of literary 'taste', which subordinated the creative and developmental functions of literature to mere matters of social status. This grouping was committed to an idea of moral seriousness, derived ultimately from provincial Nonconformity, and also to an idea of developed expertise and literary professionalism against the gentleman-amateur traditions of belles-lettres. This commitment to intellectual performance and seriousness of purpose might be thought to be an ideology functional to a new educated class claiming vocational status (especially in this case in the professions of education) on the basis not of birth but of talent. The Leavises were also notably protagonists of a morally serious and 'mature' view of (heterosexual) sexual relationships: F.R. Leavis was a principal advocate for many years of the genius of D.H. Lawrence. He had an implicit and deliberately untheorized concept of 'life' as a positive value, which he used as a measure of a writer's work as well as of the qualities depicted in its characters. This quality is chiefly reflected in literature through the 'realization' of individuals in their relation to each other: this is the main touchstone — partly a matter of literary form, but also of Leavis's idea of what is humanly most sacred. Life-bearing qualities seem to be defined chiefly by an openness to deep emotional experience of others, a rather physically discreet notion of sexual attraction which has the force of requiring sexual feelings to be bound very closely to the response to the qualities of a whole person, and a sharp dislike of merely social exclusions, in the name of status or power, over the primary valuing of persons for themselves. There is a very sharp social awareness and edge to Leavis's work, which was initially deployed largely from the left. His concept of a 'Benthamite-utilitarian civiliz-ation' is, as Raymond Williams pointed out in an obituary, capitalism by another name; and he also displayed great intransigence and pointedness in the critique of aristocratic claims to superiority. Later, however, the concern with cultural 'standards' became more defensive, perhaps as the hopefulness that society could be remade through the medium of education in English literature diminished. Leavis had never liked Marxism because of its subordination of the values of individual experience, but much more important than any overt hostility to the politics of the left, which he mostly avoided, were his increasing identification with the values of a beleaguered cultural minority and his pessi-mistic anxieties about the encroachments of mass society on cultural standards.

Ideologies of the New Middle Class?

The parallel between this and my view of Kleinian work will perhaps be evident. For one thing, there is a certain common moral intransigence — almost a puritanism of purpose — which has caused a considerable cultural hostility towards both tendencies. There is a common moral seriousness, and also a shared stress on the value of the disciplined pursuit of new specialized callings: respectively literary criticism and psychoanalysis. One might say that the actual practices of criticism — which the Leavisites say should be based on a kind of emotional and empathetic sensitivity explicated through language — and analysis, which has some of these same prescribed qualities, are not all that far apart. Alan Shuttleworth (1966) has written about Leavis's affinities with some of Max Weber's work, drawing attention to the interpretative methods and centrality of moral concerns of both. In connecting the Kleinian school with this pair, we can add the common preoccupation with the concept of a rational vocation — a general quality of the capitalist ethic in Weber's work, here a specific recommendation for the new vocations of teacher-critic and analyst. And we can also add the fit between Weber's idea of the rational differentiation of social function — a characteristic feature of modern industrial society, he thought — and the notion of named and differentiated parts of the self, and also of differentiated social settings, which it seems to me are central to the mental universe of Kleinian work. Between the *Scrutiny* group and the Kleinians there is also a certain common evasion of existing ideological pigeonholes. Both oppositional and radical in one way, neither school of thought has found affiliation with wider social or cultural movements easy. While Leavisism has, after influencing many socialists, in the end become a position of rather conservative defence of high culture against encroachment by 'the masses', the ideological destination of the Kleinian tradition remains to be determined.

Scrutiny was uninterested in Freudian psychoanalysis in the 1930s, no doubt because of its close associations with Bloomsbury and because of the unacceptability to it of a hedonist ethic. But it is interesting in relation to this argument that the one psychoanalytic work which *Scrutiny* promoted, Ian Suttie's *The Origins of Love and Hate* (1935), was in fact a pioneer of object-relations theory, and proposed a notably more tender view of human relatedness than the liberal Freudianism of its day. Direct connections between Leavisite and analytic conceptions of personal development continued later through the work of David Holbrook, evolving from writings about the value of literature for young children into somewhat heavy-handed neo-Kleinian critiques of pornography.[14] But despite Holbrook, the key concept of 'maturity' remains generally unexplicated within Leavisism, and this theoretical failure in fact constitutes a crucial difference between these traditions. Mulhern has commented on *Scrutiny* that while its position was in many respects a radical and critical one, it was bound to fail as a progressive intellectual force specifically because of its lack of theorization. It was because the positive concept of 'life' has a wholly intuitive and self-evident basis that it was impossible to generalize the rather generous social values which the term usually signified, and also impossible to prevent a slide into pessimistic elitism when earlier cultural hopes were not fulfilled. Whether or not this explanation by theoretical deficiency holds for the case of Leavisism, it certainly points up a clear difference from the case of Kleinian analysis. Here, without doubt, there is a fully articulated basis for a social, altruistic and moral view of humankind, with all the harshly realist and anti-utopian qualifications one must make of this.

To characterize these positions in sociological terms, we might speculate that both 'Leavisism' and the 'British Psychoanalytic School' are 'ideologies' of fragments of the new middle class dependent for their income and status on higher education and on a specialized professional training. Both systems of ideas revolve around a far-reaching and rationalized concept of personal development, which we may suppose has some congruency with the needs of an advanced industrial social structure. The greater autonomy required of more educated strata of employees in advanced industrial society, and the shift from authoritarian to more consensual means of social integration, give a heightened value to both cognitive and emotional complexity and self-awareness. The main institutional 'channel' bearing the ideas of Leavisism was the expansion of the state education system and perhaps especially the grammar school. English

31

teachers here became to a degree missionaries for Romanticism. The main institutional settings for the ideas of the British psychoanalytic school have been the state health, welfare and education systems, but also private analytic practice for the professional middle class. Both tendencies have had a certain characteristic radicalism, probably imparted partly by their originating outside the dominant cultural forms. In *Scrutiny's* case, this reflected itself in its prolonged battles over several decades with what it conceived of as a 'literary establishment'. In the case of Kleinian analysis we can note, as factors making for a certain radicalizing exclusion, the hostility to psychoanalysis in Britain in general, on the part of dominant scientific and medical elites, which has given analysis the option of a rather passive enclave role (adopted by the British Psycho-Analytical Society for the most part) or working in fields carrying less prestige and financial reward and therefore more open to permeation: work with children clearly comes into this category. The unusually preponderant role of women in the generation of the key ideas of Kleinian work, and also in most psychonanalytic work with children, is another factor making for a minority and quietly oppositional definition of role.

These ideologies emphasize values — of the sensitive use of language in the one case, and the development of moral and emotional capacities in the other — which are far from dominant traits in this society. Therefore while ideologies of the 'new middle class', they are potentially, and sometimes actually, oppositional. In their more hopeful and universalizing moments, they find affinities with social forces demanding more generous and egalitarian social services; in their more limited and class-regarding moments, they confine themselves to the servicing of a narrow fragment of the educated middle class. It is still an open question, in the case of psychoanalysis, what its ultimately most important political affiliations will be. Socialist traditions have incorporated many values and conceptions of life deriving from the experience of social groups other than the industrial working class. Almost by definition in socialist theory, the life conditions of this class are so impoverished by exploitation as to be unable to generate a whole alternative culture from its own experience, central to socialism as its institutions, traditions and claims naturally are. Alliances with other social strata are politically crucial to any peaceful change or subsequent consensus. Intellectual dialogue with radical but not specifically socialist currents of thought are the ideological equivalent of this political necessity. We will now try to sketch out the positive significance of the neo-Kleinian tradition for a socialist perspective.

The Relational Vision and Socialism

I shall argue first that the relational focus of the British psychoanalytic school — the assertion that what matters most to human beings is whether they stand in loving and trusting relations to others — is the theoretical basis for a much-enlarged concept of human development. This has potential relevance to the 'social architecture' provided for the experiences of primary socialization (in the family and elsewhere); for secondary socialization, in the worlds of education and work for example; and in 'remedial socialization', the treatment of illness and social deviance. The awareness of the emotional needs of infants has already been greatly advanced in considerable part through the influence of this school of thought. In the care of babies and in the treatment of children in hospital, for example, the recognition that the fundamental relationship with parents or parent-figures is a key to healthy development is becoming wide-spread. It is notable that the findings of more experimental and positivist techniques of psychological investigation, through observational and longit-udinal studies, seem increasingly to confirm the general analytic perspective regarding the very early appearance of needs for stable relations with individual caring persons, and the disruptive effects of damaging these.

The recognition that the relational context of learning and development is crucial sometimes provides half-baked methodological premisses for much social work intervention. Attempts to meet the goals of analytic intervention without the resources or training needed for it have not of course been helpful to these ideas, though these problems could not easily have been avoided. The dependence of human development on affective relationships is one major implication of this theory, both in its account of the 'work' of normal develop-ment through the family and, even more, in what is required to make up any deficiencies of development through therapy or alternative care. In providing alternative education for disturbed or rejected children, for example, the staff requirements for schools are a factor of four or five times higher than is required for children who have been well supported in their relationships with normal schools and unpressured families. This society is becoming worried that human labour is becoming redundant. Even where industrial investment occurs, it is widely recognized that it will often intensify rather than reduce job loss. The transfer of work emphasis from machine-related to human-related activity, and the greater recognition of what can be accomplished — in emotional well-being, self-expression, culture, skill — through relationships in which development is the principal object, is therefore an appropriate one in a

33

society which could be within technological sight of the conquest of material scarcity.

This relational vision also enables Kleinian theory to make a contribution to the problems posed for socialists by the 'biological basis' of human experience. The recognition in work on bereavement, for example, that what matters to individuals is often their anxieties about the well-being of others, and the sense of their pain and loss being shared by others, constitutes a critical 'humanization' of a sphere of personal experience which industrial societies have notoriously found it hard to deal with as religious belief and practice have declined. Furthermore, the recognition that individuals identify deeply with others, and can regard themselves as to some degree living on through others, enables an idea of the primacy of the social over the individual to be created in socialist thought at a level much deeper and more emotionally significant than through the solidarities experienced through class or community alone. Biological parenthood is clearly extremely important in this regard, creating a sense of a life's contribution having been made and passed on, though there are many symbolic transferences of this formative model actually and possibly occurring. The pessimism arising from individualist philosophies comes partly from there being no meaning or reassurance in the idea of 'life after me', if the basic definition of existence, identity and meaning is the self alone. The circling of Kleinian (and psychoanalytic) theory around the experiences of the life cycle reveals its 'religious' character: that is to say, its address to questions of fundamental human experience of birth, sexuality and death, and also to the 'theodicy' of pain and evil. Socialist and humanistic perspectives cannot be silent on these matters, and if we wish to live in a secularized and humanistic world, some fundamental beliefs that enable us to live with these material and biological realities are necessary.

The great violence of contemporary society — pervasively in its military technology and preparations, but quite generally throughout its popular culture and increasingly perhaps in everyday experience — must also be attended to by socialists. The Kleinian recognition of the connection between violence and mental pain and anxiety, and its understanding of the mechanisms and techniques by which these are warded off and displayed by the self, provides a foundation for some serious address to these matters. The distinction of paranoid-schizoid and depressive positions, and the understanding of the amplifying qualities of persecution, give some leverage on the social processes by which violence and destructiveness in individuals (and groups) can be responded to. (See, for example, Segal [1987] on nuclear war.) The merit of this approach is that it does not practise an avoidance of the fact of envy and hatred, as many 'supportive' and well-meaning kinds of psychotherapeutic orientation do. It looks and is prepared, as it were, for the worst. But it also holds in mind an awareness of the pain and growth required to acknowledge the meaning and consequences of violence for the self and others, and to confront the damaged object relations from which it holds violence derives. The assumption that good object relations and reparation for past damage, in phantasy or reality, consti- tute a natural and desired condition of individuals makes possible a hopeful view of rehabilitation — though one must also say that a realistic application of this perspective would require recognizing much damage as irremediable in present conditions and knowledge.

Some consideration may usefully be given to 'law and order' issues from a psychoanalytic point of view. What has recently been happening has been a spiral of disruptive events and media responses to them, in which offences by muggers, terrorists, sex criminals or rioters are amplified into phantasies of a general persecution of the citizen. This then licenses ever more severe repres- ssion, in which it becomes permissible, because of the phantasied threat posed by wrongdoers, to remove normal legal restraints on policing. This was evident in such cases as the Iranian Embassy siege, the Yorkshire Ripper trial, and in the Southall and Brixton riots. (One could add the prosecution and wrongful imprisonment of the Guildford Four and the Birmingham Six.) While the political saliency of 'law and order' has been usefully shown to be to some degree a displacement of class conflicts, the unconscious dimensions of this process are also important.[15] Social democracy after the war offered a benign environmentalism as its main theory of deviant behaviour, arguing that if material and social conditions could be improved, criminal behaviour, especially among the young, would diminish. Little progress was achieved through this approach, except perhaps through the adoption of less inter- ventionist and therefore probably less harmful approaches to juveniles.[16] Sympathy for past and present deprivations is something less than a strategy for overcoming them, and those committed to 'social work' approaches seem to have been defined as merely 'soft' and easily pushed aside when law and order tensions have risen. It seems to me that some more rigorous theoretical consideration of these issues is required, using the more realistic approach towards destructiveness of Kleinian theory, if spirals of increasing persecution of both disaffiliated 'offenders' of various kinds and by punitive authorities are to be broken.

Central to a more radical approach is the recognition of the humiliation, rage and mental pain which lie at the roots of callous and sadistic behaviour. Deprivation sometimes imprints itself on the inner world and gives rise to effects not amenable to merely external remedy. Repression through imprisonment does nothing to modify such mental structures, and indeed often reinforces them and their consequent associations. Yet such states of mind must be attended to. What is needed is a determined commitment to effect self-understanding, and also the retention of belief that in some part of the self will persist a desire for relationships in which the self is felt to be trusted and valuable to others. How accessible and capable of growth this part of the self may be will depend on the extent of personal damage previously suffered. There is a deep pessimism in repressive approaches to crime, in which the authorities tacitly collude with prisoners' views of the normality of what they do. 'Containment' in the psychoanalytic sense is different and distinct from repression, in that while it requires that both potential victim and offender be protected from dangerous behaviour, it recognizes that safety can be achieved by means other than walls. Alcoholics Anonymous is in related matters a much more enlightened institution than most of the British custodial system.[17]

A potentially important concept in this alternative framework is that of reparation, experience of which may be important if individuals are to recover from a sense of irreparable damage inflicted on all around them. The development of community service alternatives to prison has probably come about in part through some intuitive sense of the psychological importance of this, but more important than symbolic reparation of a contractual kind may be enabling individuals to continue to remain connected and supportive to their families, and in their working capacities towards society at large, whatever their offence. The stigmatization, role-stripping and enforced uselessness of the prison system work in wholly negative directions, attacking all sense of worth and provoking antisocial reprisal. While these facts are no doubt obvious enough, it does seem that the absence of a developed theoretical account of human socialization that is adequate to understand the failures of the penal system has been a major lacuna of social policy. Much recent socialist criminology has tended simply to define a different set of problems — the class relations and biases of law, for example. While these are valid, this work also evades to a degree certain difficult realities of behaviour.

A more general conclusion can be drawn from these tentative applications of Kleinian theory to social concerns: that socialists must address themselves not only to material deprivation and its redress, but also to the quality and intensity of social relationships as prime criteria of value. Human powers and capacities are developed principally through relationships with others. In childhood, in creative work, in the attempted repair of personal damage, development is sustained by relationships which can recognize and absorb pain, and thus make possible growth and integration. Such insights into the social nature of human-kind, even of highly individual beings, have flowed into the socialist tradition from many sources — Marxist, Romantic, and even religious. The object-relations tradition in psychoanalysis offers a theorized view of these preconditions for human development, based on its particular understanding of infancy.

The utopian ideal of a simple undifferentiated community, in which alien-ation is overcome by virtue of allowing free development of each individual's powers, is incompatible with the qualities of performance, in many respects, that we have come to want in advanced industrial society. Specialization of function, for reasons of aesthetic choice and preference but also for reasons of technology, is an unavoidable and indeed beneficial fact. The most fortunate are sometimes the more specialized, not all those whose working skills could be learned by any adult in three weeks. Yet some contrary recognition of essential human equality is also needed if this is ever to be a social order providing a fulfilling life for all. The value placed on common human experiences, on the unavoidability of pain, and on the essential human importance of love and attention to others in Kleinian theory seems to be one version of such a universal ethic. Hegelian and Marxist views of human creativity are another and not incompatible version, connecting with object-relations theory through common interest in the preconditions of creativity. The realism of a perspective which makes us recognize the consequences and costs of our own actions — and especially in Kleinian theory, the pervasive presence of negative emotions in them — also has relevance to the problems of constructing a feasible socialist theory for this society. There will be competition and conflict in any conceiv-able social arrangement. Hostility must be contained and managed — if we attempt to deny its existence it will become more dangerous, not less. Individual and social differentiation is necessary and has positive consequences, as well as imposing limitations on us.

This outlook might suggest to socialists rather serious difficulties in the way of replacing the family as an institution. This is because of the emphasis Kleinian work places on depth of emotional commitment and understanding as the basis for containing the pain of development, both in infancy and in sub-sequent stages of life. A sufficient quality of care for children and also, for example, in illness and old age, is not easy to reproduce outside the lifelong commitments of the family. The paradox is felt by many socialists today that belief in intensity of commitment to others often leads back to rather than away from family connections, even though political convictions might suggest a preference for less ascriptive and less narrow attachments. The values placed on difference in Kleinian theory (difference of generation, life stage and gender as sources of growth) also casts doubt on ideological commitments to banish differentiation as divisive in some communal utopia. The Kleinian tradition is prone to view hostility to differentiation as mainly a defence against the pains of separation, jealousy and envy, at one lever or another.[18]

This is not, however, to argue for any ascriptive imposition of social attributes, such as those defined by gender. The commitment to the value of intense affective life is compatible with the view that it should be unconstrained by social convention and chosen by individual commitment. Both Freud's and Klein's researches into sexuality led not only to a forceful differentiation of male and female attributes, but also to the recognition that both were lodged to varying degrees within each individual. Commitment to the nurturing processes now sustained mostly by families is consistent with stronger social and institutional support for these processes, through the suffusion of other institutions — hospitals, schools, work-groups, and political and neighbour-hood associations — with the qualities of understanding and attachment for which procreative and parental relationships are taken by object-relations theory as the original model. The task of providing care, membership and identity in society plainly cannot be met through the restoration of some religious or ideological myth of the family, and such attempts at a conservative reaction as can now be seen (for example, to enforce parental discipline by law or to recriminalize abortion) are merely likely to worsen the problems to which they are a response. Commitments to the processes of familial relationship found in object-relations theory need not be regressive in these ways, but can instead enrich socialist ideas of what should be asked of wider social relationships and institutions.

These are unutopian assertions, needed if socialism is to face up to its present ideological crisis in responding (in a non-regressive way) to the conditions of advanced industrial and post-industrial life. But there is a utopian content also in object-relations theory: a commitment to the values of life, of relationship, of membership in a social community from birth, of creative development, and of a normal care for others, which properly form part of a socialist conception of humankind.

Notes

1. Raymond Williams's essay on 'The Bloomsbury Fraction' in his *Problems in Materialism and Culture*, NLB/Verso London 1980, indicates some of the roots of this connection.

2. In his 'The Idea of Equality', in P. Laslett and W.G. Runciman, eds, *Philosophy, Politics and Society*, Second series.

3. See W. Reich, *Character Analysis*, 1950.

4. H. Marcuse, *Eros and Civilization*, 1956.

5. For an account of Lacan's role in the recent development of psychoanalysis in France, see Sherry Turkle, *Psychoanalytic Politics*, New York 1978.

6. Cf. Nancy Chodorow, *The Reproduction of Mothering*, Berkeley 1978; and Dorothy Dinnerstein, *The Mermaid and the Minotaur*, New York 1976.

7. In the essay 'Problems of Materialism', in *Problems in Materialism and Culture* (1980).

8. There is a substantial and sympathetic account of the development of object-relations theory, including Klein's, in Harry Guntrip's *Personality Structure and Human Interaction* (1961). These object-relations approaches develop from the elements of Freud's work that had progressed furthest from its instinct-theory beginnings. Mrs Klein and her colleagues developed a theory of an 'internal world' of mental process in which phantasies of parental figures in their various parts and bodily functions, and as whole persons, are the principal elements. The work is distinguished by its attention to early infancy and its mental states; by its attention to the interrelationship of infancy and mother or mother-figure, in reality and fantasy; by a corresponding interest in the phenomena of the transference and the countertransference in psychoanalysis; by its exploration of psychotic states of mind, related to exploration of the primitive mental experiences of infants; by the autonomy it attributes to unconscious phantasy in development; and by its attention to envy and destructiveness as inescapable elements, to some degree, in development. Later work in this tradition, for example by W.R. Bion, developed further the phenomenological direction of Klein's work. His *Second Thoughts* (1978) is a particularly brilliant collection of papers on primitive mental states as they are observed in analysis. Another analyst, Donald Meltzer, has sought to systematize this evolution of psychoanalysis from Freud to Bion in *The Kleinian Development* (1978). Hanna Segal's *Introduction to the Work of Melanie Klein* (1975) and Isca Salzberger-Wittenberg's *Psycho-Analytic Insight and Relationships: a Kleinian Approach* (1970) are brief introductions to Kleinian ideas, though the Guntrip volume has a fuller discussion of the intellectual context. He also discusses in this volume other British work in the object-relations tradition. The emphasis of this, especially the work of D.W. Winnicott, is more environmental; the concept of 'good enough mother', for example, suggests a more externalist explanation (in terms of environmental failure) of mental pain and pathology than the Kleinians'. These are, however, in large part differences of emphasis; the object-relations school has absorbed many of Klein's idea even though some issues — for example, the importance of envy and hate — remain matters of contention. Bibliographies of Melanie Klein's own work are given in the secondary sources noted above.

9. Interest in the processes and disorders of thought have been a major emphasis of later Kleinian work, for example by H. Rosenfeld in *Psychotic States* (1965), in many works by W.R. Bion, and by Meltzer and his colleagues; for example, Meltzer *et al., Explorations in Autism* (1975). This interest develops from Melanie Klein's own work on very early mental states, and the extreme psychological disorders which they provide a means of understanding.

10. Melanie Klein's book *Envy and Gratitude* (1975b) is one of the clearest statements of her later views. Further exploration of Klein's own work might be made through *Our Adult World and its Roots in Infancy* (1963), *Narrative of a Child Analysis* (1961), and the collection of Klein's papers published as *The Selected Melanie Klein*, ed. Juliet Mitchell (1986).

11. Most substantially in the work of Adrian Stokes, published complete as *Critical Writings*, vols 1–3 (1978) and as a Penguin selection as *The Image in Form* (1972). There are also a number of important theoretical papers: for example, Segal's *A Psychoanalytical Approach to Aesthetics*, reprinted in M. Klein, P. Heimann and R. Money-Kyrle, eds, *New Directions in Psycho-Analysis* (1985). Other object-relations theory has also been fertile in this field; see, for example, M. Milner's *On Not Being Able to Paint* (1957) and D.W. Winnicott's *Playing and Reality* (1971).

12. Raymond Williams's *Culture and Society* (1958) is still the most important attempt to recover these various pre-socialist critiques of industrial capitalism, and relate them to a contemporary socialism.

13. See H.V. Dicks's *Fifty Years of the Tavistock Clinic* (1970).

14. David Holbrook's *English for Maturity* (1961) and *English for the Rejected* (1964) argue for a creative use of literature in the secondary modern school, the latter work making some use of Kleinian theory. His argument about pornography is in *The Masks of Hate* (1972).

15. For example in Stuart Hall *et al.*, eds, *Policing the Crisis* (1978).

16. See J. Packman, *The Child's Generation* (1976) and also J. Clarke, 'Social Democratic Delinquents and Fabian Families', in M. Fitzgerald *et al.*, eds, *Permissiveness and Control* (1979).

17. An interesting theoretical approach to AA is given in Gregory Bateson's essay, 'The Cybernetics of Self: a Theory of Alcoholism', in his *Steps Towards an Ecology of Mind* (1972).

18. It should be acknowledged that psychoanalytic ideas of all kinds undoubtedly emerge from traditions which might be described as some of the most enlightened and creative aspects of liberal individualism. While object-relations theory in Britain has a particularly familial and therefore social inflection, it does not by this means escape its bourgeois inheritance. The relations between bourgeois and socialist theory are often not simple, however, and attitudes to this legacy raise problems similar to those arriving from other achievements of bourgeois culture which socialists do not have the option of 'replacing' except with enormous loss.

2

Psychoanalysis and Social Justice*

The questions I want to deal with in this chapter concern whether psychoanalysis contributes or can contribute anything to our idea of a good society. Is it, as some people think, merely a privilege that only a minority could possibly have, the indulgence of having personal problems examined and thought about at great expense of time and money, a really *Hampstead* kind of activity? How could the non-availability of psychoanalysis possibly be considered an *injustice*, when it seems so difficult to imagine psychoanalysis in any form as a common experience?

This issue was given a particular focus by press reports *à propos* threats to the funding of the Tavistock Clinic, which suggested that it was difficult to justify the priority given to psychoanalytically based treatment at a time of National Health Service economies. The implication in these reports was that psychoanalysis is too expensive; that it treats too few people for the resources involved; and perhaps also that the people it does treat are not those most needing or deserving of treatment — 'merely a few hundred neurotics', one report in the *Observer* said.

But there is a more general reason why this is an appropriate place to be discussing the question of the social value of psychoanalytic psychotherapy. This is because the Tavistock is unusual in being an institution where psychoanalytic methods are practised and taught, to a variety of different professional disciplines, within the National Health Service. Patients are accepted, like others in the NHS, on grounds of need, and the treatment services provided are

---

*This chapter originated as a talk in the Tavistock Winter Lecture Series, in November 1983.

free to those who receive them. I'm told that even people who are referred as patients to the Tavistock sometimes find this hard to believe. The NHS is an area of national life in Britain in which a particular egalitarian idea of justice — 'to each according to his need' — has been widely implemented and believed in. It has been built on the principle that it is socially just for those needing medical treatment to receive it, regardless of ability to pay. In this entitlement at least, the NHS defines all people as equal. Richard Titmuss, in his inspiring book *The Gift Relationship* (1970) — which is about the system of blood-donorship, and unfavourably compares systems in which blood is *sold* with our system in which blood is *given* — drew attention to the element of altruism, of moral identification with others, which is involved in this wider national health system for which we all pay without regard to our immediate and personal benefit. This public commitment to a national health service provided in response to need seems to have survived the attrition of the Thatcher era, to judge from many public opinion surveys.

Psychoanalytic treatment at the Tavistock and similar institutions now finds a small place in the total provision of free health care, in accordance with an egalitarian conception of social justice. Is it right that it should be so provided? If it is, should there be more of it? What conceptions of health, development, and the social good does psychoanalysis presuppose? These are the questions I want to look at.

Social justice and injustice are pretty strong concepts. When we talk about justice and injustice we are talking about rights and wrongs, not just about conditions that might be vaguely desirable or undesirable. There is an important distinction, brought out in an interesting article on these themes some years ago by an American sociologist, Ralph H. Turner (1969), between *injustice* and *misfortune*. A misfortune is a lack or a happening against which we have no right to seek remedy. An injustice, on the other hand, is a condition which should not occur, and which we can make claims on others to see put right, if it does. Turner points out that what counts as a misfortune or an injustice in society is subject to historical change, and redefinition over time. For example, slavery was once defined by most people in England merely as a misfortune for the slave, but later became redefined as an injustice against which all civilized people were expected to act. Turner argues that we can see a general enlarge-ment and shift in the recent history of Western society in the meanings of justice and injustice. First, from the seventeenth century onwards, it came to be argued that political subjection was an injustice, and not an inevitable human condition. The absence of the rights of free assembly and speech, and to participate in choosing governments, became gradually elevated to the status of an injustice, as a 'just society' (sometimes going back to the model of the Ancient Greeks) was defined as a society which conferred rights of political equality on all its citizens. Then, as the next great stage in this evolution, poverty and economic subjection became defined as injustices. This happened partly because the concept of freedom that liberals had been using was extended to include a material dimension. Freedom under the law was perceived to be of little use to those who were so poor that they lacked the means to exercise it. Under the pressure of this enlarged definition of freedom and justice, governments began to take responsibility for guaranteeing minimum living standards as the condition of a just society — for example in the provision of different kinds of social security, minimum housing standards, and the like.

Ralph Turner described these two earlier conceptions of injustice as liberal-humanitarian and socialist, and traced their respective influence on the politics of the United States. The post-Depression and subsequently post-war era was mainly dominated, he argued, by economic or what he called socialist ideas, until the 1960s brought another change of emphasis. In the late 1960s, when Turner's article was written, concerns with questions of identity and personal fulfilment rose to a new prominence. 'Alienation' became a much-used concept in social criticism, and the state and other social institutions like the universities were denounced for their depersonalizing and demoralizing effects. Where the bourgeoisie had been the class most prominent in the social movement for liberal rights, and the working class had been the main bearer of demands for economic rights, claims for enhanced personal meaning and identity were advanced first by movements of students and the young. Since Turner's article was written, the rise of feminist, 'green', ethnic and other social movements has vastly widened this agenda of 'qualitative' demands.

The ideas of the major British theorist of the concept of social citizenship, T.H. Marshall (1963), also clarify these mutable definitions of human rights and claims. Marshall's subtle and complex account of the development of rights in Britain also offered a three-stage historical model, although since he wrote before Turner, his final stage is in effect Turner's second. Marshall, influenced by the functionalist ideas dominant in British sociology after the war, describes how civil, political and social conceptions of citizenship become differentiated in industrial societies, as institutional functions become distinct from one another. Rights and powers became functionally separated but geographically unified, with the rise of the nation-state. Marshall locates the rise of civil, political and social citizenship in Britain in the eighteenth, nineteenth and twentieth centuries, respectively. He thus gives Turner's 'liberal humanitarian' concept of injustice two components: the first concerned with civil rights – or what Isaiah Berlin calls 'negative freedoms' – and the second with political rights, or 'positive freedoms'. (This reflects the fact that in Britain individual freedom under the law long preceded an inclusive democracy, if indeed the latter has yet been fully achieved.) Marshall's concept of 'social' rights is close to Turner's 'socialist' idea of injustice, though in Marshall's account it is used to describe and explain the rise of the British welfare state. Marshall sees the development of rights – for example, to a minimum income, to education, to improved housing, and to health care – as social rights intended to remove unjustified inequalities, but still within the framework of a class-stratified society, with whose market principles these ideas of social citizenship remain in continuing tension. Whilst Marshall is describing some 'rights' of a diffuse and qualitative kind (to education and health care, for example), his own main concern, before the rise of the new social movements of the late 1960s, was with the redress of economic inequalities.

Nevertheless, qualitative claims cannot be separated from the thinking and practice which underlay the development of the British welfare state. Claims made for desirable standards of health care, education and childcare already placed 'qualitative' claims on the agenda, albeit within a less individualistic and libertarian social order in which support for the family was a primary goal of public policy. Psychoanalysts such as Bowlby had some influence in this earlier phase of welfare policy, just as one can argue for the centrality of psychoanalytic concepts at the present time, as I do here.

One person's right of entitlement must be someone or some institution's obligation, if it is to be a right at all. The issue arises: how can rights of such a diffuse kind as the rights to enabling conditions of life described here be capable of being enforced, of being made into any institution's duties? It is clearly much easier to make an entitlement to a material benefit enforceable than a right to experience a process of care, or personal development, or human consideration. The possibility of quantifying and standardizing a benefit brings it within the potential scope of legal justice more readily than services such as physical or mental health, where what is appropriate or good unavoidably requires professional judgement.

But the state already assumes responsibility for many 'qualitative' services, and long ago developed procedures of measurement, monitoring and inspection to ensure their standard. Mostly these procedures are made the responsibility of officials, not ordinary citizens. Even when things go wrong – for example, in the spheres of health or childcare — it is other professionals or judges, not juries of ordinary citizens, who are usually asked to investigate and report, by means of committee or court or inquiry. There is scope and need for a much larger involvement of citizens not merely in making laws or administering policy, through decentralized government or an enlarged voluntary sector, but also in a quasi-judicial role of inspection and review of the delivery of services. In this way, citizens' rights to appropriate standards of service or treatment might be become more enforceable, and public providers be exposed to judgements concerning the adequacy of what they provide. I have developed these ideas more fully elsewhere (Rustin, 1991).

Another way of looking at the issue of social justice which is relevant to the question of identity and meaning has been developed by Michael Walzer in his book *Spheres of Justice: A Defence of Pluralism and Equality* (1983). Walzer argues that the essence of justice is respect for the values of each distinctive sphere of life, and preventing their invasion by the one-dimensional values of wealth or political ideology. As society becomes more complex and differentiated, so the range of values and human possibilities also extends. Within this framework, which stresses a trend towards increasing social variety and complexity, we can see that the needs of personal development claim increasing attention and become one of the goals which people seek through relationships of kinship or friendship, through education, through work and culture. Psychoanalysis thus has its place as one such 'sphere of justice', with its own criteria of value.

One problem in the contemporary debates about social justice is the way in which the concept of 'fraternity' has often been squeezed out in the battles between the advocates of 'liberty' (which often turns out to mean mainly economic liberty) and 'equality'. The danger is that a predominantly material and acquisitive definition of human ends is assumed or taken for granted, and the political argument is then only about the rules governing acquisition, about how the weak or strong are to be protected or guaranteed access to material benefits. Once the argument seems to be only about relative claims to the same material goods and opportunities, and no longer about a different and more fraternal or caring conception of society, it becomes difficult to maintain any active commitment to the idea of equality. The current backlash against equalitarian notions by the supporters of individualism and acquisitiveness has occurred in part because of the failure of implementation, and the consequent erosion, of normative conceptions of social justice. It was because *political* strategies for achieving greater equality failed during successive governments that there was a reversion to more sectional and economistic strategies by trade unions.

Ultimately, these demands became open to appropriation by the Thatcherites, one of whose most potent appeals in 1979 was to skilled workers, for a restoration of 'free collective bargaining'. The failure of collectivism was symbolized in the public service workers' strike, during the 'winter of discontent' of 1978–9. While the revolt of low-paid workers might be fully justified by the burdens unfairly placed on them by Labour's counter-inflation policies, it also in certain instances struck cruelly at the idea that public services should represent some more altruistic mode of organization.

Now I regard one of the main contributions of psychoanalysis and especially psychoanalysis of the object-relations or British School, which predominates in the Tavistock, to be its contribution to a more social, interdependent and fraternal view of human nature and human ends. I suppose 'familial' might be a more accurate word than fraternal; there is more stress in this way of thinking on the importance of parenting and containing roles, both within families and out of them, than on relationships between siblings. Freud himself, especially in his social and cultural writings, was preoccupied with the poor 'fit' between innate human appetites and impulses and the social structure; and his writing leaves little scope for an optimistic outcome, except in fortunate individual cases, from the tragic contradictions between unconscious wish and social possibility. But some of his successors — and especially psychoanalysts following Melanie Klein, who studied the emotional developments of infants — were able to outline in a more positive way the preconditions for human development. Even the exploration of the extreme conditions which arise when these conditions are lacking — through the inability of a mother to bear the feelings evoked in her by a baby, for example — has enabled us to understand better the preconditions of health. An example of such work is *Psychotherapy with Severely Deprived Children*, edited by Mary Boston and Rolene Szur (1983). What all this work has done is to install as its central concept of human life an idea of a capacity for development, which can be either nurtured or aborted. The ability of care-givers, whether parents or others, to tolerate or contain painful feelings, and to think about their experience, has been shown to be critical to the support of development. The concep;t of 'maternal reverie' (a brilliantly evocative description of the intense preoccupation of mothers with their young babies, of heightened sensitivity and identification) is an example of this necessary absorption in the experience of the infant, from an early stage of life.

Interest in what happens in the relationships of infants and their mothers, from the moments of birth onwards (Miller *et al.*, 1989) has given the idea of emotional and psychic development a central place in the psychoanalytic account of human life. The process of growth of cognitive, emotional and moral capacities has been found to depend above all on the quality of relationship between the infant and those who care for him or her. While subsequent research in other psychological traditions has usefully measured the stages of growth, the earliest moments of recognition and interaction, and so on, it was psychoanalysts who first insisted that the infant was a 'person', so to speak, almost from the beginning. The psychoanalytic study of infancy, especially through the direct observation of mothers and babies in the infants' first two years of life, has given its distinctive attention to feelings and unconscious conceptions, but argues that these inner states are the keys to more outward changes.

The emotional developments which occur during infancy are, of course, not only within the child but also, and sometimes to a frightening degree, in the parent or other care-givers. Psychoanalysts and psychotherapists have thus been led by these observations of infancy to an interest in development in other phases of the life cycle. The experience of parenthood is one such extension, but since analytic therapists are called upon to treat people who are ill or in emotional pain of various kinds, other phases of life have also been investigated — for example, states of bereavement, and the understanding of the ageing process as one which requires the acceptance of loss, and depends for its tolerability on identification with persons and values which can survive an individual's departure or death. The work of Colin Murray Parkes (1975) and of Lily Pincus (1981b) on these questions are well-known examples.

So psychoanalytic research has helped to identify the social conditions — that is to say, the relationships — within which psychic development and integration can take place, and those in which it will be likely to fail, sometimes with catastrophic results. This research has focused especially on critical events within the life cycle — childbirth, infancy, adolescence, ageing and loss — which are biologically determined in the first instance, but depend for their human quality and meaning on the conditions of relationship and understanding within which they occur.

The idea of development and fulfilment of the person through relationship, both internal and external, which is implicit in this psychoanalytic account, is a distinctively *social* one. I want to stress this point — it might seem obvious — because it goes against the widespread idea that society will be better when and if we merely give more opportunity and goods to the *individual*. It is the quality of relationships that individuals can generally have with others around them — and we must include phantasied and symbolic others — which make for contentment and creativity, not merely gratifications of various kinds. The most beautiful house with a swimming pool is obtained at a serious psychic price when there has to be an armed man at the gate to keep out intruders. Serious damage must also be done to the quality of experience of 'liberty' when its defence depends on threats to inflict total destruction.

It is often easier for people to recognize the dependence of children on the relationships that surround them than to see that this is also true of adults. The National Heath Service's greater generosity towards the psychoanalytic treatment of children and families, through child guidance clinics and the like, than of adults, is an instance of this particular commitment to the young. Another partial exception is made for the family by the believers in individualism; it is held by some to be the proper place for care and altruism in a world otherwise to be run on competitive principles. But these 'concessions' to humankind's social nature don't, for me, go far enough. They don't sufficiently recognize that adults too develop through relationship, and that families work best — perhaps only work at all — when the environment they depend on fits their needs: needs for safe neighbourhoods, for available work, for understanding received in childbirth or from their doctor, for help when the children are small. Families, especially the small families of today, can't provide all these things for their members unaided, and if we are committed to a high quality of family relationships of different kinds, we also need to be concerned about the conditions on which these depend.

Especially in recent years, through the influence of Wilfred Bion and others, psychoanalysts in this British tradition have come to stress the importance of emotional understanding in development (see Meltzer, 1978). Of course the understanding of unconscious meaning is what psychoanalysis has always been about, since Freud, but what has particularly grown in recent times is a recognition that it is mental states in the here and now, not merely in the traces and unconscious residues of the past, that have to be borne and attended to if learning of any kind is to take place. This working principle of the consulting room can be transferred into other settings. The distinctive quality of a setting — a classroom, a nursery or a family — is that if people are to learn and grow, someone needs to be there who is capable of *thinking* about what is going on, and of helping others to do so. Psychoanalytic education at the Tavistock Clinic — especially those activities whose purpose is to enhance ordinary working skills, and not to train clinical therapists as such — is substantially devoted to developing these capacities. The pre-clinical psychoanalytic observation course for childcare workers of various kinds, or the Tavistock–Leicester Group Relations conferences, are examples of what I mean.

What is the connection between all these ideas and social justice? I suggest that we can begin to define justice as the provision of opportunities for emotional and psychic, as well as other kinds of development. Psychoanalysis has already taught us a lot about what these opportunities depend on, and I shall give some examples of conditions of this kind — mainly concerning the development of children — which we are beginning to know with reasonable certainty. When one defines these as conditions of 'social justice', it means of course that we can protest at the society or its institutions which fail to meet them. They cease to be misfortunes once they are well enough understood to be within human powers to remedy.

One example (Menzies Lyth, 1983) can be taken from the treatment of young children in hospital and the importance of the parents' role in this. Psychoanalytic observations and findings, as well as other long-term studies of outcomes, have been important in showing that separation from parental care through hospitalization is liable to produce subsequent setbacks to development, as well as immediate unnecessary pain. It turns out that even with newborn premature babies, whose needs might seem to lie exclusively in the physical and medical domain, the damage to early relationships that can come about if parents are not involved in frequent contact with their baby often leads to long-term harm. Interestingly, in relation to our argument that psychic development is important for adults as well as children, this separation at a critical time can lead to impairment of the bonding capacity of the mother as well as the child.

Another example — regrettably by no means widely accepted or implemented — is the understanding of the need for constancy and stability in the care of young children. Research at the Tavistock (Menzies Lyth, 1988a) has shown that improvements could be achieved by institutions devoted to the care of infants — day nurseries, for example — if they understood the importance of personal attachments to one or two care-givers, and the harm that results when care is indiscriminate or impersonal. It seems clear that for children under three, the care of mother and/or mother-substitute is normally best. But we also need to understand the pressures that sometimes prevent this from being the method of care chosen — which may be material, or the result of loneliness, distress or isolation — and devise, as social workers have sometimes done with single mothers, ways of alleviating these difficulties and of supporting parents' relationships with their young children.

We might still regard it as merely a misfortune if a young child finds itself hospitalized without its mother, or in a day nursery where it has no stable relationship with anyone. But we should perhaps regard it as a social injustice, and hope that this will be widely recognized as such when such understanding has been more widely assimilated.

This reminds us that one of the most important contributions of psychoanalysis is to the understanding of why individuals or institutions often *don't* make use of their knowledge, or even act in accordance with what is apparently perfectly obvious. Isobel Menzies Lyth's (1960) work on institutional defences against pain, in the nursing procedures of hospitals, is well known, and Melanie Klein described the destructive effects of the envy of new knowledge as an obstruction of learning and development within psychoanalysis. The Tavistock's counselling courses for teachers explore these issues in relation to school and college education. More generally, we can say that learning involves exposure to the necessity for change, and requires a giving-up of omnipotence by individuals or groups for whom 'not knowing' may be a source of fear and threat. Sociologists tend perhaps to overstress the social aspects of these issues, and thus lean towards an environmentalist view – the idea that if the institutional arrangements are all right, then development can take place. But the particular contribution of Kleinian psychoanalysis has been to show that there are internal resistances to development too – sometimes unconscious ones. This obliges us to recognize that development can be made possible, but cannot be programmed or forced.

We have to recognize that these are difficult elaborations of the idea of justice extending into these subtle areas of relationship and understanding. (But of course all the previous enlargements of the idea of justice were difficult in their time too.) The 'goods' we are talking about are not as measurable as economic commodities, nor as definite and codifiable as legal rights. Even though we can assert that human beings do have common qualities – the vulnerability to mental pain and the capacity for learning are universal and don't depend on wealth or status or educational qualifications – it is not easy to lay down uniform standards in these areas, as it is for a balanced diet or so much house-room per person. I will now explore some of the difficulties of enlarging the concept of 'social justice' in these ways.

Once we start to define human needs and possibilities in more than material terms, we have to recognize that the 'equality' with which we are concerned is the equal opportunity to be different, to find one's own personal and original way of being a child, a parent, or a creative worker of some kind. The problem is to clarify the social conditions and practices which will alow for such individuality and differentiation, and will not then be consumed by the *individualism* — the self-centredness and disregard of the needs of others — which is easily confused with it. The National Heath Service, with all its imperfections and attrition, is still the finest practical example in this country of an attempt to assert such a minimum condition of citizenship as one necessary condition for making possible individual experience.

Another difficulty in implementing such a diffuse conception of social justice is that the nurturing of development through relationship and understanding — whether in families and schools, or through psychotherapy — requires above all sensitivity to the individual case. It must be a very delicate and complicated social mechanism which both asserts a common principle — the right to care and development for all in a good society — yet can actualize it only by allowing discretion, autonomy and variation in each instance. This is, however, the situation when children are sent to school. We expect them to be given opportunities to grow, but have to leave it to the teachers to create these conditions in the way they know best. Standards can change over time: to take an extreme case, children were once expected to work in mines and factories. But norms can also change to accommodate more subtle understandings of what children's and parents' needs are, and institutions gradually learn to assimilate these different and more 'human' ways of thinking. I've already given some examples of this, for example in the treatment of children in hospital. We might hope that institutions would generally become more sensitive to the effects of sudden changes and separations, and would take care over them, as many already do. An example is the provision which good schools make for the settling-in of new pupils.

Not least, if any real development is to take place for individuals, we have to recognize the importance of choice and responsibility. Even the best and most responsive care doesn't automatically lead to good results; its recipients, sometimes for reasons best explained by psychoanalysis, don't always make a benign introjection of and identification with the good object. This freedom just has to be accepted — perhaps real learning cannot be programmed. In the case of psychoanalysis or psychotherapy, for example, development can't be made to take place, and there has to be a right not to come, or to walk out, as a condition of genuine co-operation.

One might be tempted to think that other kinds of 'social justice' could more easily be introduced by legislation or fiat than could a social environment favourable to growth. But it is probably more true to say that complicated kinds of shared learning have been necessary for all social advances. The right to vote was conceded after many decades of campaigning, and the meaningful exercise of political rights takes dedication and co-operation by many people too. Legislation requiring compulsory schooling also only provides a framework, within which teachers and pupils and families have to make something. The law also provides a framework, but it is shared understandings and standards of practice that give the rights we acquire under the law a real substance. The same will be true — even more so — in these more subtle areas of relationship and institutional practice.

I've been trying to suggest, then, that the understandings achieved by psycho-analytic work into the conditions for favourable development of children and adults can be incorporated into the working of social institutions, and become part of our legitimate expectations of them. But what about the provision of psychoanalysis itself? Is it reasonable to imagine that psychoanalytic treatment — whether classical psychoanalysis, or less intensive forms of analytic psycho-therapy — could be widely available as a right, in the way that we might now expect the best medical treatments for physical illnesses to be? Or to put this another way: how much of an injustice is it that psychoanalysis — certainly for adults — is now much more easily available for those who can afford to pay for it privately than for those who cannot?

One difficulty here is that psychoanalysis is valuable as a means of achieving further development in individuals who would not normally be regarded as 'mentally ill', as well as in the treatment of those who without it cannot live anything like normal lives. Psychoanalytic thinking has helpfully blurred the boundary between the 'ill' and the 'healthy', recognizing that most people have more-or-less healthy and more-or-less ill aspects to their personality, and seeing that these change in their balance with life circumstances. This has been helpful, in that it has made possible a more understanding and compassionate view of mental illness, and greater confidence in the treatment of it. But it can also lead to the idea within certain social groups (it seems to be so in parts of the United States, for example) that 'therapies' of various kinds should be routinely available as aids to living and development. I think this is a less helpful idea.

It is certainly true that in Britain the availability of psychoanalytic therapy, especially outside the London area, is much too restricted. There is a great disparity between the quality and kinds of care available to children and families, for example, who live in the Home Counties and in a very few other cities, and the rest of the country. The same is true of adult psychoanalysis. For those who believe in the value of analytic psychotherapy it should be a high priority to see other centres like the Tavistock set up outside London: public discussion should be about this, rather than about reducing the little that exists.

Nevertheless, we also have to face up to the real limitations of what would ever be possible, and perhaps desirable, in regard to the wide provision of psychoanalysis. This is partly a consequence of its extreme labour-intensiveness. Intensive psychoanalysis involves, according to classic procedures, five sessions per week of fifty minutes each. A personal analysis might be expected to take at a minimum three years, and perhaps six or seven. Simple calculation shows that a single psychoanalyst would have been working hard to have treated ten intensive patients in a three-year period. This potential 'output' can be multiplied quite a bit if one allows for short-term and less frequent analytic therapies which, in the Tavistock Clinic and elsewhere, have been developed with considerable success. Nor should one be too formalistic about what is to count as 'psychoanalysis', so far as frequency of treatment is concerned. The insistence on 'orthodox' methods can be a means of defending the prestige and power of professional psychoanalytic institutions as well as of maintaining high standards of work. Psychoanalytic methods can be used in treatments of different frequency and intensity, and patients differ in regard to those which they can use with most benefit. Nevertheless, when all is said and done, it is still very costly compared, for example, with the throughput and patient caseload that is expected of the GP's surgery.[1]

A further limitation seems to me to be in the delicacy and difficulty of the work of psychoanalysis and analytic psychotherapy, and the real difficulties of expanding the numbers of persons capable of doing it to a sufficient standard. While there are hundreds of thousands of schoolteachers, and tens of thousands of lecturers in higher education, there are currently in Britain merely a few hundred psychoanalysts and psychoanalytic psychotherapists, whether for children or adults. Training is very slow, and the base from which it begins is very small. There should be more. But it isn't likely — perhaps not even possible — that there will be *that* many more. Perhaps one should hope mainly for the establishment of a few other centres for this work in other major cities.

Does this then make one resigned to a pessimistic or elitist view that psycho-analysis must just be for the fortunate and privileged minority, and has little value for the rest of society? I don't think so. The fortunate thing about changes in understanding brought about by the social sciences — and in this I include psychoanalysis — is that they can be and are assimilated over time into everyday knowledge and understanding. They become part of our common sense. It took exceptional knowledge and skill to discover, for example, that premature babies can suffer in their later development from early separation from their mothers, if cared for without human contact in incubators, and so on. (This was a matter of detailed observation and statistical research, and also of the psychoanalytic understanding of the relationship of mother and baby in the first weeks, which explained why its interruption could be so devastating.) But once discovered and recognized, this finding could be readily assimilated into practice. This is to draw attention to the important research function of psychoanalytic work.

It is also important to distinguish between prevention and treatment. In emotional and mental illnesses, as in other kinds, damage is usually hard to repair once it has become well established. If everyday practice can be improved — for example, in the care of children, and support for their parents and others in carrying it out — there will be fewer casualties. The deepest and most far-reaching improvements that are likely to come from psychoanalytic work are in the prevention rather than the treatment of illness, including the preventive measures that come from a wider everyday awareness of emotional needs and vulnerabilities.

This is not to say that even costly treatments may not sometimes be the most effective and most economical available. The costs of containing individuals who have suffered permanent emotional damage — in children's homes, or in prisons, or through long-term incapacity and medication, or in hospitals — are, as we all know, enormous, and the improvement shown for all this effort is very little. The recent study of *Psychotherapy with Severely Deprived Children* (Boston and Szur, 1983) referred to earlier has some moving examples of personal development that can be achieved by psychoanalytic work, even with the most difficult and hostile young patients. Some of this work may make a lifetime's difference to the fate of these children.

Change can be diffused at the level of personal skills, as well as institutional practice. One can imagine a greater level of emotional awareness — partly through the influence of psychoanalytic work — becoming more widely diffused in everyday life, without this leading to a general desperation or mere fashion for 'therapy'. Where people experience their society as being more 'in touch' with their needs, most of them will manage to grow and develop, and professional help should be needed only for small numbers with particular difficulties.

Psychoanalysis is not the only form of knowledge which is leading in the direction of a greater emotional understanding. It would be surprising if such a substantial movement for the improvement of lives in qualitative and emotional respects were being sustained by psychoanalytic ideas alone. We can note, for example, as parallels, changes in attitude that are occurring towards childbirth, through the Natural Childbirth Trust, and the emotional support more widely expected, in some social milieux at least, from husbands in the experience of birth. We can see the development of the pre-school playgroup movement as a recognition of mothers' needs to share with each other the responsibilities of looking after young children, given also the wider commitment to maintaining independence and working identities among women. This movement has also been a means of creating or re-creating communities in modern urban settings where they are often lacking. The idea of development through play and contact with other children is one which the playgroup movement shares with the nursery school and the infant school. This educational philosophy has some links with the approach to development of child analysis, in its origins as well as in current practice.

So in conclusion, I think that psychoanalysis *has* contributed towards a broader and richer conception of 'social justice' in many important and often indirect ways. It has been a source of crucial research findings which — as in the work of John Bowlby, for example — enable us to redefine the ways in which institutions can best meet human needs. Capacities for emotional understanding can be extended well beyond the individual work of psychoanalysts and psychotherapists themselves; for example, through the programmes for members of other 'helping professions' which the Tavistock Clinic has offered over the years. Such emotional capacities can be more widely learned, as people are formed in their own lives by the experience of more understanding relationships and by work settings which are adapted to their development.

And where psychoanalysis and analytic therapies provide the best forms of treatment to repair damage that has been done, or to treat individuals or families who are in great pain and difficulty, it is right that such treatment should be available on the same basis of entitlement by need as other forms of medicine. A 'right to health care' implies that individuals should be able to receive the available form of care and treatment which is most appropriate to their needs. I've suggested reasons why analytic psychotherapy is always likely to be a scarce resource. Considerations of social justice thus suggest that a good proportion of it should be provided either to those who most need it, because of illness or incapacity, or to those whose use of analysis in training will help them to contribute to the welfare of others. The alleviation and overcoming of mental pain makes claims of the same kind as the relief of physical pain: it should be given in relation to the degree of suffering, and the possibility of help, not the possession of wealth or privilege. The latter are invasions, in Michael Walzer's terms, of this specific 'sphere of justice'. The commitment of institutions such as the Tavistock Clinic and Institute over many years to such needs, both of individuals and communities, which it has expressed through its research work, its training programmes and its provision of treatment, have been unusual and exemplary, and its work should be vigorously defended.

Notes

1. It would be beneficial to extend the GP's role and training to include recognition of the emotional aspects of illness, which contribute to a significant proportion of presented symptoms. This work has also been pioneered in the Tavistock Clinic's catchment area.

3

Psychoanalysis, Racism and Anti-Racism

Race in Social Science

'Race' is both an empty category and one of the most destructive and powerful forms of social categorization. How is this paradox to be explained, and how are its negative consequences for human lives to be resisted? These are the central issues to be explored in this chapter.

Amongst the attributes that can be chosen as grounds for categorizing people, those of race are widely recognized to have the least power to explain any significant differences between them.[1] The distinctions of national culture, religion and class mark out some significant properties and differences between members of groups defined in these terms.[2] To share the assumptions of the dominant culture of France, in regard to such matters as the meaning of 'culture', the proper role of the state, or the significance of food, is to think differently from English middle-class society about these aspects of life. To be brought up as a member of a Nonconformist Protestant community is to share beliefs, habits of thought, a particular cast of moral feeling, distinct from those of a Roman Catholic, a Jew, or a humanistic atheist. Equally, to share the values of a class or status group is to hold some set of implicit attitudes, derived ultimately from the common economic situation of those similarly positioned.

Such differences are likely to be expressed by the choice of distinct principles and habits of classification, expressing not so much a clear opposition to other groups as different principles of cognitive and moral selection. Of course, where groups are antagonistically placed in relation to one another (Protestants and Catholics; rival nationalities; opposed social classes) there will also be disagreements of an explicit kind — members of one group will be forced to take note, in a negating way, of the dominant definitions of the other's existence. But even in such cases of open antagonism, there will probably be positive as well as negative grounds of identity. A Protestant is not merely a bundle of non-Catholic characteristics; even more obviously this is true of national identities; class identities, even if formed in relation to antagonistic classes, usually develop some positive values and categorizations of their own, which do not need the threat of the other class to keep them in being.

In most imaginable societies, one might expect there to be structured differences based on shared membership of a specific community, over a period of time and generations, and shared geographical space.[3] One would expect some clustering of individuals around shared views of the sacred or transcendental, which can clearly take very divergent forms. Economically stratified or divided societies (so far there are hardly any societies except the simplest kinds which are not so divided) are likely to generate different ways of thinking among those differently placed in them. One could add other axes of differentiation, based on other characteristics which have major effects on human experience — gender or age, for example.

By contrast with this series of attributes, differences of biological race are largely lacking in substance. Racial differences go no further, in their essence, than superficial variations in bodily appearance and shape — modal tallness of different groups, colour of skin, facial shape, hair, etc. Given the variations that occur within so-called racial groups, and give rise to no general categorizations or clusterings (the physically stronger, more symmetrically featured, larger, leaner, etc.), it is hard to find any significance in these differences except those which are quite arbitrarily assigned to them. (As Van den Berghe points out,[4] even physical visibility has been lacking in important cases of racism as a ground of distinction — the Nazis compelled Jews to wear the Star of David because they were not readily identifiable as Jews. Their methods of categorizing Jews [by criteria of descent] were thus as bureaucratic as their procedures for extermination.) Racial differences depend on the definition given to them by the other — that is to say, on the definition of the other — and the most powerful definitions of these kinds are those which are negative — definitions that we can call racist. Because the differences marked out by race are inherently so trivial (in terms of the human capacities they describe) they are to be explained largely as a myth, or counter-myth, in a sense that does not in the main apply to the other dimensions of difference discussed above, though these can be — and often are — also turned into myths.

Of course, these 'empty' categories of race are nevertheless immensely powerful as markers and boundaries in many human societies. Identification with one 'racial group' and against another, oppression of one racial group by another, and resistance to such racial oppression by groups who define themselves in racial terms for this purpose, are among the most important forms of social cleavage, domination and resistance. Sociologists, being concerned to understand and explain the world as it is, note this line of cleavage as a social fact, and have been able to demonstrate its prevalence, its origins, its relation to other lines of division (especially those of class, nation, and empire) and its dire human effects. But in so doing they tend to lose sight of an important issue: how is it that a categorization that is so empty and arbitrary can nevertheless give rise to such powerful, oppressive, and even catastrophic social effects? What is the mechanism or principle that can explain how a nothing, an objectively insignificant no-thing, can become and remain so disastrously and dismally important in its effects on human lives?

It is significant that supposedly 'natural' differences of race appear to be insignificant or unnoticed in the discriminations of others made by small children, whether of adults or others of their own age. Very young children, shaped in this presumably by their genetic inheritance, relate to adults in terms of their familiarity or friendliness, not in terms of their superficial bodily characteristics. It is mainly at the age of latency — both when cultural definitions are gaining greater influence in children's minds, and when there are powerful positive and negative feelings making themselves felt outside the holding setting of the immediate family — that racial patterns emerge in thinking and social behaviour. The more negative feeling and anxiety that is having to be processed by children and adolescents in their social milieu (such as school), the more likely this is to be projected in persecutory ways into negatively defined 'out-groups'. Racial feeling among children seems to be a product of group life and culture, not instinctual nature.

From a sociological point of view, this may not seem a very interesting question. A social fact is a social fact. Among the most causally important of social facts are shared beliefs about the world, whatever their justification or otherwise from the viewpoint of the scientific observer. Sociologists often seem to be committed to a kind of epistemological neutrality about the beliefs they study.[5] Their interest in beliefs is in their facticity and causal potency; it seems to them to be some other discipline's job to explain where this potency comes from. Other disciplines have not, in the particular case of beliefs in the significance of race — what we can thus accurately describe as race-ism — come forward with very powerful explanations.

Clarifying the differences between beliefs which have rational grounds, and those which do not, and explaining how each come to be held, nevertheless seems to me to be a crucial task for the social sciences. It is hard to imagine a distinction between good societies and bad ones, or tolerable ones and intolerable ones, which doesn't turn on the pervasiveness or otherwise of rational, well-informed and intelligent ways of thinking, and their opposites — irrational, ignorant and stupid ways. These distinctions may have as much application in the moral sphere as in the scientific, and it is a mistake to assume that these different domains of thought always advance congruently with one another. Societies which are relatively rational in their ways of adjudicating human claims and of responding to human needs may be ill-informed in their understanding of nature. Conversely, societies which are highly rational in their technical understanding and practices may be completely deluded in their social beliefs. The Azande (as they were described by Evans-Pritchard [1976]) might thus be regarded as mostly sensible and well ordered in their social practices, but limited in their scientific understanding. The Nazis, on the other hand, were rational in their organizational and technical methods, but maniacs in their thinking about and dealings with human beings. These distinctions do not follow merely from arbitrary cultural and ethical preferences. Consistency and inconsistency in thought, respect and disrespect for contextually known facts, are empirically observable attributes of practices and beliefs about the social world, as well as about the natural. Simple societies may be rationally well ordered, in their everyday social actions, or not. On the other hand, whilst technological progress may be, empirically, a precondition of many morally desirable states of affairs (less suffering, longer life spans, etc.),[6] it does not necessarily bring these into existence, and can indeed enlarge rather than reduce the scale of human suffering.

It is important to retain the criterion of rationality as discriminating between different kinds of individual and social behaviour, if there is to be any ground for making moral judgements, whether of acts, individuals, or societies. If one recognizes that the categories of 'rational' and 'irrational' are separately applicable to many different spheres of life, it is possible to avoid the privileging of 'Eurocentric' and 'Western' world-views which has followed from post-Enlightenment faith in reason, and has made Western rationality sometimes seem like one ideological face of imperialism. By the criteria of embodied reason, Western societies do not rate high on all possible and important dimensions, even if a dimension on which they do rank highest, that of technological rationality, is crucial to removing some of the major causes of human misery.

Similarly, Freud's stance of scepticism towards the claims to unquestionable rationality of those he analysed — and indeed, of society in general — led him not to indifference to the value of human reason but to a life's work designed to strengthen its sway in all human lives.

Since beliefs in racial difference are among the most irrational that men and women hold, it seems that the science of the irrational, psychoanalysis (that is to say, the science which seeks to understand the sources of the irrational in the human mind), is one science to which we ought to look for their explanation. It is surprising that this field of theory and practice has not had more to say about it, especially considering that Freud and several of his followers were Jewish. As Carl Schorske has pointed out,[7] anti-Semitism was pervasive in Vienna during Freud's early career, and posed considerable problems for him. He was later forced to flee from Nazi persecution which of course led, after Freud's death, to the Holocaust, the most concentrated and purposeful catastrophe brought about by human racism, though there have been many others, such as the slave trade and the extermination of indigenous populations by European colonists.

Psychoanalysis and Racism

A valuable starting point for thinking about a psychoanalytic approach to race and racism is Sartre's brilliant essay *Anti-Semite and Jew*.[8] Though he makes no reference to psychoanalytic ideas in this piece of writing, the core of Sartre's argument immediately grasps what in psychoanalytic terms is the key phenomenon to be understood. 'Anti-Semitism', he says, 'is a passion.' What he means by this is that the attitudes of the anti-Semite are made up of opposite and inconsistent attributions, involve sensations of physical repulsion and disgust, and explicitly deny any reason or need to be ordinarily logical:

> I noted earlier that anti-Semitism is a passion. Everybody understands that emotions of hate or anger are involved. But ordinarily, hate and anger have a provocation: I hate someone who has made me suffer, someone who contemns or insults me. We have just seen that anti-Semitic passion could not have such a character. It precedes the facts that are supposed to call it forth; it seeks them out to nourish itself upon them; it must even interpret them in a special way so that they may become truly offensive. Indeed, if you so much as mention a Jew to an anti-Semite, he will show signs of a lively irritation. If we recall that we must always consent to anger before it can manifest itself and that, as is indicated so accurately by the French idiom, we

'put ourselves' into anger, we shall have to agree that the anti-Semite has chosen to live on the plane of passion.

> The anti-Semite has chosen hate because hate is a faith; at the outset he has chosen to devalue words and reasons. How entirely at ease he feels as a result. How futile and frivolous discussions about the rights of the Jew appear to him. He has placed himself on other ground from the beginning. If out of courtesy he consents for a moment to defend his point of view, he lends himself but does not give himself. He tries simply to project his intuitive certainty on to the plane of discourse.
> (*Anti-Semite and Jew*, pp. 17, 19)

What Sartre calls 'a passion' (the opposite, in his view of the world, of reason, linked indissolubly with compulsion; as, conversely, reason is the means and expression of freedom) we might in psychoanalytic terms describe as a psychotic state. The essence of the argument that follows is that beliefs about race, when they are suffused with intense feeling, are akin to psychotic states of mind. This is not, of course, to say that they are beliefs only or mainly held by a particular category of psychotics — how much that would simplify the matter if it were so! The psychoanalytic argument is a different one. It is that psychotic attributes of mind are universal, original and latent components of human mentality; never wholly banished from the self; liable to become more salient in conditions of fear and anxiety than in more benign settings; and of course more central and pathogenic in some individuals than in others, sometimes for explicable reasons in an individual's psychic history.[9]

The mechanisms of psychotic thought find in racial categorizations an ideal container. These mechanisms include the paranoid splitting of objects into the loved and hated, the suffusion of thinking processes by intense, unrecognized emotion, confusion between self and object due to the splitting of the self and massive projective identification, and hatred of reality and truth. The arbitrariness and baselessness of racial categories, their embodiment of a pure spirit of otherness, are an advantage if one 'wants to think' (as Sartre would see it, from his perspective of unlimited individual responsibility for acts of self), or is compelled to think (as psychoanalysts would be more likely to see it), in a psychotic way. There is nothing, in reality, to think about; no real external object (at least, none that wouldn't cut across these organizing categories if its real properties were recognized) to impede the free flow of projected feelings, or the projective identifications of different and unwanted parts of the self. The emptiness of racial categories renders them particularly good vehicles for pseudo-thinking, and for what Bion calls lies — that is, pseudo-thinking intended to defend against the apprehension of reality.[10] Concepts that are useless for the purposes of understanding anything are effective enough for the transfer of Sartre's 'passions' — that is, unwanted states of feeling.

Of course, many other systems of categories will do for the same purpose. Religion, class, nationality can all provide blank screens, or crude outlines, on which the phantasies of the unconscious can be written. Mental constructions of animal species will do as well, and racial categorizations have often been represented through the metaphors of the bestiary, as Leo Kuper has pointed out.[11] (Who isn't irrationally afraid, in some part of themselves, of some animal or other, whether spider, snake, or rat?) But in these other cases of social discrimination there is more real difference to intrude, more complications to consider, in making any descriptive use of these categories. In the racial case, virtually no differences are caught by 'black' or 'white', except those which are the effects of something else — culture, nationality, the experience of discrimination or of oppression; the result of hostility to the racial category as such. These differences are in the main the product, perhaps over a long period of history, of the irrational regard (and actions) of the other. This is paradoxically the source of racism's power. It is the fact that this category means nothing in itself that makes it able to bear so much meaning — mostly psychologically primitive in character — with so little innate resistance from the conscious mind.

One unconscious source of these projections, underestimated in Sartre's unduly rationalist view of the mind, may, however, be the significance of bodily sensation in early infancy. In physical contact between parents and infants, sensations of touch, smell, the feel of hair, the perception of family resemblance, become suffused with intense feeling. In so far as early attachment is textured in these ways, physical characteristics remain potential objects of powerful emotions, both positive and negative. (Such physical characteristics are subsequently given typical or idealized form in cultural representations, tapping and reinforcing the early identifications of dominant groups and alienating or severing contact with those of subordinate or marginalized ones, which is why argument over the diffused range and plurality of representations is an important one.) This is not to say that human beings naturally remain fixated for life on these dimensions of similarity and difference. If this were the case, attachment would be exclusively within family groups, and incest would be the norm. It does, however, suggest that the 'passions' Sartre so brilliantly denounces are more firmly rooted in human identities than he might wish.

Rationality and the capacity to enjoy differences depend on a continuing developmental struggle within each individual and social group, and cannot be accomplished by a simple act of rational will. This is consistent with Freud's more general view of the possibility and precariousness of reason and the reality principle in human life.

The Relevance of the Kleinian Tradition in Psychoanalysis

The psychoanalytic ideas from which these characterizations of racial categorizations are drawn are those of Melanie Klein and analysts influenced by her.[12] Klein's distinctive interest was in the earliest stages of psychic development, in the first two years of life, and she constructed a theory of the 'paranoid-schizoid position' to describe early mental development in which feelings of persecution dominate the psyche. She described primitive psychic mechanisms by which good and bad experiences of the external world — above all experiences of intense intimacy, dependency, and passion, evoked by contact with mother or primary care-taker — are dealt with by splitting of the ego, one part of the self becoming identified with the good object, and one with the bad.[13] Klein saw the parts of the self formed by identification with external objects, in the process which Freud had called introjection. She conceived the existence of an 'inner world' of the mind, populated by phantasies of others (by no means identical with the qualities of *real* others), and saw the infantile self as evolving through these identifications. As well as taking attributes of others into the self ('introjective identifications') she saw the infant self also as getting rid of unwanted feelings into others, through the process which she called projective identification. In the earliest years, and in residues of these kinds of primitive mental functioning in later life, the boundary between self and others is highly volatile and fluid. Others are sometimes perceived as possessing qualities which in reality belong to the self; the self is sometimes experienced as possessing qualities put into it by others (if bad qualities) or stolen from them (if good ones). One function of projective identification is to enable the infant to deal with conflicts between good and bad internal objects within the self by projecting them into others, and then relating to them, so to speak, through hatred or fear, externally and in a relatively objectified form.

Kleinian analysts have come to see this process of projective identification not merely as a phantasy of the infant, or of the infantile part of their adult analysands, but as an interactive process in which the objects of projective identification do sometimes unconsciously absorb some of these phantasies, in a transitive process. One major function of parenting in infancy is deemed to be a capacity for bearing the impact of these exploded parts of the infant's self, and by doing so rendering them more tolerable for the infant. Maternal reverie[14] and primary maternal preoccupation[15] are defined as states of mind functional for the healthy development of babies, since they enable the mother or other primary care-taker to share the work of psychic and emotional integration. The development of the understanding of the 'countertransference' in Kleinian and post-Kleinian psychoanalysis is connected to these ideas too, since much of what is taken note of and used in the countertransference are the mental phenomena associated with projective identification. That is to say, the countertransference provides the evidence, in the form of effects on the analyst's thinking and feeling, of patients' states of mind and being. These may be states of fear, anxiety, guilt, or whatever, but what is significant is that analysts see their mental processes in certain circumstances as liable to be unconsciously 'taken over' by their analysands. In everyday life, individuals may sometimes feel that an aspect of themselves has been 'taken over' by someone significant to them, and may find themselves acting out roles which in part derive from projective identifications into them.

The 'schizoid mechanisms' described by Klein include splitting, idealization and denigration, and she refers to these processes as liable to be wholly un-restrained by considerations of logic and rationality. These psychotic mechanisms do not usually take the form of artfully disguised rationalizations, of thought processes merely distorted or biased by the pressure of unconscious impulse in the matter of neurotic symptoms. In this more primitive field of mental operations, reason does not merely become rationalization, it may cease to operate at all, or be in evidence only in episodic moments.

Bion's work has further developed these ideas, through his closer attention to the mechanisms and preconditions of thought and disorders of thought.[16] He identified the desire for knowledge and understanding as an innate human need, parallel in its functional importance to the desires of love and the aversions of hate. This developed Klein's idea of an 'epistemophilic instinct', or innate appetite for knowledge, with which she explained the infant's interest in and phantasies about parental intercourse in writings on the early stages of the Oedipus complex. Where Klein's model of the mind was mainly constructed around the antonyms of love and hate, Bion adds a third dimension of knowledge.[17] Attacks on the understanding (sometimes called 'attacks on linking' in his writing[18]) form a specific dimension of malfunction and perversion, taking the form sometimes of lies (minus K) or of total refusal to enter the treacherous field of communication through language. Perversions of thought thus become in Bion's view — and in that of Donald Meltzer, who has further developed some of these ideas[19] — a specific kind of individual and social pathology.

The relevance of these conceptions to the phenomena of racism derives from the importance of irrational projections and states of projective identification in racial attributions. Dichotomous versions of racial difference are paranoid in their structure, since they function mainly not as cognitive mapping devices intended to identify facts, but as ways of channelling and condensing basic feelings of positive and negative identification. They are modes of mental splitting, idealization, and denigration (Leo Kuper points out the significant etymology of this last term[20]) *par excellence.*

Explicit vilification seems to be a more prominent element in the racism of dominant groups than self-idealization, even though idealization and its opposite are usually linked. The effect of getting rid of bad feelings into the other is to allow the self to perceive itself as wholly good. The idea that the subject- or subordinate- or pariah-race (whether blacks or Jews in different contexts) is inferior or repellent nevertheless seems to carry more intuitive conviction than triumphalist assertions of the perfection of the dominant group, though these occur too. The most active process at work in such racisms is the projection of negative, repressed, or inaccessible aspects of the individual and social self. Cultures of racial domination, since they are founded on greed, cruelty and the exploitation of weakness, will have many such hateful states of mind to get rid of somewhere. This process can have a self-reinforcing dynamic, in which the evidence of damage inflicted on projected internal objects generates still more violent persecution, which is again projected on to powerless victims.

One location in which the other side of this psychic coin, idealization, is to be found at the present time is in the form of practices and ideologies intended to attach positive value to attributes deemed to be inherent in the subordinate group. Here the emphasis, so far as racial definition is concerned, is on positive, not negative, feelings in the propagation of ideologies and sentiments of racial pride. One hardly wishes to call in question practices whose purpose is to improve the self-esteem of members of oppressed or stigmatized groups, and to defend them against hostile attributions. But there are possible costs here, too, in subordination of the vital and virtuous habits of mind of truth-seeking, and in the unnoticed negative side of all idealizing modes of thought. Ideological attributions of goodness to a group defined as falling on one side of a dividing line tend to involve implicit attributions of badness to those on the other.

Other evidence of the psychotic roots of racism are to be found in the primitive mental associations and accompaniments of racist thinking. Enoch Powell gave expression to one symptom of this when he referred in his infamous Birmingham speech[21] to excrement being pushed through an old lady's letter-box. Deep psychic confusion is revealed when faeces become such important carriers of meaning as they have been in the mythology of race relations in Britain. It is clear that disgusting and degraded aspects of the self are here being dealt with by being either ascribed to, or literally dumped on, the unwanted group. Anxieties about fecundity and sexual potency of other racial groups are an indication of another source of primitive disturbance. Oral phantasies of cannibalism lie deep in the colonialist memory — Caliban is a near-anagram of cannibal,[22] and Robinson Crusoe rescues the slave/servant he names Friday from being eaten by pursuers of a different tribe. While the idea of cannibalism as such has often been treated in modern times as a joke (giving rise to a standard cartoon format of persons about to be cooked in large cauldrons with some witty caption) the lasting preoccupation with the idea of cannibalism (out of all proportion to its historical or anthropological significance) seems to indicate deeper unconscious roots. (The idea comes nearer to the surface in the classic fairy tales and in some more recent children's fiction.[23]) The connection between primitive oral phantasy and contemporary racism can be seen in the way emotions and anxieties about food suffuse racial prejudice today. The *Observer* of 22 November 1987 reported (among many other incidents) severe harassment and attacks on an Asian family in Thamesmead initiated when 'the next-door neighbour banged on the door and said: "Your curry is making the whole street stink."' The passions and disgusts thus evoked by food habits reveal deep preoccupations with, and probable confusions about, bodily functions and their inner meanings. (There are mythologies about what other races and peoples eat.) All the three levels of bodily fixation described by Freud — oral, anal and genital — seem to be conspicuously in evidence in the everyday mythologies of racism.

The schizoid mechanisms described by Klein in the context of infantile life, and in their manifestation in the experience of individual psychoanalysis, have also been described as processes in the mental life of groups, by Bion and others.[24] This idea can be extended to a societal level, to explain the processes by which powerful transitive communications take place between members of imaginary collectivities; what is thus communicated are emotions or aspects of identity of high negative valency. What is expelled by the group expressing prejudice or hatred, and what has to be borne (or resisted, or got rid of, if that is possible) by their recipients, are powerful doses of bad psychic stuff. Such transactions are more potent, psychologically primitive, and damaging than the mere mental definitions or images that are usually written about in this context. It is just because these communications do not operate merely at a cognitive level, as statements of opinion, that they are so hard for their recipients to deal with. Expressions of prejudice, rejection, or distaste fulfil active, albeit unconscious, emotional needs for those who make them — they get rid of something unwanted or uncomfortable out of the self, where they cause mental conflict and pain, into some external container, whose pain is either disregarded as of no account or, worse still, has a perverse value for those who project it in its visible existence outside the self. One can easily see how social groups made to receive the projections of collectivities superior to them will be filled with the desire to push them on to some group still more vulnerable than they, and thus how maltreatment is passed down the social status ladder from group to group. Racism can thus be seen to involve states of projective identification, in which hated self-attributes of members of the group gripped by prejudice are phantasied to exist in members of the stigmatized race. An example of this mechanism is to be found in Jeremy Seabrook's account of racist attitudes in Blackburn in the 1960s, in his *City Close-up*.[25] The paradox of the hostility expressed by members of the white working class to Asians was that the Asians then, in Seabrook's view, had come to embody in reality many of the virtues of solid working-class family life, while it was the prejudiced white community that was experiencing a shaming loss of these qualities in the context of its economic and social disintegration. What the white community described by Seabrook did was to project on to the Asians the demoralized and disintegrated state which was being acutely experienced as a degradation by the depleted white working class.

Theories which don't take note of these psychic roots of racist practices can't adequately account either for the deep pain and damage they cause to their victims, or for their persistence as a social pathology. The tendency to see racism as a system of ideological or false beliefs, to be banished by anti-racist teaching and propaganda, fails to see that its main power lies at an unconscious level. Racist ways of thinking may be so resistant to argument precisely because they don't derive from or really engage with these levels of mental functioning.

They derive from preconceptions, not observed facts, and pay little regard to rules of consistency or rational inference in the formation of judgements and strong opinions. The racist, as Sartre said of the anti-Semite, 'takes his stand from the start on the ground of irrationalism'.[26] Rather than attending, as much recent writing about racism does, to the prejudiced content of thoughts about race and their historical and social origins, perhaps we should pay more attention to their psychic form, to the process rather than the product of thoughts and feelings about race.

These psychoanalytic insights suggest how processes of thoughts are driven and overdetermined by unconscious emotional forces. Splitting between positive and negative feelings, and corresponding processes of idealization and denigration, are inherent in racist attributions. Klein and her early colleagues gave most attention to the power of the emotions of love and hate unconsciously to shape states of mind and relationships to internal and external objects. The later Kleinian interest in the nature of thought processes also has relevance to racist beliefs, however. What Bion, Rosenfeld, Meltzer, and others came to understand was that sadistic attacks on absent or lost external objects could lead to a perverse idealization of the 'bad self' — that is, the self as the author of denigratory and sadistic attacks. Such destructive narcissism could extend to the self's own pathological and destructive ways of thinking. The 'lie' in this system of personality organization becomes positively valued, as carrying for the self an important aspect of its defences against weakness, loss, or negative judgement. The idea that negative attitudes to the truth, as well as more familiarly towards persons and objects, can become part of pathological organizations of the personality may explain something about the extraordinary tenacity of racist beliefs in certain conditions. This qualifies only to a degree the view earlier expressed that the primary hold of racism comes from the domain of sentiment rather than reason. This is because whilst this view acknowledges that kinds of 'reasoning' may be clung to as important defences of identity and motives to action, the 'reasoning' in question is itself a representative of hatred of the truth, and the reciprocal exchanges and relationships on which truthful apprehension of reality must be based. The gangster's stylized mockery of 'conventional' values and morality, and of 'straight' ways of thinking, and the Nazi's frenzied denunciations of 'alien' kinds of thinking, indicate a deep hatred of rational processes as such. This is what explains the almost arrogant indifference to reason or evidence described by Sartre in his discussion of anti-Semitism.

There is a parallel between the arguments made here about the relevance of psychoanalysis to the understanding of racism and those of some feminists on the implications of psychoanalysis for women's oppression. In each case, the psychoanalytic argument draws attention to the unconscious roots of mechanisms of domination and subordination, and suggests that reasoning about the issues — that is, discourse on a level of superficial rationality — is unlikely to shift the balance of social relations very much. Feminists like Mitchell, Dinnerstein and Chodorow[27] argued that gender identities were established by unconscious processes of repression and identification during infancy. Only by radically altering the family (Mitchell) or in a more reformist vein by altering the balance of male and female parental responsibility within it (Dinnerstein and Chodorow) could more equal gender identities be forged — more equal but nevertheless different in general pattern, I would say.

There is, however, an important difference between the psychoanalytic view advanced here in regard to race, and the above argument as it has addressed feminist issues. Feminist writers on this topic have tended to think of women — feminists even — as their principal readership, drawing attention to obstacles to emancipation lodged inside themselves, and trying to describe and account for some deep-rooted conservative attachments among women to traditional identities (for example those of mother and wife) even where these conflict with feminist ideals. The psychoanalytic view of racism is not, however, intended to be principally addressed to racism's victims — as a way of reflecting on how hard it is to overcome negative self-definitions, for example. It is worth drawing attention to the emotional damage caused by projections of the kind referred to above, but more important to think about their causes and possible removal. Racism is primarily to be located as a problem of those who perpetrate its practices, not of its victims.

Obviously racism is not wholly explicable by reference to the operation of social sentiments, or by psychoanalysis's analysis of these in terms of unconscious mental processes. It would be crassly reductionist not to recognize the interaction of racial oppression with the oppression of class, or to fail to acknowledge the enormous role of imperialist domination in creating conditions for, and legitimizing, racial domination. It can even be argued that rational-choice theories have some leverage on this (and other) forms of social cleavage. That is to say, for members of a social category, however constituted, the use of membership of that category as a criterion of inclusion or exclusion, advantage or disadvantage, clearly potentially serves to advance the interests of individuals favourably classified. For white South Africans competing for scarce resources, power and status, it is clearly advantageous, by many common-sense definitions, to be able a priori to exclude blacks from virtually all competition. Similarly, exclusions by gender, or status group, benefit some by restricting competition from others, and indeed by the idea of superiority embodied in the principles of exclusion.

The point that is being made here is not that these forms of exclusion or domination do not exist, or do not count. Patently they do, and the social forces that contribute to them obviously need to be understood as well as possible, and vigorously challenged. What is being argued is that societies or groups that commit themselves to enforcing discriminations and disadvantages on a racial basis *ipso facto* commit themselves to irrational ways of conducting their affairs. Gains in material or other interest by particular groups are achieved at the expense of a denial of truth and reason — in effect, by adopting the strategy of the 'useful' lie. Imperialist doctrines of 'natural' inferiority, or more opportunistic exclusionary practices based on more blatant kinds of self-interest, are founded on misrepresentations, and inevitably invade the capacity of those who hold them to cling on to rational mental functions and the respect these demand for the apprehension of reality and for the reciprocal conversations by which this is sustained. Projections, splittings of good and bad, and delusional phantasies are inevitably engendered by such commitments to lies, even where they do not provide their primary source.

It is not, of course, being argued that these social and political levels of oppression have no reality. The point is rather that a crucial means by which such structures are upheld is through irrational mental process, and that this dimension needs to be recognized and confronted as such. Above all, it is vital for those opposed to racist definitions not to fall victim to similar delusional and wilfully untruthful systems of thought as those which dominate the worlds of their oppressors.

Anti-Racism as a Strategy for Overcoming Racism

Nevertheless, it does seem vital to assess correctly what racism is, before deciding upon anti-racist strategies. Theories which characterize racism primarily as an ideology, as a system of false beliefs derived from imperialist history and as representing in a displaced form the interests of conflicting social classes,[28] may in part misrepresent the nature of the phenomenon, and therefore generate mistaken strategies for dealing with it.

This now-influential view has emerged in part from recent approaches to popular culture, which have extended the understanding of ideologies and their functioning. Where an earlier 'sociology of knowledge' and its Marxist cognate, the theory of ideology, viewed 'knowledge' as formalized, systematic bodies of ideas, more recent approaches — for example, those developed at the Centre for Contemporary Cultural Studies in Birmingham — have instead devoted attention to popular, everyday beliefs.[29] Just as the definition of culture has been extended from a narrow conception of 'high culture' to a more inclusive idea of 'popular culture', so the idea of 'the common sense of an age', taking up some ideas of Gramsci and applying them to contemporary society, has to some extent supplanted formalized political and social theory as the mode of ideology deemed most worthy of critical attention. While systematic social theories remain important to neo-Marxist analyses of culture, it is argued that popularly held beliefs do more work, so to speak.

Popular racist mentalities, however, have proved more tenacious and hard to uproot than scientific or quasi-scientific theories of racial difference had earlier been. Whilst theories of racial superiority and inferiority, influenced by Social Darwinist ideas, enjoyed great influence in the West in the latter part of the nineteenth and the early twentieth century (in the period of the maximum extent and power of the European empires)[30] they have in recent years been eclipsed by theories critical of biological explanations of human behaviour. Whilst some attempts have been made to revive theories supporting notions of racial difference, these do not seem to have acquired much scientific influence. It has been hard to find sound evidence of biologically given differences between racially defined groups, in contrast to the relatively large and obvious differences traceable to cultural and social causes. It is hard to know what significance could be attached to such differences as have been asserted (even if they could be proved to exist), given the much greater range of attributes found within every so-called racial group.

Unfortunately, however, the intellectual strength or weakness of racist scientific theories seems to bear little relationship to the corresponding pervasiveness and vigour of popular racism. Intense forms of nationalism have also seemed able to thrive without benefit of rational support, as one would expect from the view of the unconscious sources of prejudice being presented here. It has turned out to be much more difficult to change popular definitions of the situation than it was to modify ideas in their more systematized form. The popular press is one reason for this, since it often serves as a transmitter and relay for currents of unconscious anxiety and hatred. Strong feelings are aroused by the press's attention to violent, distressing, or perverse events in its news coverage, and by the powerful images which dominate it, but seldom is anything written in the *Sun* or its equivalents which helps readers to respond to such events in reflective ways. Mrs Thatcher has recently proved a more successful exponent of the strategies of transforming common sense than her left-wing opponents, despite the fact that it was the left in the 1960s which initiated new forms of popular social movement — civil rights, peace campaigns, women's liberation, green movements, etc. — and the New Right which subsequently sought to emulate them. Philip Cohen[31] has described, in the specific context of anti-racist teaching, how tenaciously 'common-sense' world-views are defended by working-class pupils against the more 'rational' anti-racist approaches of their liberal-minded teachers. Conflict between 'racist' and 'anti-racist' definitions are, he shows, subordinated to a more deeply structured contest in working-class comprehensive schools between the 'middle-class' ideas of those in authority, and the 'culture of resistance' of working-class pupils among whom the educational transmission system of the school often fails.

Racist ideas may unwittingly be given an intellectual weight and plausibility they do not in reality justify, if racism is defined by anti-racists mainly as an ideological formation. Once racism is defined as a set of beliefs, it seems obligatory to explore their origins and affinities, and by implication to assign them intellectual significance. Thus biological theories of racial difference, eugenicist programmes of selective breeding, racial theories in cognitive psychology, are dredged up for scrupulous study, even though their current intellectual importance in the relevant social sciences may be trivial. Given the hypothesis that racism is a system of false beliefs, if these theories did not exist it would almost be necessary to invent them in order to demonstrate their falsehood. If, however, the major roots of racism in society have little to do with rationally held beliefs, a strategy which identifies their critique and refutation as a primary aim may be somewhat beside the point. To explain how and why false beliefs arise and are sustained may be a more vital matter than the repeated slaying by logic of ideas that may, to all intents and purposes, be already dead.

Whilst there may be good reason for vigilance to prevent the unchallenged re-emergence of racist theories (which might be more likely to occur without it), there is also a danger that concerns over legitimation or proscription may take the place of objective concerns for the truth. The politicized habits of thought thus induced, though they may seem harmless and even beneficial in the specific sphere of hostility to the pariah-field of racist theory, are hard to combine with the retention of a spirit of truth-seeking and open-mindedness in general. Such a rational and non-repressive climate is broadly the one in which racist thinking is least likely to thrive, and in which, conversely, positive perspectives of social improvement are most likely to develop.

There may be related problems with regard to certain other methods currently adopted to combat racist beliefs, if the argument that racial prejudices are psychologically primitive in origin has validity. In this case, what may be most significant for individuals, including those who hold them, to understand about them is their quality as states of mind rather than their phenomenal content. It seems likely that everyone, without exception, operates in a 'paranoid-schizoid' mode some of the time, though of course with varying objects into or on to which fear, hatred, frustration, etc., are projected. Such bad feelings are likely to be dealt with unconsciously — as Bion pointed out, merely knowing about such feelings is very different from knowing them in an emotionally real way.[32] Classroom teaching aimed at changing attitudes may therefore do no more than ruffle the surface, for psychological reasons as well as because of the conflicts between the class cultures of teachers and children discussed so insightfully by Cohen. Worse than this, it can have the effect of increasing defensive kinds of psychological organization.

This psychological dimension to racist attitudes also raises questions about what is likely to be appropriate or helpful in teaching 'racism awareness' in educational settings. It seems important to distinguish between states of irrational hatred and projection *per se*, which are virtually universal in their incidence (though varying greatly in degree and intensity both for biographical and social reasons) and need to be understood and contained as such, and their particular manifestation in racial attitudes. Persecutory and guilt-inducing procedures may not be helpful as a technique for dealing with states of mind that are at root paranoid and persecutory in nature. Evoking feelings of guilt and shame in white students may not necessarily throw much light on where irrational antagonisms between groups come from, or in reality help individuals to deal with them.

From a psychoanalytic point of view, persecution seems ill-advised as a technique for dealing with states of mind that are at root paranoid and persecutory. (Persecutory here means deriving from the feeling of being persecuted.) This procedure would seem closely analogous to trying to deal with neurotic or psychotic symptoms (or, say, troubling personality disorders such as sexual sadism) by repression. Some apparent success might be achieved by such means, in that individuals susceptible to group pressure will be led to hide their inclinations or find relief in persecuting them (through projective identification) in someone else. But such change will be superficial, brought about wholly through a strengthened superego and group-mindedness (part of the constituting problem of racism in the first place). Lasting change requires an experience of thinking about states of mind and their origins and meanings, in relatively free and non-accusatory settings. This is why psychoanalysis developed the technique of free association, and works in the mode of understanding rather than moral judgement. Psychoanalysis also makes the assumption that human beings in principle share the same latent dispositions and habits of mind, and that pathologies are not the monopoly of the other. It would seem to follow that in order for learning to take place at any depth, some mental tolerance has to be extended to what is contemplated, in order that it can become an object of conscious reflection and choice. The psychoanalytic assumption that primitive and 'bad' states of mind are universal dispositions seems a necessity for transformative learning.

On this view, racist states of mind are only one of many possible forms of irrational and negative projections of group feeling, whatever one might say about their specific historical and current social power. These states of feeling, in their general form, are not the monopoly of particular national or ethnic groups. Black racism or counter-racism, as well as white, is clearly both conceivable and actual. It seems to me that such states of mind, and their harmful consequences for the relations of individuals and groups, should be the larger subject of 'awareness' teaching, and should be thought about in whatever form they are manifested. It is hard to see how people of different 'races' can learn together about themselves if the fundamental assumption is that members of one group are guilty and members of the other are innocent.

Some related considerations may apply to more politicized versions of anti-racist teaching, in which racism is viewed straightforwardly as an ideological formation to be rooted out wherever it is found. On the surface, such anti-racist movements identify a wholly bad and non-racial object to attack. Since it is hard to find any rational basis for defending this object, the campaigns seem unchallengeably to have both morality and reason on their side. Even here, however, the form of mobilization of group sentiment in this movement, and the apparently overwhelming and self-evident correctness of the argument it makes, should raise some critical questions.

On the surface, anti-racism does not represent a simple reversal of racist feeling. Since its negative object is racism itself, not a racial group, anti-racism seems to invite an inclusive and clearly non-racist form of support. In reality, however, the position is a little more complicated. The 'racism' attacked by the anti-racist movement is not racism in all its forms, but mainly the racism of white society. Its pervasiveness is usually explained in this context by reference to the history of imperialism, and to the class dynamics of capitalism. This is importantly qualified in more sophisticated accounts by the insistence that racial inequalities and conflicts are not reducible to those of class, and have a separate causal weight within a more complex but still unified theoretical model.[33] The 'universalist' frame of reference which implicitly holds all this together is a socialist or neo-Marxist theory, and this framework enables an alliance to be constructed (fragile as it may be) between black radicals concerned mainly with questions of racial disadvantage, and white anti-racists concerned, among other things, with threats from the radical right. Whites identified with racism, or blacks deemed insufficiently hostile towards it, are the primary objects of criticism, not those subscribing to racist definitions of any kind. There is evidently a current of 'counter-racism' among blacks (insisting, for example, in social work on the enforcement of racial uniformity in fostering and adoption policies[34]) which is not subjected to critical reflection within this broadly anti-racist movement. 'Anti-racism' thus seems to allow both for the conduct of a universalist critique of racial discrimination, prejudice, domination, etc., and for claims by black spokespersons to obtain control on a racial basis of what is deemed to be 'their own' social space. The ambiguity and slippage in this context between anti-racist and counter-racist arguments perhaps follows from the necessity to win multiracial support in Britain if any action on behalf of racial minorities is to succeed.

The existence in Britain of powerful forms of racism, resistance to attempts at remedy, and the need for a deliberate redress of ethnic disavantage is not in doubt in this argument. What does need to be reflected on is what forms of investigation, advocacy and political response are most beneficial. On the whole, mere inversions of persecutory ways of thinking by dominant groups, in those few settings where minorities have some local control, may not be the most effective in the long run. Even the apparently righteous inversion inherent in the concept of 'anti-racism' may have its serious drawbacks, in being both manifestly the direct antithesis of racism, yet also bound by it as the central object of thought and feeling. What this concept does not encourage is the dissolution of the empty object of signifier 'race' into more real and individuated kinds of difference. A good society would be one which was not anti-racist but non-racial in its identities.

The danger lies in the powerful feelings of 'unity-in-conflict' evoked by negativistic campaigns, however justified their apparent object. While these states of mind may not be at all racist, they are persecutory in direction and conformity-inducing in their internal structure. The underlying state of mind they induce is massifying and deindividualizing. They are therefore liable to produce unconscious states of mind and hostility psychologically analogous to those of racism, even though they may well have a quite different content.

One might hypothesize further that a function of such antagonistic movements (one which defines itself as 'anti-' cannot be anything else) is to deal with the hostility suffered by victim groups by pushing it outwards, back in the direction of its perpetrators (Fanon's idea of cathartic liberation through acts of revolutionary violence[35] was a more extreme version of the same idea). One can see that this has helped to mobilize black people — and in other circumstances other victims of racial, class, national, or indeed gender domination — to fight to improve their situation, and why this is necessary. The psychic pain brought about by racial discrimination cannot simply be endlessly absorbed without deep damage to individuals' positive feelings and hopefulness about themselves and the world.

On the other hand, there are potential costs in the self-assertion of racial (or national) identities against other groups around them. If the assertion takes (implicitly or explicitly) a racial or communal form, it defines other groups antagonistically and exclusively. The terms of the relationship between insurgent and dominant group are cast in what Bion called, in his work on the psychodynamics of groups,[36] the 'basic assumption' (that is, dominant unconscious definition) of 'fight-flight', the behaviour appropriate in the face of enemies. While concessions may, and ideally will, be made by dominant groups in the face of such conflicts, increased contact and racial integration may be less likely, in part because of the strength of group hostility aroused by the conflict itself.

Those differently placed among the dominant ethnic groups may respond in different ways. Concessions at the topmost levels of power, where political integration is most valued, may not be regarded with sympathy lower down the social scale. The response of liberals sympathetic to — and perhaps less directly threatened by — minority claims may be different from those more directly competing with minorities. Local victories may be more evident than the antagonisms evoked at a greater distance. Greater solidarity among the subordinate group may generate counter-solidarity in response. Counter-attack (so-called white backlash or militant white ethnic mobilization, as in some American cities) is one possible outcome. Another is withdrawal — social flight — and greater social and physical separation, for example through the emergence of even more racially segregated residential patterns. It is possible that movements whose objective is to dismantle racial barriers will unwittingly strengthen them, even though they will achieve some real gains in power, material and social self-respect in doing so. A review article by Andrew Hacker in the *New York Review of Books*[37] suggests that this has been the recent pattern in the United States. While blacks have gained some greater opportunities and powers, residential segregation has been growing. This is serious in its consequences for blacks in that segregation has the effect of perpetuating disadvantage among the subordinate groups, and also negates the idea of a community defined other than by race. At some point the emergence of non-racial rather than anti-racist identities and claims seems vital if one wishes to see a society that is not to remain deeply racist in its definitions and modes of organization.

It may even be that definitions and exposures of racism as part of the dominant ideology may exaggerate its general extent and scope in Britain, seeming to prove its intractability and pervasiveness not least to members of minority groups themselves. The hypothesis that racism is a general state of mind for which all whites should feel themselves responsible, regardless of their individual attitudes, experience and actions, makes a non-racist society seem a utopian idea, and makes it seem rational to avoid the risks of any close inter-racial contact. Anti-racism can become a counter-racism, whose natural outcome is a situation where members of different racial groups choose an uncomfortable racial separation. In the same way, attributions of incorrigible anti-Semitism have been used as arguments within the Jewish community for the maintenance of an exclusive Jewish collective identity, leading to a repudiation of close relations with non-Jews, morally enforced with at least the intensity of the converse rejections from the non-Jewish side.

Such a pessimistic view of the prospects of lessening the salience of race in British life may not, however, be justified. After all, beliefs in racial difference, *per se*, are now difficult to defend in any public form in most liberal capitalist or, indeed, Communist countries. The careers of Powell and Le Pen indicate in the end the unwillingness of the major political formations to tolerate an overt racism, though they make many covert concessions to its pressures. The irrational basis of racial distinctions is widely recognized both politically and in daily life. Communities that don't (or didn't) recognize this, such as the majority of the white community of South Africa, have been seen by the rest of the world to be living in a condition of suicidal delusion, supported by the abuse of power.

Individuals should certainly be made aware of the pain and damage caused by racial attributions. But it should also be acknowledged that much prejudice is unwitting, a conductor for inner states of hostility whose origin and mental function need as much attention as their substantive object. Such superficial attitudes may be modified by experience and reflection. Some weight must be given, in the assessment of the strength of racism in British society, to its vigorous rejection by many of the young (as well as its adoption as a badge of threatened identity by others). Even the failure of the right to make significant public headway in its programmes of repatriation, etc., despite long-standing and dire predictions to the contrary, suggests a more rooted refusal of racism than is sometimes represented.

Given that black people encounter the daily prospect of insult, injury, discrimination and abuse — in a way that Jews in Britain, for example, now seldom do — this may seem an unduly complacent view to take. There is also, of course, abundant evidence of the effects of social discrimination in the fields of policing, employment, the enforcement of immigration laws, and education. It is easy enough to see how an unpredictable hazard of racial abuse, arising when it is least expected, may be best defended against by a general wariness and scepticism, if not outright hostility towards the intentions and mentalities of white people in general. Nevertheless, a negative political judgement of the prospects for a non-racist society in Britain may not be a correct one to make. The widest support for anti-racist positions needs to be sought and maintained. Neither the language of racial separatism, nor an alliance cast in revolutionary terms between the white and black opponents of imperialist capitalism, is likely to be able to deliver a broad constituency or consensus for anti-racist action. The idea of rights of citizenship for all, unqualified by race, would probably provide the strongest support for the aims of a non-discriminatory society, in which life chances are not determined by ethnic attributes. Addressing that sane part of most individuals which is not racist may be a better basis for advance towards a non-racial society than a generalized attribution of racism.

Racial, Cultural, and National Definitions of Identity

The argument so far is that 'race', as such, is an empty signifier. Its use as an attribution of negative identity has no rational foundation, and some doubts seem to follow as to its ultimate counter-value as a positive signifier, though one can see well enough how important it has been to insist on challenging the dominant — indeed, almost exclusive — presence of 'white' cultural representations of attractiveness, beauty and positive identity.

However, cultural, religious and national differences have a more positive existence than those of race. Regard for differences of history, social memory, and values should be the essence of a democratic society. The ideas of biological race and cultural difference are often difficult to separate. Anti-racists on the whole prefer the cultural category of ethnicity[38] but are prevented from discounting biological categories altogether by their factual weight and importance in patterns of oppression and discrimination. They are made inescapable facts by the attributions of others, and especially by others holding power. Nevertheless, much of the work that is done to affirm racial difference and identity is more cultural than racial in character — for example, the identification of African or Caribbean traditions, and cultures of resistance to slavery and oppression, as the foundations of a distinct social identity.

The idea of differentiated social identities, based on continuity of settlement, shared beliefs, common ways of life, is a positive one.[39] Neither the homogenization of societies through the pervasiveness of mass consumer markets, nor their more forceful massification through the agency of central political decision, seems an attractive model of development for humankind. Nor does the idea of individual freedom and difference seem a sufficient counter-ideal to these uniformitarian tendencies — some differentiating microstructures are necessary in order for individuals to find the resources from which differential identities can be constructed.[40] Gifted and distinctive individuals usually emerge from within powerful micro-traditions — whether those of music or writing — not from isolated acts of total self-generation.

Even so, there is a danger of misunderstanding what a social or subcultural identity is. If too 'social' and conformist a view is taken of what it is to hold a social identity, the paranoid formations which are readily identified with racist attitudes (according to the argument above) are liable to become projected on to nationalist and culturalist social self-definitions also. Collective identities should be seen as no more than symbolic resources out of which individual identities can be made through specific interactions with others. Existence, in Sartre's terms — that is to say, choice — is or should be prior to essence, or fixed social being. An ethnic identity has to be made and continually remade by an individual; it isn't naturally given to him or her, nor should it be prescribed. If social differences — that is, differences of living practice between communities — are tolerated and celebrated, then the symbolic resources available to individual members (and non-members) with which to construct their own way of life and sense of self will be richer and more varied. But differences marked out between social practices, if these are conceived as strict obligations of membership, can produce communities that are little better than tyrannies, of majorities or otherwise, in which individual exploration and choice are rendered impossible.

Individuals in plural societies define their identities through an unending succession of particular choices: choices, for example, of whom to be friends with at school; which member of an extended family one likes or dislikes; which aspects of parental attitudes are admired or adopted, and which are argued with; which, if any, religious or political belief to embrace; ultimately in choice of sexual partner and in decisions on how to bring up children. Individuals with parents of different origin, or whose parents' national culture of origin is at some remove from the local culture, have particularly radical and explicit choices to make — to assimilate to the dominant local culture more or less than parents have, for example, or to remain committed members of a minority community. Of course, for members of some groups, especially those defined by race, such choices will to some extent feel forced, but even so it is unlikely that for any individual there will be a complete absence of freedom. Cultural differences are symbolic resources, available possibilities, in making such continuous choices of an identity; they should not be blueprints. The process of self-definition has the shape of a branching tree, in which options chosen at one stage of life select the choices most easily available at later stages. It will probably be much more difficult to unmake a significant life choice, and do it differently, than it would have been to choose differently in the first place. (A marriage or choice of education or job are cases in point.)

What follows from this model is that ambiguities of role and allegiance, and idiosyncratic differences between individuals, are inherent in the nature of any plural society. It is individuals' difference from one another, the unique mixes of qualities and capacities they learn in their specific settings, that make them interesting and distinctive persons in the first place. (Observing the great range of national backgrounds among friendship networks in both primary and comprehensive schools in London makes this diversity seem a great potential strength and benefit to everyone.) The forcing of prescribed identities on to individuals negates the truth of their lives. This is why it is misguided to seek to define children of mixed race as 'black' (or 'white', for that matter) when in fact they have an undeniably double genetic origin, and cannot avoid at some level coming to terms with both parts of it. It is psychologically necessary and inescapable for individuals to establish some sense of their relationship to their parents (positive or otherwise), and it is through this rather than through political or racial identification that primary definitions of self are likely in most cases to be formed.

On the whole, it seems that cultural definitions — those which identify as a symbolic resource a distinctive social history, relation to place, and forebears — are likely to be a more textured ground of identity than racial definitions *per se*. There seem to be severe drawbacks in choosing, as a ground of identification, biological characteristics whose undoubted social potency depends on primitive and irrational kinds of collective mental process. The mobilization of racial feeling (I don't mean by this anti-racism, or the development of ethnic cultural identity) seems unavoidably likely to provoke other, polarized racial feeling as its dialectical response. Only the recognition of racial categories as the empty, reductive and malign definitions they are seems likely to provide the base for an interracial rejection of racism.

The psychoanalytic tradition discussed above places a primary value on providing space in which reflection and choice are possible. It identifies, both in infancy and in later life, emotional preconditions for such thought — under certain preconditions of benign containment and security, even aggressive and anxious feelings can be tolerated in a group without provoking rejection or reprisal, and can themselves become a topic for reflection. Recognition of the close relationship between thought and feeling — and consequently the view that intense relationships with individuals are the necessary condition for most kinds of personal development — are distinctive of this psychoanalytic view of social practices. The understanding of organizational dynamics (preferring consultative to authoritarian forms of co-ordination and control), of the relational and emotional preconditions of learning, and of the psychological conditions in which pain can best be borne, are some fields of attempted social application of these insights.[41]

There is of course need for conflict and challenge to racist attitudes, and out of this learning and change do take place. But it is probably best that such conflicts of attitude are contained by structures that are not themselves excessively threatening, and that individuals are brought into touch with realities of other persons, including their capacity for pain and sympathy, rather than driven back on phantasy as their primary means for making sense of the world.

Racism, as a system of distortions and lies, can be successfully fought only through a commitment to the truth, concerning both inner and outer realities. Only societies (and smaller institutions within them) in which habits of reason and individuation are cultivated will be able to resist the sway of states of mind such as racial and communal hatred, which are rooted in paranoia and collective phantasy.

Notes

1. See P.L. Van den Berghe, *Race and Racism: a Comparative Perspective*, John Wiley, 2nd edn, 1978, ch. 1.

2. See Benedict Anderson, *Imagined Communities: Reflections on the Origin and Spread of Nationalism*, Verso, 1983.

3. M.J. Rustin, 'Place and Time in Socialist Theory', *Radical Philosophy* 47, 1987.

4. Van den Berghe, p. 24.

5. See the essays in Martin Hollis and Steven Lukes, eds, *Rationality and Relativism*, Oxford University Press, 1982; and Ernest Gellner, *Cause and Meaning in the Social Sciences*, Routledge, 1973.

6. This argument is central to both Marxist and liberal conceptions of progress. For the former, see G.A. Cohen, *Karl Marx's Theory of History*, Oxford University Press, 1980: and for a version of the latter, see Ernest Gellner, *Thought and Change*, Weidenfeld & Nicolson, 1964. A more complex view of the cognitive aspects of modernization and their consequences is presented in Gellner's later *Plough, Sword and Book: The Structure of Human History*, Collins Harvill, 1988.

7. Carl Schorske, *Fin-de-Siècle Vienna*, Knopf, 1980.

8. Jean-Paul Sartre, *Anti-Semite and Jew*, Schocken, 1948 (Paris, 1946).

9. The relation of these modes of thought to prejudice is touched on in Hanna Segal, 'Schizoid Mechanisms Underlying Phobia Formation', in *The Work of Hanna Segal*, Free Association Books/Maresfield Library, 1986.

10. W.R. Bion, *Attention and Interpretation*, 1970; republished Maresfield Reprints, 1984, ch. 11,

11. Leo Kuper, 'Ideologies of Cultural Difference in Race Relations', in *Race, Class and Power*, Duckworth, 1974.

12. See J. Mitchell, ed., *The Selected Melanie Klein*, Penguin, 1986; H. Segal, *An Introduction to the Work of Melanie Klein*, Heinemann, 1975.

13. M. Klein, 'Notes on Some Schizoid Mechanisms', in J. Mitchell, ed.

14. This concept is developed by W.R. Bion in chapter 11 of his *Learning from Experience* (1962); Maresfield Reprints, 1984.

15. D.W. Winnicott, 'Primary Maternal Preoccupation' (1956), in D.W. Winnicott, *Through Paediatrics to Psychoanalysis*, Hogarth Press/Institute of Psycho-Analysis, 1975.

16. W.R. Bion, *Second Thoughts*, Heinemann, 1978.

17. Bion writes on the processes by which meaning is constructed from the raw material of sensation and emotion in *Learning from Experience*. This issue, and its relevance to the psychoanalytic process, is also central to his subsequent works, *Elements of Psychoanalysis* (1963), *Transformations* (1965), and *Attention and Interpretation* (1970), all republished as Maresfield Reprints, 1984. Melanie Klein's idea of the epistemophilic instinct is developed in various papers to be found in M. Klein, *The Psycho-Analysis of Children* (1932), republished Hogarth Press, 1975(c). Her 1928 paper 'The Early Stages of the Oedipus Complex' is reprinted in J. Mitchell, ed.

18. W.R. Bion, *Learning from Experience*.

19. D. Meltzer, *The Kleinian Development*, Part 3, Clunie Press, 1978, and *Studies in Extended Metapsychology: Clinical Applications of Bion's Ideas*, Clunie Press, 1986.

20. Leo Kuper, p. 96, n. 16.

21. Powell's speech was delivered in Birmingham on 29 April 1968. For a discussion of Powell,

see Tom Nairn, *The Break-Up of Britain*, Verso, 1981, ch. 6.

22. See Octave Mannoni, *Prospero and Caliban*, Methuen, 1956.

23. See Bruno Bettelheim, *The Uses of Enchantment*, Penguin, 1978; and on more modern writing for children, M.J. and M.E. Rustin, *Narratives of Love and Loss*, Verso, 1987, esp. ch. 7.

24. See W.R.Bion, *Experiences in Groups*, Tavistock, 1981; and for a later Kleinian view, R. Hinshelwood, *What Happens in Groups*, Free Association Books, 1987.

25. Jeremy Seabrook, *City Close-Up*, Penguin, 1973.

26. J.-P. Sartre, p. 25.

27. J. Mitchell, *Psychoanalysis and Feminism*, Penguin, 1975; D. Dinnerstein, *The Mermaid and the Minotaur: The Rocking of the Cradle and the Ruling of the World*, Souvenir Press, 1976; Nancy Chodorow, *The Reproduction of Mothering*, University of California Press, 1978.

28. Centre for Contemporary Cultural Studies, *The Empire Strikes Back*, Hutchinson, 1982; for a more complex view, see Paul Gilroy, *There Ain't No Black in the Union Jack*, Hutchinson, 1987, esp. ch. 1.

29. See, for example, S. Hall and T. Jefferson, eds, *Resistance through Rituals*, Hutchinson, 1976; and S. Hall *et al.*, *Policing the Crisis*, Macmillan, 1978. For work which relates this approach more specifically to racism, see Philip Cohen, *Racism and Popular Culture: a Cultural Studies Approach*, London University Institute of Education, 1987.

30. See Van den Berghe, ch. 1.

31. Philip Cohen, *The Perversions of Inheritance: Studies in the Making of Multi-Racial Britain*, forthcoming.

32. Bion develops the distinction between 'knowing' and 'knowing about' in *Learning from Experience*.

33. For example, in *The Empire Strikes Back*.

34. A review of research on transracial adoption which does not support making race an over-riding condition in deciding placements is reported in Barbara Tizard and Ann Phoenix (1989).

35. Frantz Fanon, *The Wretched of the Earth*, Grove Press, New York, 1963.

36. W.R. Bion, *Experiences in Groups*.

37. Andrew Hacker, 'American Apartheid', in *New York Review of Books*, vol. 34, no. 19, 3 December 1987. See also Wilson, W.J. 1975 and 1987.

38. See John Rex, *Race and Ethnicity*, Open University Press, 1986.

39. See Michael Walzer, *Spheres of Justice*, Martin Robertson, 1983, for a persuasive exposition of a pluralist view of the good society. There is a discussion of this in M.J. Rustin, *For a Pluralist Socialism*, Verso, 1985. p. 39. See also Charles Taylor, *Philosophy and the Human Sciences*, vol. 2, part II, Cambridge University Press, 1985. Some of these issues are also raised in M.J. Rustin, 'Place and Time in Socialist Theory'.

40. The conclusion of J. Rex makes a plea for voluntarism in the context of multiculturalism.

41. See Rustin and Rustin (1985) and I. Salzberger-Wittenberg *et al.*, *The Emotional Experience of Learning and Teaching*, Faber, 1981; Isabel Menzies Lyth, *Containing Anxiety in Institutions: Selected Essays, Vol. 1*; and *The Dynamics of the Social: Selected Essays, Vol. 2*, Free Association Books, 1988-9.

PART II

Sociological Approaches to Kleinian Practice

4

The Social Organization of Secrets:
Towards a Sociology of Psychoanalysis*

This chapter attempts to characterize the organization of psychoanalysis, and especially its training systems, in sociological terms, It situates the distinctive purposes of psychoanalytic work in relation to the kinds of social structure in which they have developed and continued to flourish. It explores why the unusual features of psychoanalytic organizations are functional for the practice of psychoanalysis, and examines different ways in which the goals of psychoanalysis can be defended and pursued by its professional institutions.

Intrinsic Goals of Psychoanalysis

The main emphasis of this account will be on the intrinsic goals and values of psychoanalysis, and not on psychoanalysis as a means to the more universal ends of wealth, status and power. Psychoanalysts undoubtedly share the pursuit of high incomes and comfortable lifestyles with other professionals — and indeed many other occupations. Within the psychoanalytic profession, the same strategies of individual and collective advancement — via credentialism, personal patronage, exploitation of scarcity, seniority, and so on — are to be found as occur in professions everywhere. Light has been thrown on the professions by a critical sociological approach which has emphasized precisely

---

*An earlier version of this chapter was presented to a seminar of the New Imago Group in London in 1982. I am grateful to the members of this seminar, and in particular to Donald Meltzer, for their encouragement and helpful comments.

these universal objectives of wealth and status-maximization, and has viewed claims to distinctive expertise, restricted entry, altruistic self-regulation, as means to more mundane materialist and status-enhancing ends, rather than accepting them at their own self-regarding valuation. Indeed, one influential argument of the critical neo-Weberian sociology of professions (Johnson, 1972; Parkin, 1979) has been precisely that 'professionalism' has often been a strategy for 'talking up' the value of services, and of excluding competitors in the market. This has been, as far as it goes, an illuminating approach, making clear that professionalism is more similar in its strategies to craft unionism than its representatives usually like to admit, and providing some grounds for a critique of privileged monopolies.

However, this approach would leave out of account what is of most interest to psychoanalysts themselves — namely, what makes their calling distinct and different from others in its non-material ends. What are its distinctive goals, sociologically speaking, and how do they determine its specific forms of organization? Psychoanalysis constitutes a moral and cultural community as well as a way of making a living. So do the natural sciences, or the various fields of art, or sport. All these have a material dimension, and constitute one among many fields of competition for universally regarded goods of wealth and social honour. But each of them also supports distinctive values of its own, and will on occasion defend these against the corrosive effects of money or 'exchange values'. It is important to the diversity of goods and values in society that this should be so, and that separate universes of value should be sustained (Walzer, 1983). It is therefore a question of general sociological and ethical interest to understand how the values of distinctive callings, such as psychoanalysis, are in practice maintained and reproduced over time.

The Modern Individual and Psychoanalysis

The classical nineteenth-century German sociologist Georg Simmel (1950) drew attention to a contradiction in modern societies between the development of individuality, which is advanced by processes of social differentiation and ever-greater social complexity, and the divisive and alienating pressures of the social structure upon the individual. In a brilliant series of essays, Simmel wrote of the psychological consequences of the life of the city, in fragmenting personal experience and segmenting the individual's life into a set of roles which could become largely discrete from one another in space and time. This increased the psychological freedom within which individuality as a subjective condition could be incubated, but could also deny the intensity and intimacy of relationship necessary for the development and support of such complex mental states. Relationship and membership were needed as an essential support for the self, and yet resisted and rejected for the constraint they imposed upon it. The most intense forms of personal relationship – in romantic love, marriage, and friendship – were pursued for the intensity of experience they gave to their participants, but also risked the dangers of mutual exhaustion or painful rejection. Simmel was exploring in a formal sociological language states of experience which were the subject matter of much 'modernist' literature (Bradbury, 1971), which was equally preoccupied with the psychological consequences of metropolitan life.

We can understand psychoanalysis (as I am sure Simmel would have done if he had lived long enough to see it established) as a form of social interaction characteristic of this extreme differentiation and complexity. A personal analysis provides precisely a relationship within which forms of individuality can be explored and elaborated, as the purpose of the interaction. As, for Simmel, the party was an occasion where the pure form of sociability could be experienced, without other content or purpose, so we might say that in psycho-analysis a pure form of exploration of self is pursued. It is pursued, of course, through relationship with another, but it is a relationship of a peculiar kind in that the relationship has no other purpose, and in that the experience of only one of the two participants is directly presented for discussion and investigation.

The 'artificiality' of this relationship is often difficult for non-participants to understand, since it seems a contradiction to obtain so intimate a relationship by the means of an hourly fee. Psychoanalysis is often thus misunderstood as a hired substitute for other relationships – of love or friendship – normally entered through mutual affection and not explicit contract. But while it may be given these latent and substitute functions, it is important to be clear that the psychoanalyst no more aims to substitute for the intimate friend than does, in a different culture, the priest. The latter is typically concerned in his pastoral care of individuals to mediate critical life-transitions such as serious illness or death, within a fixed framework of beliefs; this is itself a specialized role. The psycho-analyst is concerned with the more long-term and unscripted transitions involved in the development of the person and her or his self-understanding. This becomes a recurring issue for individuals when societies, and especially certain milieux within them, have achieved a high degree of sophistication and complexity. Probably those most exposed to pressures for individual change –

through failures in particular roles — or whose work demands a particularly high degree of self-reflectiveness (in the arts or human relations professions, for example) — are those who most often become clients of psychoanalysis.

Institutional Aspects of Psychoanalysis

We may see it as characteristic of psychoanalysis that it combines great intimacy and exposure of the self with a formal and regulated institutional pattern. Psychoanalytic relationships are entered by explicit contract, whether privately or by professional decision as a form of public health treatment. They are tightly bound, in the case of the 'orthodox' kinds of psychoanalytic work with which I am here concerned, within a framework of time, space, and indeed behavioural constraint. Analyst and patient communicate through talking and through many other less explicit modes of conveying meaning and feeling, but they do not eat together, go out together or have physical contact, even in these permissive times. The analytic relationship takes place only in fifty-minute slots, in conditions rigorously separated from the rest of everyday life (except in so far as this is a subject for reflection and communication). In these respects psychoanalysis represents an extreme point of social differentiation, locating its highly personal content within what to the outsider appears a strikingly impersonal, contractual, and limited-liability kind of situation. The combination of forms of experience which are highly individual and personal, yet are also organized through a specialized division of labour, was seen by Simmel as a typical consequence of modern social organization.

Psychoanalytic organizations, as well as two-person psychoanalytic relationships, have to combine these opposed characteristics of highly personal and idiosyncratic modes of work — each analysis being different from every other — with the need to maintain a permanent and predictable institutional form. Psychoanalytic organizations have to provide a dependable and consistent professional training, and usually an associated clinical service. They also have to create conditions within which their own modes of understanding and practice can be questioned and thus enabled to develop. These desired goals of predictability and originality are somewhat contrary in the demands they make of an organization. One might expect, given this model, to find a recurrent oscillation in the history of psychoanalysis between the pressures exerted from either polarity — that is, from the claims of instrumental, rational and rule-bound organization on the one hand, and the claims of personal feeling, intuition and creative originality on the other.

There is evidence that this is indeed the case. The history of psychoanalysis is regettably racked by distressing intrusions of the most intense forms of personal and private emotion into public spheres in which they are thought properly not to belong, and which they embarrass and even discredit. The history of Freud's own relationships with his colleagues is the most well-known and maliciously mined of these instances, and Melanie Klein's life provides others (Grosskurth, 1985). The fact that candidates are trained and enter this profession through analysis and personal supervision with senior analysts has the effect generally of conjoining the acquisition of professional skill and commitment with unusually personal and individual attachments to senior members of the profession. It is inevitable, given this necessary pattern of training, that the public life of the analytic community, with its unavoidable intellectual and political debates about its collective affairs will be influenced by the pressures of the more primitive loyalties and claims on loyalty which arise from the particular relationships in which analysts are trained. Factional and personal career battles will inevitably sometimes impinge on analytic practice, and will be fought out by means of influence on 'followings' of trainees and supervisees. According to the highest ideals of psychoanalysis, this ought not to happen (both analyst and analysand are seeking to understand, not act out, trans-ferential and countertransferential bonds, and thus to become more capable of rational judgement and discrimination). But while, no doubt, most try hard to see that it doesn't, the interpenetration of the personal and public spheres of analytic life seems an unavoidable phenomenon in these conditions. Another factor which must contribute to this is the element of clientelism which arises from the referral system by which cases are matched to analysts. Referral networks tend naturally to be centred on the more senior and prestigious professional figures, to whom intending analysands will first go or be sent. Junior analysts will therefore be to some degree dependent on these senior figures. Such relationships between senior and junior professionals of course have analogues in many professional fields, but they derive a particular intensity from the nature of psychoanalytic work.

There is a converse to this problem of the invasion of the public life of psychoanalysis by the more primitive emotions of its members, or what some analysts might call the influence of the 'basic assumption group' (Bion, 1981). This is the unavoidable consequence of institutionalization itself. The necessity to regulate, to standardize, to achieve professional respectability and recog-nition, imposes an external discipline on the primary work of psychoanalysis, which is capable of becoming antithetical to its inner life and development. And for psychoanalytic institutes there are always alarming lessons at hand of how high a price might be paid if the imperatives of safe institutionalization are not obeyed — the spectacle of eccentric and ephemeral therapeutic sects emitting their primal screams and other heresies on the fringes of respectability and, no doubt, of economic security as well.

The necessity for institutionalization arises from the desire to stabilize and reproduce the practice of psychoanalysis in a more or less reliable and consistent way. While psychoanalysis was originally an act of heroic discovery — and especially self-discovery — by an exceptionally original man and his immediate circle of followers and collaborators, it must for later generations be at least to some degree contained by precedent and by established routines. Of course the nucleus of discovery and creative life remains a potential for each personal analysis, and a reality in many, but institutions must worry about more than such primary processes. These are even to some degree to be feared for their disruptive and revolutionary potential, which cannot be wholly precluded while the creative aspect of the work exists. Institutions must worry about their recruitment, their public standing, their relations with rival institutions, and create some roles in which these political and administrative functions, rather than analytic activity, are the principal work. In this respect psychoanalysis has to solve the same problems as churches which must reconcile spirituality with institutional survival, or artistic organizations which have to solve many practical and economic problems in order to facilitate the making of art. There have been a number of intimations by eminent psychoanalysts — in Britain notably W.R. Bion (1971) — which have drawn attention to the high costs to creative work of such institutionalization and routine. Bion even went so far as to wonder whether analysis could be contained within conventional social structures at all, rather than constituting a revolutionary antithesis of all such structures. The problem with this tension between the creative and the rule-ful, the private and the public, the work of the analytic dyad and the institutional structure in which it is contained, is that it seems impossible to resolve it wholly in favour of either pole, tempting as the contending claims of institutionalization and individual freedom will sometimes be. Without a containing structure, there is no chance that the delicate and differentiated capacities needed to conduct analysis will be consistently nurtured. Yet such institutions are all too likely to fear the originality inherent in the process they are intended to further, and discriminate in favour not of the most alive, but of the most orthodox and safe representatives of institutional continuity.

The Necessity for Privacy

A more specific problem is presented for the psychoanalytic profession by its distinctive function in society. We have suggested that psychoanalysis is a social form dedicated to allowing a particular intimacy of individual experience within the framework of a contractual relationship. Personal knowledge of individuals is thus its stock in trade, the material on which its professional skills are performed. Supervision and clinical research depend on consideration of case material, and may also require considerable self-revelation by analysts themselves, since their own mental states, given the importance of transference and countertransference processes, are important to the development and understanding of their clinical findings. Thus the task of managing personal knowledge, and making it available for examination in ways which do not threaten to spill out of psychoanalytic relationships, is central to all analytic work.

Simmel characterized institutions in society by kinds of mutual knowledge of their participants which they routinely made available. Institutions can be placed on a continuum of intimacy and distance: love, marriage and friendship fall at one extreme, and merely casual instrumental contacts between persons — for example in shops — fall at the other. The degree of openness and trust that prevails in a relationship is one of its most significant attributes, and access to social groups or networks is virtually coincident with the flow of information across their boundaries. For formal organizations, the management of knowledge may also constitute a primary problem — for example where knowledge is the main competitive resource of an organization, as may be the case in manufacture or trade; or where the clandestine character of activity — in conditions of political repression, for example — requires that membership of an organization and its proceedings must be kept secret. Simmel was interested in the distinctive forms of organization that arose where the maintenance of secrecy was an important precondition of activity. His formulations on the secret society are thus unexpectedly illuminating in relation to psychoanalytic institutions.

The reasons for this are clear, and derive from the distinctive importance of the spheres of intimate and private experience in a differentiated modern society. As society becomes more complex, we find our lives segmented in space and time. Relationships in one sphere or period of our lives may be quite segregated from those belonging to another, although each set may be important in itself. Created by this multiplicity of partial relationships is a measure of individual choice, and the possibility and perhaps the need to cultivate the private space and individuality which 'makes sense' of each person's particular experience. The more complex the individual's roles, the more we might suppose this personal space will be felt to be needed. The more complicated the psychological development required of the individual through time, the more settings and subcultures will be devised which can support such development. This is the sociological location and function of the professions of psychoanalysis and counselling in their various forms, and of the 'personal growth' movement more generally. This situation also has its reflections in curricula and teaching methods in schools and colleges, as Basil Bernstein (1975) has shown.

As a consequence of their role in these processes, psychoanalysts are privileged witnesses of, and in a sense participants in, the secrets in intimate personal life and imagination. Psychoanalysis necessarily shares the features of what Simmel called mutual confidence — that is, of shared but restricted knowledge — with the conventions of intimate personal life. But since psychoanalysis is a contractual and professional relationship, it must be able to 'guarantee' the confidentiality and trust appropriate to such communications even though it departs from the other conditions — for example reciprocity of knowledge — which normally accompany intimate self-revelation. It thus becomes an essential part of the institutional practice of psychoanalysis to bring this about in a dependable manner. A significant part of the long professional socialization of psychoanalysts is devoted to securing this outcome.

So taken-for-granted are these boundaries of personal knowledge in much of the psychoanalytic world that analysts may be unaware that their existence is an institutional and cultural achievement. There are by contrast other settings in which psychoanalytic ideas are used more loosely and with less professional training available, where the consequence of a less bounded structure — or in our technical sense the absence of 'secrecy' — can be observed. Where 'interpretations' become utilized in everyday life to control individuals or groups, they are often experienced as invasions of privacy, and inhibit instead of supporting the development of individual autonomy. Social work after its rapid expansion in the 1960s was a common setting for such diffused psychoanalytic language, and reputable psychodynamic casework suffered from the hostile reactions to it.

Analysis may explore and reveal any aspect of the analysand's experience, both past and present. Any qualities of 'confidentiality' inhering in the family are *ipso facto* enjoined on the analytic process, as an investigation of a member of a family and therefore potentially of 'family secrets'. This is especially the case since within the analytic relationship there must be no inhibitions of confidence on the part of the analysand: the goal to be aimed for is wholly uncensored free association. Patients would hardly submit themselves to psychoanalysis without a particular trust in the confidentiality of their exchanges with their psychoanalysts. This is a much more intense and less partial version of the confidentiality incumbent on other kinds of private professional adviser to families – whether clergymen, solicitors, or doctors.

Another quality of psychoanalysis enjoins a norm of what we might describe as confidence or 'secrecy' in Simmel's terms. This is the requirement that the analytic relationship be segregated from everyday life, so that the transference of the analysand (and in more recent psychoanalytic thinking the counter-transference of the analyst) be enabled to develop in the segregated setting of the analytic relationship, without the impediment of circumstantial knowledge of the daily reality of the analyst's life and character. Since much depends on the feelings of need and dependence evoked by this transference relationship, it is also important, at any rate to orthodox analytic schools, that these feelings be observable within the fixed frame of analytic sessions, rather than being confused by the possibilities of other forms of day-to-day relationship. It is thus a condition of being able to recognize and interpret transference phenomena – projections of the analysand's phantasies on to the analyst and the analytic relationship – that the analyst does not have contact with the analysand's daily life. Not only, therefore, must the patient's experience be an object of confidence for the analyst, and secluded from the knowledge of others, but in a sense the analyst's whole life, apart from his or her clinical contact with each separate analysand, must be completely secluded from theirs. These requirements seem to go beyond what might be required in most other professional callings. While other professionals might wish to keep their non-professional lives or even their other professional activities distant from any particular client, to protect their privacy or to heighten the mystique, privilege, and scarcity-value of contact with them, in other cases this role-segregation does not seem to be a *technical* requirement of their work. Psychoanalysis appears to depend on the analysand knowing, ideally, nothing more of the analyst than what he or she learns, mainly through the analyst's voice, in analytic sessions.

The Regulation of Analytic Knowledge

This clarifies the imperative need for a particularly rigid form of control of mutual knowledge in the practice of psychoanalysis. Yet matters are even more complicated than this, in ways which make impossible actual secrecy while simultaneously, and probably consequentially, increasing the moral and cultural emphasis upon it. The particular complication arises from the fact that while *between* different analytic relationships there is meant to be no transfer of knowledge, *within* each of them there is meant to be a wholly uninhibited flow of it, from analysand to analyst. There is no secrecy there at all — indeed, the injunction to free association and the goal of rendering conscious the repressed and unconscious constitute its direct contrary. However, analytic relationships are not and cannot be completely sealed off from one another. Analysts in training, and sometimes afterwards, themselves have analysis. Their own analyses also depend upon free association, and they may include reports of work with their own analysands. Analysts are taught by means of supervision: in these sessions case material must be discussed outside the analytic relationship. They are taught in clinical seminars, in which supervision is conducted in a group setting.

How to deal with this situation in a way which preserves and protects the various essential conditions of psychoanalytic activity becomes, we may suppose, an implicit preoccupation of the psychoanalytic community. It is this sociological imperative to ensure that these boundaries of intimacy — involving, of course, normally unspoken phantasy and desire as well as actual behaviour — are carefully respected that perhaps explains why psychoanalytic societies do appear to have some of the attributes of the 'secret society'. The imperative need of these, in Simmel's argument, is to regulate the flow of knowledge, and especially knowledge about members. The conventions of exclusiveness exist because there are boundaries that *have* to be maintained. The reasons for this vary in different instances. In the case of psychoanalysis it is largely an implication of the right of personal privacy for its particular professional activity which of its nature invades this domain. But the forms of institution which result show similarities, whatever the reason why personal knowledge is so critical to them.

It may be argued that the analogy between the 'secrecy' described in Simmel's 'formal sociology' and the privacy characteristic of psychoanalysis is false because members of a 'secret society' share knowledge in common, whereas members of a psychoanalytic society do not share their knowledge about analysands. Simmel, however, suggests that the nature of a secret society may be such that knowledge is not routinely shared within it — the only invariant rule is that it is never communicated outside. And in psychoanalysis there is some necessary communication within the protected bounds of the qualified membership. Knowledge of what goes on in one analysis will some-times be given in carefully specified settings — for example, in a trainee's own analysis, in supervision, or in clinical seminars. It would be an idealization of the facts to suppose that information about persons never travels by such methods, even though propriety will prohibit unguarded acknowledgement of this, and the greatest pains are generally taken to control its flow. Those responsible for supervising trainees, especially if they are responsible for programmes of clinical treatment and for the health and welfare of patients, *must* exchange information on these matters.

It may be suggested that this imperfection, measured against an ideal of perfect segregation, at least applies only to the training function. An 'imperfec-tion' which affects only the experience of novices might be thought to leave unaffected and uncompromised the norms of the qualified professional. This, however, would be too simple a view. Even the qualified continue in analysis or return to it, seek supervision, and attend seminars, often for many years. In so far as they wish to advance knowledge in the field, and to make use of clinical experience — the major form of empirical knowledge in psychoanalysis — they have to engage in communication, about their own and other people's patients, in these various professional settings. This system of 'secrecy' is therefore unavoidably full of 'leaks', and must be so.

It is a remarkable achievement of this community that it succeeds in containing and controlling all this out-of-place information in such a way that it can be used when necessary without destroying the confidence and limits on which analysis depends. This is achieved both by strict procedures and by a strong internalized sense of propriety. Analytic relationships are maintained in a segregated mode, and role confusions are avoided. Confidentiality and dis-cretion in the use of names are widely observed. (Indeed, one's impression of the analytic community is of a contrast between the intensity of feeling and communication located within analytic and supervisory relationships, and a relative inhibition of the mode of relationship in all other professional and social settings.)

This overriding importance of safely containing knowledge in the practice of psychoanalysis is not only a matter of preventing it from spilling outside specific analytic relationships; it is also a precondition of the analyst's work within the analytic relationship. While 'free association' is enjoined on the analysand (actually this is rather a complicated concept in which a particular kind of receptive attention to mental phenomena is valued) a very different state of mind is required of the analyst. Psychoanalysts — especially following the influence of Klein and Bion, and the growing importance of the understanding of the countertransference in analysis — are encouraged to be open and receptive to the feelings that may be evoked in them by patients. This is analogous to the free association encouraged in analysands. But they are also required to be able to reflect, consciously and explicitly, on the meaning of the phenomena presented to them by their analysands and also by their own flow of feelings and associations. They are required, after all, to *interpret* to the patient, to characterize and explain the meaning of his or her communications. This requires a consideration of alternative possible utterances, and of their likely meaning and consequences for the patient. Questions of timing and context, learning from past experience about which forms of interpretation bring about the development of understanding and which do not, are essential to the successful conduct of analysis. This is a highly self-reflective activity, and one which must by and large take place as a solitary process in the analyst's mind, only its outcome in decisions to say this or that being known to the patient. The relationship between analyst and analysand is thus asymmetrical. In the conduct of analysis, the analyst has in effect to keep a great deal of what she or he is thinking 'secret' from the patient, even while the patient is enjoined to keep nothing secret from the analyst and while the analyst devotes effort to overcoming the 'resistance' by which he or she might attempt to do so. The practice of containment of knowledge (in our sociological sense a form of secrecy) is thus inherent in the relationship between analyst and analysand, as well as being an essential boundary-condition for it.

A 'culture of secrecy' thus appears to derive from the technical requirements of conducting psychoanalytic work. Similar procedures and conventions seem to be followed in these respects by the two largest institutions in Britain which are concerned with education in this field: in one case with the training of psychoanalysts (the Institute of Psycho-Analysis) and in the other with training in psychoanalytically orientated therapies of various kinds (the Tavistock Clinic).

But there is another problem which psychoanalysis has to resolve: the question of what attitude to take to the role of psychoanalytic knowledge in society. Psychoanalysis is a form of knowledge capable of effecting radical transformations in individual experience. It is thought by some of its practitioners to constitute a kind of visionary prophecy, in Max Weber's terms, having a potential for effecting deep and disturbing changes in human self-knowledge and creative potential. The psychoanalytic community has had — still has — to decide how this precious kind of knowledge is to be transmitted, and to whom.

Two 'Ideal Types' of Psychoanalytic Institution

We now turn to a consideration of how psychoanalysis as an ordered body of knowledge is regulated and institutionalized. We discover that Simmel's reflections on the social form of the secret society are illuminating in this regard too.

In the solutions adopted to meet this wider problem, more substantial differences are to be observed in institutional strategies than are to be found in regard to technical analytic procedures, about which there appears to be a considerable measure of consensus among the various psychoanalytically orientated institutions in Britain. In exploring these differences, two 'ideal types' will be set out, which bear some relationship to the different strategies adopted by the British Psycho-Analytical Society and its Training Institute on the one hand, and by the Tavistock Clinic on the other. These institutions of course differ in their role and function. While the former is concerned with (and guards its monopoly of) psychoanalytic training in Britain, the latter is engaged in the training of clinical and educational psychologists, social workers, psychiatrists, and adult and child psychotherapists, not of psychoanalysts. Nevertheless the orientation of the Tavistock is to a large extent psychoanalytic, and at one end of the wide spectrum of its activities (the training of analytic child psychotherapists) the specifications of its training (length of required personal analysis, number of supervised cases, curriculum) follows closely the pattern one might expect of a formal training in child analysis. One significant difference lies in a reluctance on the part of the child psychotherapists to distinguish the purpose and methods of a 'training' from a 'personal' analysis. They also have a less formal designation of analysts deemed suitable for trainees. But in most respects, the similarities with a child analytic training seem greater than the differences. (The adult psychotherapy training at the Tavistock diverges more from this model, being concerned on the whole to give training in less intensive forms of analytic therapy.)

The differences of approach which we will note occur within a field which from most points of view ought to be regarded as one. They may therefore be regarded in part as a division of labour. While the Tavistock will be characterized as having a distinctively open and 'community' orientation, nevertheless those of its staff who are formally psychoanalytically qualified must be trained as analysts at the Institute (which alone confers the qualification of psychoanalyst) and its various trainees often undertake psychoanalysis with analysts who are members of the British Psycho-Analytical Society. On the other hand, while the British Psycho-Analytical Society will be characterized as a more closed and conservative institution, many of its members in their individual work take up positions as psychiatrists and consultant psychotherapists in psychiatric hospitals and clinics, and work as consultants in other community settings. In practice there are substantial overlaps of persons and working styles between the two institutions and their memberships. One way of characterizing their differences is to say that whereas the 'proselytizing' work of Institute members is undertaken in their individual capacity, in the case of the Tavistock this community orientation is a general commitment and policy of the institution. Its dependence on National Health Service funding, compared with the British Psycho-Analytical Society's role as an institution of mainly private professional practice, is another aspect of this difference. Despite the important areas of convergence, the contrast between the cultures and conventions of the two structures seems to be real, and can indicate the general consequences for other institutions and settings, as well as those discussed, of adopting one priority and institutional strategy rather than another for the transmission of psychoanalytic understanding.

In ideal-type terms, the differences being described are between an approach which principally seeks to conserve and maintain the essence of psychoanalytic insight in the safekeeping of those proved fit to be trusted with it, and one which seeks a more active diffusion of this form of insight into as many settings as will receive it. The concern with the former approach is with maintaining standards and the purity of the analytic essence, even if this means renouncing any substantial attempt to convert a wider circle to psychoanalytic approaches. The latter approach gives higher priority to missionary efforts, and is prepared to incur risks of diluting and contaminating the analytic essence to do so. The institutional form best adapted to preserving the essence of a teaching or prophecy appears to have similarities to what Simmel described as the form of the 'secret society'.

Simmel's Concept of the Secret Society

For Simmel, the secret society was a type of social organization characterized by certain structural attributes. It was the essence of his sociological method to look for common forms in institutions whose overt substantive goals (for example, whether they be religious, political or criminal) were very different. In this case the most general attribute was the holding in common of knowledge by those within an institution and its concealment from those outside it. Simmel described the form of the secret society in terms of a number of typical features. These, with possible applications to psychoanalytic organization, are given in Table 1.

It seems clear that all psychoanalytic organization gets a hefty push in the direction of secrecy from the functional considerations described above, and therefore all Simmel's variables seem to have some application to psycho-analytic organization. It seems also that the more restrictive the psychoanalytic institution in its conception of the 'purity' of psychoanalytic practice, the more it will correspond to Simmel's model. More 'missionary' or 'community-orientated' institutions will necessarily have to tolerate less hierarchy, more relations with other professionals, and more sharing of information with them. These differences are discussed more fully below.

Cultural Factors Affecting British Psychoanalysis

It seems also that special factors in the history of psychoanalysis in Britain must have inclined the analytic community to perceive itself as a small enclave of moral or cultural enlightenment in an indifferent or hostile society. Freud's own discoveries were, after all, received with shock and disbelief by the society in which he worked. The British lack of sympathy in regard to discussion of matters either sexual or theoretical — and therefore especially the two in combination — made this an *intellectually* inhospitable climate, even while the civility of British life no doubt made life in north-west London comfortable enough. The Bloomsbury circle, psychoanalysis's first British friends, provided an indigenous model of enlightened aloofness for the new movement, and while there was a great interest in Freud's ideas between the wars among literary intellectuals, this seems to have been confined to a fairly narrow social stratum. And the number of continental exiles in the early analytic movement, in a homogeneous culture unlike that of the United States, where exiles could

Table 1

Attributes of the Secret Society	Relevant Attributes of Psychoanalytic Institutions
(a) A rule of silence.	Strict principle of confidentiality.
(b) Preference for oral over necessarily more public written forms of communication.	Psychoanalysis and supervision take place in oral mode. Publication often regarded as inferior account of the analytic process.
(c) The intense mutual relation encouraged by the sharing of secrets. Whatever the content of a secret, the fact that it is a secret engenders stronger bonds between those who are parties to it.	Special conventions of confidentiality in analytic work restrict the possibility of communication with non-analysts, and thus create special bonds between members of this community.
(d) Hierarchy; democracy is a more open and permeable form of organization.	Orthodox forms of analysis and also supervision require a 'structured inequality' of relationships. The more orthodox the analytic practice, the more hierarchical the organizations through which it takes place.
(e) The role of ritual as a means of enforcing commonality among members.	Analytic techniques (lying down on the couch, the neutrality of the setting, etc.) might be understood as having some ritual force in establishing a stable and familiar context for analytic work. But the commitment to rational understanding works against mere ritualization.

(f) Freedom *within* the boundary established by secrecy, as the reciprocal of limits across this boundary.

The deep exposure of self within the analytic relationship is an instance of this.

(g) A strongly intentional and self-conscious quality in the mode of life of any 'secret' group, brought about by a heightened awareness of its difference from the outside world.

A more self-aware subculture than that of psychoanalysis would be hard to find.

(h) A concept of aristocracy, or of leadership by those with some special essence of values of the group.

The relationships between leading analysts and their analysands become something like 'lines of descent', through which the analytic essence is held to be transmitted.

(i) The existence of degrees and stages of initiation into the mysteries of a secret society.

A long process of socialization through training analysis and supervision has to be undergone before individuals can practise as psychoanalysts or analytic psychotherapists. This, and initial entry, is regulated by highly personal judgements about the capacity and disposition of a candidate. Analysts will have a high degree of autonomy in their work with individuals once qualified; thus a lengthy training is needed to ensure their trustworthiness.

easily lose their sense of strangeness in a whole country of strangers, must also have made seclusion seem the most comfortable option. The unremitting hostility of some of the academic disciplines most crucial for the acceptance of psychoanalysis into British intellectual life, especially academic psychology and its scientific friends, also succeeded in excluding psychoanalysis from the university system. The avenues that remained open for the penetration of psychoanalytic practice were in the less prestigious caring professions – the paediatric branch of medicine, social work, and to a degree education – and among avant-garde elements of the intelligentsia, who could not, however, offer psychoanalysis much of a public institutional foothold. All this should make it clear that the forms of psychoanalytic organization which have evolved in Britain were by no means an unforced choice. (But one benefit of the anti-theoretical British intellectual climate has been that psychoanalysis has developed here with a mainly clinical and not theoretical emphasis. More recent literary enthusiasm for psychoanalytic ideas received from France was notably unrelated to any clinical practice here.)

Qualities of Psychoanalytic Organizations: 'Orthodox Psychoanalysis'

Simmel's characterization of the secret society draws attention to the import-ance of the sacredness or specialness of the knowledge held in common within the society, and made available to those outside only in restricted ways. Entry into the 'secret society' is difficult, and initiation is only after meticulous selection and through a long process of guided instruction. The process of socialization into this calling is unusually intense and pervasive. Candidates are subjected to a continuous process of judgement which is necessarily experi-enced as a judgement of themselves as persons rather than only of their specific skills, as would be the case with most occupations. Internal organization is hier-archical: the protection and conservation of the essence of knowledge is best entrusted to its oldest and most faithful adherents. Such organizations appear highly traditional in their forms. It does seem that some of these descriptions apply to the most orthodox psychoanalytic organizations. One notes, for example, that their growth has been slow – it seems doubtful if the present rate of recruitment to psychoanalytic training (about twelve *per annum*) does much more than ensure the net replacement of those who leave the calling through retirement or death (Sandler, 1982). Training requirements are exceedingly strict, and training functions, including training analysis, are confined to a highly selected and restricted group of training analysts, even for candidates who have already had or are still in analysis with another qualified psycho-analyst.

The combination in orthodox training analysis of the idea of personal analysis with a supervised induction into analytic practice appears to be a very powerful form of control of new entrants to this profession. Apart from the hierarchical implications of the stratification of analysts into an 'inner' and an 'outer' group, it is open to question whether authentic analytic experience is not liable to be constrained by the requirement that training analysts make periodic reports on their trainee analysands' progress.

The fact that the essence of analytic understanding is passed on principally through personal analysis establishes a particularly close filiation or 'line of descent' from the original founders of the movement, and from later prophetic figures. The concept of analytic descent or pedigree gains a peculiar aptness from the way psychoanalysis sets out to explore the analysand's relations with his internal parents through a transference relationship with an analytic quasi-parent. The phantasy parent–child aspects of this transference relationship can be very concretely emphasized, especially in the work of some analytic schools and in the context of the psychoanalysis of children, which of course has been a very important development in some psychoanalytic schools, especially the Kleinian. The world of psychoanalysis seems to be like an aristocracy whose members are selected by potentiality and performance rather than by blood, but in which 'lines of descent' are symbolically established and remain important markers of status. It is not necessarily to criticize an organization to describe it as having this 'closed' form. It is important to stress that we here seek only an accurate sociological characterization of psychoanalytic organization, and do not intend an a priori moral judgement based on common-sense democratic notions. Just as for Simmel some societies were necessarily secret, perhaps for pressing political reasons, so it may be that some forms of knowledge can be sustained and developed only within a boundary which demarcates and sanctions the sacred and the profane. We wish to do no more, in this account, than indicate what might be the various consequences, both positive and negative, of choosing one kind of institutional form rather than another. While the benefits of the closed form of organization might appear to be stability and the preservation of an essence of knowledge and practice, the cost appears to be a failure to extend or propagate this essence very widely, and perhaps also a certain conservatism and inertia in regard to its intellectual development, which may have to do with a pervasive weight of seniority.

In possible contradiction to any suggestion of 'exclusiveness' is the British Psycho-Analytical Society's extensive programme of publication over many years, which since the 1920s has extended from the Hogarth Press and the International Psycho-Analytic Library to the two international journals. However, this seems to have been publication aimed at a particularly well-educated and restricted readership. It is only recently that cheap paperback editions even of Freud's work have been available in Britain — although, since the first publication of this essay, there has been an explosion of publication of classic psychoanalytic writings.

The Society strictly limits one of its journals, the *Scientific Bulletin*, to members only. The sensible purpose of this rule is to allow the preliminary discussion of work-in-progress prior to full publication, but it may also facilitate a certain discretion over what is ultimately published for a wider audience. The application of this rule to the past archive has until this year kept from public view some important controversies in the history of the British psychoanalytic movement, and has made the past proceedings of the Society more difficult to research than the thirty-year-old proceedings of the British Cabinet.

A somewhat similar impression of the internal culture of orthodox psycho-analysis in the United States has been reported by Janet Malcolm in less theoretical terms in *The Impossible Profession* (1981). There, however, the popular diffusion of psychoanalytic ideas has been more extensive, as one can even see, for example, from the films of Woody Allen. Such 'popularization' has probably been a mixed blessing so far as the values of psychoanalysis are concerned.

Some sociologists might seek to 'reduce' such choices by professional organizations to their function in maintaining relative power, status and wealth. Restriction of entry, from this standpoint, is chiefly significant in its effect on the price of analytic services. While such an approach clearly cannot be discounted — psychoanalytic societies in general seem vigorously to defend their professional monopoly of analytic qualification and practice — my argu-ment draws attention to different factors. It is suggested that the institutional-ization of knowledge is an autonomous — or relatively autonomous — function, with imperatives and consequences which are not reducible to the economic. Indeed, from the economic point of view there is no simple way of deciding whether a policy which curtails supply but also does little to expand demand is likely to generate more or fewer resources than a strategy which is more expansionist in both directions. Since the balance of economic advantage is so unclear — it might well lie more in the latter direction — these characteristics may be better explained as consequences of particular values and a distinctive culture. What psychoanalytic organizations are defending, in sum, when they adopt a strategy of relative 'closure', is an intrinsic conception and practice of psychoanalysis, not merely instrumental interests of other kinds.

Missionary Approaches

An alternative institutional model for the propagation of psychoanalytic work is provided by the Tavistock Institute and Clinic, whose development (consistent with its greater outward orientation) has been described in H.V. Dicks's (1970) informative history. This institution has been explicitly missionary in its attitudes to psychoanalysis, and has sought to devise many different means of diffusing and transmitting psychoanalytic knowledge. Among these have been the use of group experience for therapy and training; the modification of psychoanalytic techniques to facilitate brief psychotherapy and analytic psychotherapy on a once or twice-a-week rather than the classical five-times-a-week basis; the use of analytic insights to guide and support professional work by non-clinical workers, for example in day care, counselling or teaching; the encouragement of more psychoanalytically informed understanding in general practitioners and other medical personnel; the development of analytically orientated action research in order to modify organizational process and structure; the use of group-therapy techniques with large numbers to develop understanding of unconscious processes within organizations as well as small groups; the use of psychoanalytically informed observational methods both as means of learning outside clinical settings and in order to develop capacities for 'containment' of anxiety for subsequent work in non-clinical settings. There are no doubt many other variants and developments of psychoanalytic work of these kinds, including attempted syntheses with other theoretical approaches such as systems theory, and in family therapy. They have in common a commitment to extend analytic methods and insights into a variety of social and community settings; and an experimental and innovative approach to the possible uses of psychoanalytic insight through different and non-orthodox methods of work. Within the Tavistock there is a great diversity and indeed conflict of view between these different approaches which echo some of the differences between the Tavistock and more orthodox analytic institutions. It is even possible to combine quite orthodox attitudes to classical psychoanalysis with experimental and open-minded approaches to other forms of work deemed and felt to contain something less than the real essence. But the whole institution of the Tavistock, despite its internal differences, seems committed to unorthodoxy and 'extension' in one or other of these forms.

Clearly the technical requirements of 'discretion' and segregation of the pathways through which mutual knowledge is conveyed are placed in some jeopardy by such outwardly orientated and missionary conceptions. For example, the method of large group-relations exercises among the staff of an institution will seek to make use of group-transference feelings towards individuals who will also have other roles — as supervisors, for example — for group members. Work discussion groups which take as their object of study not only the work experience of students outside the seminar, but interactions within it, may combine supervisory with transference techniques. The daily existence of a large, multidisciplinary clinical and teaching institution based on psychoanalytic practice must necessarily bring to the surface a good deal of unconscious emotion which must to some degree be put into public circulation and explicitly confronted from time to time.

The commitment to taking psychoanalytic insight out into the community also has the consequence that many different kinds of workers are brought into some contact with psychoanalytic ideas and methods, both within and without the institution. Such work involves short courses, group training exercises and weekly supervisions in outside institutions, as well as longer-term training programmes for a large variety of professionals, and this means that many different versions of psychoanalytic teaching are being attempted. Those taught will themselves be attempting to use these methods in their own work — which, if not teaching work as such, can still be seen as ways of passing on psychoanalytic insight. This process is bounded — or unbounded — in very different ways from the procedures of an orthodox psychoanalytic training institute, which doesn't attempt this scale and variety of experience. From a purist standpoint of psychoanalytic work, much of the work with a missionary orientation such as this must seem somewhat superficial. There is a wide spectrum of methods ranging from individual child and adult psychotherapy training which remains close in its methods to analytic training, to forms of group-analysis and group-relations work which are more distant. Perhaps the most paradoxical combination is the form of work which simultaneously seeks to extend the scope of analytic work in the community — in setting, in frequency of treatment, in guidance of other professionals — while also insisting on strict boundaries and procedures in its actual training process. This model — that of the analytic child psychotherapy training at the Tavistock Clinic — seems to suggest that 'secrecy' can be retained as a necessary technical principle, without giving rise to an ethos of psychoanalysis as a sacred substance which can be nurtured only in conditions of jealously guarded seclusion.

One can point to certain possibly negative consequences of a more exclusive conception of analytic organization. These include a possible restrictiveness and conservatism and also, following Simmel's model, a susceptibility to rumour and gossip, natural forms of communication when information is scarce. The boundary of exclusion — a fear of its being undermined or invaded — may also be a potent focus of attention, should it be felt to be in any danger.

But one can also identify hypothetical costs of a more 'open' approach. The encouragement of many styles of work, and of a very permeable boundary between a psychoanalytic institution and the surrounding world, may place analytic values under some threat. Especially because of the disciplines required of those who would practise psychoanalytic work (in regard to self-knowledge and the exposure to mental pain, for example), many may be tempted towards short cuts, or indeed to subtle denigrations and attacks on fundamental assumptions. Even within an institution supposedly orientated towards psycho-analytic approaches there may therefore be real difficulty in defending basic tenets and procedures against other fashions. There are always instrumental as well as intrinsic reasons for pursuing professional careers, and the guardians of a professional calling, especially after it becomes well established and is past the period of pioneering sacrifice (which nurtures strong group solidarities and commitments), will have difficulty in maintaining a consistent purity of purpose from new entrants. An institution cannot encourage an infinity of experiments and adherents, and simultaneously maintain the control of standards of a closed institution.

The problem of the control of psychoanalytic knowledge, and the impera-tives of secrecy, are also significant for psychoanalytic research. In clinical research, based on individual work with patients, there are great technical diffi-culties in providing publicly verifiable data when the analytic process itself has to be secluded from observation. Reports by psychoanalysts of what they observed and said in an analysis cannot be corroborated, and thus fall short of the classical norms of replicable scientific investigation. Institutional research on psychodynamic lines encounters similar difficulties, and has further suffered from the constraints of private institutional consultancy in which it has mostly been pursued. Relationships with institutional clients generate the demand for a kind of 'secrecy' analogous to work with individual analysands, but of a more doubtful necessity. The transmission of social knowledge — of organizations and their functioning — can be impeded if it is regarded as the exclusive property of the paying client. There seems to be evidence that the advance of psychoanalytically based knowledge in the organizational field has been held back by a pervasive culture of private consultancy (in the Tavistock Institute of Human Relations, for example) which has led to very restricted publication of research findings, and thus little wider dissemination of them.

There are therefore possible hazards and drawbacks in the more missionary and community-orientated model of psychoanalytic work, which may make its practitioners long for the more controlled conditions characteristic of the opposite organizational type. (They may also remain in deferential awe of it, as the custodian of the true spirit and status of psychoanalysis.) There is a balance of advantage and disadvantage in each strategy, and it seems realistic, if one values the fundamental methods of psychoanalysis, to see them as to a degree complementary and mutually necessary.

Unconscious Definitions of the Psychoanalytic Field

One may finally consider the unconscious definitions which each of these ideal types of psychoanalytic institution may hold, both of their own occupational community and of the surrounding society. We attempt to relate the socio-logical models here being explored to the models of understanding used by psychoanalysis itself. Since many psychoanalysts see themselves as witnessing the re-creation in the transference of relations between patients and their internal parental objects, we suggest that they will inwardly perceive their own communities as having collective parental functions. Our suggestion is that the Tavistock as a missionary institution has an unconscious conception of itself as bring surrounded by a world of needy children and also of ill-supported parents and quasi-parents in the caring professions. The Tavistock programmes bring a democratic zeal to the task of taking enlightenment, and therefore potential comfort, to all these innumerable infants. The contribution to the early work of the Tavistock of concern with evacuated wartime children is in this regard expressive of its more general later orientation.

It may be that the internal collective world of an orthodox psychoanalytic society corresponds more to the restricted obligations of the conventional middle-class family to its members, both favoured and otherwise, than to the more indiscriminate responsibilities of the missionary. Perhaps, it is permissible to add, even a particularly Jewish family, in view of the emphasis placed by analysis on a form of intimate familial care, as opposed to the more public and exterior forms of socialization (in boarding schools, colleges and clubs) favoured by the majority of the English upper middle classes.

These definitions may perhaps be compared to alternative forms of religious community, in regard to who is seen as a member or potential member, and can therefore exert claims for attention. One has in mind, of course, the attitudes of psychoanalytic organizations to believers and non-believers, in their own terms, not in relation to any actual religious belief or background *per se*. Both forms of psychoanalytic organization share a commitment to enlightenment through the experience of language and commonly experienced feeling. In that respect British psychoanalysis is basically rationalistic and Protestant in form, though there are some more Platonistic (Bion, 1977) and in Jung's work mystical conceptions too. But the orthodox analytic organizations are characteristically not very interested in expansion or conversion, and take as their primary object of concern those who seek out membership from their own chosen identification with the truth, without persuasion or advocacy. Whereas the other ideal type is committed to active conversion and to offering some form of psychoanalytic service — for example in child guidance clinics — to families whose own definition of their difficulties may be innocent of any knowledge of psychoanalysis. One wonders if a significant self-definition of orthodox psychoanalytic practice is not the provision of help to individuals who are otherwise potentially gifted and capable of relatively successful lives, in over-coming particular personal difficulties, internal conflicts, and inhibitions. One sees such kinds of patient, often young men, referred to with more than random frequency in the literature. The commonest identifications (though of course there are many others) are therefore perhaps with family members not too distant from the community of psychoanalysis itself. The high status accorded to the training analysis of future members — which can be conducted only by the most senior analysts — is consistent with this model. Clearly the organization of psychoanalysis as private practice must in any case push it in this direction — whereas by contrast, one priority kind of Tavistock child patient in terms of the preoccupations and commitments of the child psycho-therapists has recently been the deprived child (Boston and Szur, 1983) from the children's home or institution who is to be rescued by therapy, if possible, from a future of institutionalization, prostitution or violent crime. Such individuals represent the furthest possible extension, in *social* terms, of psychoanalytic knowledge; they therefore signify an almost limitless aspiration, in principle, for its use.

A distinction made in a recent study by Olive Banks (1981) of the feminist movement, between the divergent contributions to this movement from the traditions of the Enlightenment and from Evangelism, may have some relevance. According to Banks, Evangelism contributed to feminism a militant moralism and campaigning approach to social evils such as prostitution, and idealized both missionary celibacy and motherhood. The Enlightenment, on the other hand, contributed a more rationalist commitment to equal rights, but also to liberation from undue familial or sexual constraint. One may see the familially orientated object-relations school as a transformation of aspects of Evangelical religion, and the more individually and libidinally orientated orthodox Freudianism as reflecting aspects of the rationalist Enlightenment. These differences do to some degree correspond to the institutional differences discussed here, though because of the breadth of the British Psycho-Analytical Society the correspondence is by no means perfect.

Conclusion

Finally, we should consider what prescriptive conclusions, if any, follow from the above sociological account. It seems that many of the attributes of the secret society, in Simmel's sense of this term, are necessary for the production and reproduction of psychoanalytic practice.[1] The 'essence' of psychoanalysis does need to be nurtured in these special conditions of carefully regulated entry, prolonged professional socialization, and extremely subtle and complex forms of internal and external control. Work with the unconscious calls for elaborate safety precautions on the part of the individuals and institutions that would do it, for their clients and themselves. There are, however, inherent tendencies in these social mechanisms towards conservatism, institutionalization, and indeed stasis. Simmel's sociological method can teach us that every form of social organization has its costs and benefits, creating some possibilities and fore-closing others by its very nature. Assessment must therefore be balanced. The more outward and community-orientated approaches to the transmission of analytic knowledge, both in widening its clinical base and in preventive appli-cations, have the possibility of greatly enlarging the scope and influence of analytic ideas, at a time when a rapidly changing and increasingly differentiated society should be receptive to them. The opening up of analysis to a variety of professional and social experiences, despite its risks to the 'essence' of analytic goals and methods, also seems likely to provide intellectual stimulus and cross-fertilization to psychoanalysis, without which it is unlikely to develop intellectually. It did after all emerge as an original synthesis, not a received orthodoxy. The problem is to combine these two forms of analytic activity: that devoted to maintaining the standard and purity of the fundamental analytical work, and that which seeks to extend its scope and social influence.

Notes

1. According to Peter Gay's (1988) account, this was the case from the very beginnings of the psychoanalytic movement. He refers to Freud's clandestine 'Committee' of intimate colleagues formed in 1912. The first requirement, Freud thought, was that 'this committee had to be strictly secret' in its existence and its actions.

5

Psychoanalysis, Philosophical Realism, and the New Sociology of Science*

In this chapter I propose to consider three influential accounts of psycho-analysis as a form of knowledge. These are the empiricist critique, the hermen-eutic defence, and the alternative 'realist' account of psychoanalysis that can be constructed using the resources of recent philosophical and sociological studies of science. This is not intended to be simply an apologia for psychoanalysis as a prototypically deep-structured or emancipatory form of knowledge. One of the positive lessons to be drawn from recent work in the sociology of science is that it is more productive to describe what scientists of different sorts actually do than to legislate philosophically about what they ought to do. In this spirit, I will try to characterize the practices of one network of psychoanalysts and analytic therapists (work mainly connected to the Tavistock Clinic in London), describing both their painstaking efforts to ground their knowledge in reality and the difficulties which they unavoidably encounter, considering the nature of their object of study.

Empiricism

One might imagine that the demarcation criteria established in the empiricist tradition of the philosophy of science were devised with the specific intent of excluding psychoanalysis and Marxism from the domain of legitimate human

---

*Earlier versions of this chapter were presented during 1986 at seminars of History Workshop in London, of the Sociology Department, Manchester University, and at a conference on 'Realism and Human Sciences' held in the Architecture Department, Glasgow University.

sciences. Certainly both these fields are prominent negative cases in the work of Karl Popper (1963, 1974), and recent writers in this tradition such as Adolf Grunbaum (1984) and Ernest Gellner (1985) have continued to argue the case against psychoanalysis for failing to meet, in their view, the necessary standards of rational scientific inquiry. Gellner attempts to characterize and explain the rise of psychoanalysis as a successful social movement, and is concerned more with its institutional modes of self-justification and defence than with the validity of its theories as such. His book rather unexpectedly conjoins a perceptive acknowledgement that psychoanalysis accurately addresses real problems of modern life, and a denunciation of the falsity of its solution. ('In brief, the news of the plague which is upon us and of its character is, in rough outline, true. The news brought us about the cure is not': p. 223.) He thus seems to combine a view reminiscent of the early Sartre — of the treacherousness of human purposes and motivations — with A.J. Ayer's plain man's approach to knowledge and verification. As Iris Murdoch (1953) has pointed out, there seems to be an unavoidable core of anomie and irrationalism at the heart of moral individualism, a state of moral chaos which Gellner confronts with a distinctive stoicism.

Gellner's clinching argument against psychoanalysis is directed at its claim to be a privileged source of knowledge of the unconscious. He says this claim fails for lack of acceptable evidence of clinical efficacy. If it worked, he says, psychoanalysis would certainly by now have been able to demonstrate the fact in conventional scientific terms. The methodological failings he identifies in psychoanalysis seem to follow ineluctably from his own view of human behaviour as inherently given to cunning and self-deception, though this is not an implication he acknowledges. I do not find his characterization of the psychoanalytic community as self-serving, intellectually dishonest and fundamentally uninterested in the empirical foundations of its world-view to be at all consistent with my observations, as I hope to show.

Philosophically more substantial is Grunbaum's critique of psychoanalysis, which can stand as a sophisticated and representative statement of the empiricist position. He at least acknowledges the theoretical richness of Freud's ideas. He accepts that Freud did attempt to construct genuinely testable theories, whose core propositions concerned the origins (or causes) and the functions (or effects) of repression. Grunbaum incidentally rejects the hermeneutic reinterpretation of Freud in terms not dissimilar from the arguments of philosophical realists. (By hermeneutic I mean a definition of the object of psychoanalytic study as meanings and their interpretation, rather than causes and their scientific explanation. By realism I mean the idea of a transcendent 'deep structure' of reality accessible to scientific understanding.) Like the realists, Grunbaum asserts both the centrality of meanings as key phenomena in psychoanalysis and psychology generally, *and* the scientific necessity of considering them as causes. The crucial problem with psychoanalytic theory is to establish valid evidence for its key aetiological assertions. According to Grunbaum, Freud was well aware of the evidential problems inherent in his theory and attempted to meet them squarely. The critical weight — in Freud's and Grunbaum's view — rests on the demonstration of the causal connection between truthful clinical interpretation and the lifting of repression, with its consequent relief of neurotic suffering. Where clinical interpretations could be shown to have this effect, this was held by Freud to be *ipso facto* confirming evidence of the validity of the psychoanalytic theory.

Having established this (the 'tally principle') as the decisive test of psychoanalysis's status as a valid scientific theory, and quoted Freud's own endorsement of its significance, Grunbaum then sets out to demonstrate that it fails. The weightiest element in his critique is the argument from 'contamination': the idea that evidence of the patient's unconscious appears in forms which are hopelessly subject to the influence and interpretation of the analyst. Because the analytic process consists of interactions between analysand and analyst, there is no reliable way of separating the interpretative constructions of the analyst about the patient's unconscious from whatever independent object these constructions may correspond to in the patient's mind. The analyst shapes the patient's material from the beginning of an analysis, by verbal interpretations and by more implicit means of influence and suggestion. The analyst's constructions of the patient's mental world are thus, in effect, built from materials substantially supplied by him- or herself.

Analysts from Freud onwards have justified the exercise of immense imaginative freedom in the interpretation of patients' material, and have explained this as a consequence of the many-layered and metaphoric qualities of unconsciously derived material. As Gellner points out, it is the essence of repressive mechanisms in the psychoanalytic account that they disguise psychic reality. The unconscious is held to be inherently non-rational in its processes of thought. This provides psychoanalysts with infinite licence, according to empiricist critics, to defy the normal rules of logical consistency and factual reference in interpreting phenomena. Freud saw analysis as a process akin to archaeological excavation and inference performed on mental traces of early experience which were objectively observed in analysis, albeit in fragmentary, occluded and incomplete forms. Grunbaum argues that it is impossible to distinguish any distinct object of investigation that there might be in this process from the analyst's own subjective experience of it. The normal scientific procedures designed to establish validity and reliability — specified observational conditions, replicability of experiments, quantitative measurement, clearly formulated hypotheses and predictions — simply cannot be applied to data obtained through the psychoanalytic method. At any rate they have not been, so far.

Analysands are not, of course, wholly controlled by their analysts in the material they provide for analysis, even though they are bound to be influenced by the ongoing analytic conversation. Analysts may, Grunbaum admits, make conscientious efforts to think objectively about analytic material. If one 'interpretation' is not successful, either in convincing patients of its validity or in effecting some deeper shift in thought or feeling, analysts will try another. But, Grunbaum argues, analysts claim so much interpretative licence, have such private and privileged access to their material, and participate so extensively in its shaping over time that their method does not constitute a genuinely objective form of observation. Even if patients do 'get better' as a result of personal analysis, or come to accept the validity of analysts' accounts of their mental lives, it does not follow that such accounts therefore have a valid descriptive or explanatory content.

Because analysts and analysands achieve consensus, it does not follow that their agreement is evidence of the truth of analysts' theories. On the contrary, the acceptance of analysts' interpretations may be equally well explained — so these critics assert — by the nature of the analytic interaction, which confers on the analyst a superior power to define the situation. 'Cure', similarly, may as easily be a benign result of prolonged attention, self-reflection and human concern as of any truth-content of analysts' theories. Analytic procedures can from this point of view be compared sociologically with other interactive techniques used to achieve deep changes of personal attitude. Their causal effectiveness can be explained, so the argument goes, independently of any truth that these persuasive definitions might have.

Grunbaum adds that there is little evidence from the more conventional measures of developmental psychology to support psychoanalytic views of the aetiology of neurosis. Nor (he says) does evidence from outcome studies of psychoanalytic therapy support the idea that it is a causally effective means of treatment. Thus there is no independent support for Freud's theory of the origins of repression, nor for his own favoured truth-criterion of causally effective interpretation. Grunbaum's final assessment of all this is that Freud was, on the positive side, theoretically brilliant and courageous; he was further-more committed to acceptable standards of scientific truth. On these points Grunbaum is more favourable to Freud than Popper. On the negative side, however, Grunbaum concludes that the validity of the claims of psychoanalysis is wholly unproven and that these must wait to be tested by the more con-ventional scientific procedures of comparative observational and outcome studies.

This critique, like much empiricist philosophy of science, is prescriptive and normative — not to say forensic — in its method. It sets out a standard of veri-fication, demonstrates Freud's own apparent assent to it, and then proves — or attempts to prove — failure to reach it. In the process, as with Gellner's writing, little empirical interest is shown in how in reality psychoanalysts have attempted to deal with methodological issues of validity and reliability in their own terms. For writers committed as a matter of principle to the centrality of empirical evidence, these critics seem surprisingly uninterested in the actual practices and self-interpretations of their psychoanalyst subjects. These writers, we might say, conduct themselves in the mode of barristers, their commitment being largely to the strength of the prosecution's case.

Not much direct light is thrown on contemporary psychoanalytic practice by analysis of Freud's texts. Nevertheless, such critique can usefully provoke questions about what are in fact the anchorage points of psychoanalytic theories in the world of experience. Following the example of Thomas Kuhn (1970) and of the 'new sociology of science' of Barry Barnes (1977, 1982), Michael Mulkay (1972, 1979, 1983) and their colleagues, we should examine these issues descriptively, through observing and reflecting on what psychoanalysts actually do, and not merely normatively through debate about their own or their critics' idealized criteria of judgement. If we do this, I believe we can demonstrate that psychoanalytic knowledge is more multifariously and rigorously grounded in empirical and publicly shared experience than its critics assert.

We should also, however, acknowledge that some at least of the problems identified by these critics are real and do pose obstacles to the advance of psychoanalytic knowledge. Data produced by the intensely interactive methods of analysis, inherently removed from interpersonal or public inspection, are more problematic than data which exist, so to speak, in their own right at least *more* independently of the processes of investigation. Both experimental and observational methods in the sciences may require causal interaction with data, and all involve their specific categorization and selection. Nevertheless, there are important differences of kind and degree between different scientific methods, and it seems clear that psychoanalysis is a more subjective method of investigation than most of those used in the sciences. Even the sociological or oral historical interview — also an interactive research tool — or the participant observation method in social science manifests these problems of subjectively formed perceptions on a lesser scale, since the role of the investigator in such cases is usually more passive and confined than that of the analytic therapist.

Analysts are, after all, using the analysand's ongoing relationship with them as their main object of study. Clinical material emerges only within this setting. But it seems reasonable to concede that independent data on the clinical effects of analytic treatment should in principle be obtainable, using conventional social research methods, and given an appropriately informed and sensitive specification of therapeutic aims, presenting states of mind, and outcome. The sparseness of such evidence seems more likely to be the result of imperfect research designs and investigations hitherto conducted than of its a priori impossibility, or irrelevance in principle.

Nevertheless, Grunbaum mistakes the nature of this and other scientific fields when he seeks a single decisive criterion of validation. Although he is critical of Popper's falsification principle, he seems in practice to be applying a knock-down criterion which is not dissimilar in its heuristic and polemical function. From Kuhn onwards, sociologists and philosophers of science have come to appreciate that the edifices of scientific knowledge do not rest on single observational pillars. On the contrary, they are networks of interlocked and interdependent theories, supported by observational data at many different points. Major theories rarely collapse even when their major constituting propositions are empirically threatened. They seem to have more the attributes of webs, supported internally and externally in many places, than of discrete chains of reasoning liable to snap at their weakest point. Perhaps the most crucial conclusion of the sociology of science concerns the way in which theories evolve and are displaced by others. Replacement of a theory occurs usually only by process of competition from others which handle explanations of the phenomena more comprehensively or economically;[1] theories are not abandoned because they fail to meet standards set by philosophical legislation.

The Popperian model of falsification suggests an idealized state of perfect competition among scientific producers whose hypotheses, like the products of small producers in the market, succeed or fail as discrete products to meet the prevailing standards of market value in a simple and definitive way. In reality, the scientific market is usually oligopolistic, investment in ideas is 'lumpy' and long-term, and the costs of entry to a field (not least in human capital) are prohibitively high. Markets in ideas, like markets in goods, are highly segmented, and the laws of comparative advantage operate only in the long run. Gellner's admission that psychoanalysis has accurately identified burning problems of human life today thus in itself goes far to explain why it survives, since he is able to point to no viable competing theories or practices which can better explain the human condition to which it is a response.

Psychoanalysis has never depended on one single truth-criterion, and like other sciences it attempts by many different means to ground its theories in empirical reality. Whatever Freud said about the decisiveness of the test of truthful interpretation, his own practice is evidence of an intense effort to demonstrate in various ways the fit between psychoanalysis and the world of human experience. Psychoanalysts have given close attention to their modes of investigation and justification simply because of the problems inherent in the psychoanalytic clinical method. (See, for example, W.R. Bion's [1978] troubled — and needlessly self-critical — reflections in the first chapter of his brilliant collection of early papers.) This method remains central as the main source of analytic knowledge. There is no natural law that all aspects of reality must be equally amenable to investigation by the empirical methods favoured by certain philosophers of science.

Some dimensions of reality may exist yet be accessible only by particular and, in certain respects, contentious and problematic methods of investigation. In response to the problems which psychoanalytic data present for investigation, there have been developments which have sought to give greater emphasis to specific phenomenal data and their accurate categorization. There have also developed a number of modes of investigation which supplement clinical method. Analytic knowledge is thus sought in practice not by one method alone, but by using multiple sources of data in relation to the same object. This process has been described in sociology, by analogy with land surveying, as 'triangulation' (Denzin, 1970). I shall argue for a more descriptive attention to psychoanalysis in order to investigate what it does do. I hope to demonstrate that this field now conducts itself in a methodologically pluralist and self-critical way.

The Hermeneutic View of Psychoanalysis

Before doing this, however, I want to give some attention to the different account and defence of psychoanalysis which has come in recent years from advocates of hermeneutic approaches to the human sciences.[2] They have presented psychoanalysis as a hermeneutic discipline concerned with the elucidation of meanings, rather than with the determination of causes. Whilst this undoubtedly accounts better than empiricist polemic for some aspects of psychoanalytic procedure, it provides its justification only at a considerable cost to psychoanalysis's original claims to be a form of scientific knowledge. Psychoanalysts from Freud onwards have claimed to be providing theories of mental topography which characterize consistently (if not universally) occurring relations of cause and effect within postulated structures of the mind. (While these deterministic relations were subject to transformation by means of shared understanding — that, for example, achieved in the process of analytic therapy — such transformations were significant only on the assumption that they changed structures which otherwise causally constrained agents' freedom.)

Psychoanalysts believed themselves to be discovering objective conditions of human development, comparable to those imposed by biological or material limits; it was the discovery of these new 'unconscious' limits to human freedom that explained psychoanalysis's revolutionary impact on Western culture. On the other hand, hermeneutic approaches — including those related to psychoanalysis — deny the relevance of causal models in the human sphere. They are inherently voluntarist: conceiving, in place of causal factors of one kind or another, that distorted understanding and communication are the chief obstacles to the fulfilment of human purposes and desires.

This idealist approach has had some value in providing a description and clarification of the process of psychoanalysis in several respects more accurate and graphic than that previously dominant in the meta-theoretical literature. The effect of a positivist philosophical orthodoxy until the 1960s was mainly to isolate psychoanalysis as a deviant 'humanistic' discourse or, in an alternative response, to induce futile attempts to prove that the propositions of psychoanalysis could be reformulated in ways that were consistent with these norms. But positivist models of falsifiable causal relations have so far had little useful application to psychoanalytic theory and practice. It has not been possible to test psychoanalytic hypotheses at an adequate level of detail by experiment or controlled observation. The pressure to conform to this model, as David Will (1980, 1984, 1986) has pointed out, only encouraged destructively mechanistic theorizing by analysts. This ideology served mainly to expose or intimidate analytic writers, constraining them to use a misleading conceptualization of their own activity and obscuring for a considerable period the shift which had taken place in Freud's own work towards a more mentalistic and phenomenological approach, and away from his earlier scientism (Wollheim, 1971; Meltzer, 1978).

The positive explanatory contribution of the hermeneutic view arose from the fact that major postulates *are* shared by hermeneutics and psychoanalysis. The idea of systematically distorted understanding and communication is central both to hermeneutic ideas of emancipation and to psychoanalysis's therapeutic practice, as Ricoeur (1970, 1974) and Habermas (1972) have both observed. It seemed possible to translate psychoanalytic theories and practices into the idiom of counterposed meaning-systems — those of the analysand and those of the analyst — without undue loss of content. Many modern psychoanalysts have found this translation of psychoanalysis into an idealist philosophical idiom intellectually liberating. As attention within psychoanalysis has shifted from the idea of investigating the historical traces of developmental traumas and malformations in infancy as these present themselves in clinical material to the understanding of mental processes occurring in the here and now of the transference, deterministic aetiological models have come to seem mechanistic and too little supported by experience within the analytic situation to be clinically effective.

Practical interest has shifted from developmental history towards the subtleties and ambiguities of the interactions between patient and analyst, on both conscious and unconscious levels. The idea of chronological stages of development, to be 'excavated' through analytic material, has been displaced — especially in the British analytic tradition (influenced, for example, by Klein, Fairbairn, Winnicott and Bion) — by the idea of developmental 'positions' (states of internal relations or structures of the internal world). These 'positions' (for example the depressive and paranoid–schizoid positions), though still assigned a genetic origin in the development of the infant, are conceived to remain as unconscious formations or dispositions, capable of being mobilized to dominance in the 'force field' of the mind at moments or periods of later life.

It is assumed, in contemporary analytic practice, that mental structures existing and manifested in the present are more accessible and more amenable to 'mutative interpretation' (Strachey, 1934) than are structures theorized primarily as fossilizations of past experience. The question of origin is thus bracketed, to some extent. It remains important in the background as a theoretical

construct, linked through models of the aetiology of developmental difficulties, while not necessarily constituting the central focus of work with
patients. In any case, therapeutic change has to be undertaken through a shift in
an analysand's existing and actually experienced pattern of thought and feeling.
Even if the object of analysis comes to be the transformation through understanding of some rigid pattern of defence established in infancy, this process has
to be achieved, in the here and now of the analytic session, through understanding of structures of feeling and thought which are made presently real for
the patient.

In conjunction with this shift in clinical practice, psychoanalytic meta-
theory has also evolved from the initially mechanical model of the mind which
Freud took from the orthodox neurology and psychiatry of his day towards
more phenomenological approaches to mental — interpreted as meaningful —
phenomena *per se*. Donald Meltzer's *The Kleinian Development* (1978) traces this
path, culminating in his exposition and advocacy of the phenomenological and
idealist (some would say latterly mystical) approaches to psychoanalysis of
Bion (1977).

Nevertheless, while hermeneutic approaches have been helpful in characterizing psychoanalysts' distinctive attention to the phenomena of subjective and
interactive meanings, they risk obscuring the distinctive concern of psychoanalysis with the idea of determining mental structures. Psychoanalysis is more
than a phenomenology in the sense that it posits levels of reality not immediately evident in everyday experience, and seeks to name and characterize these
modalities in abstract theoretical terms. These ulterior dimensions of mental
life, lying beneath and giving form to subjective, phenomenal experience, are
no less prominent in the writings of the hermeneutically inclined school of
post-Kleinians and Bion than they were in Freud's own work.

This school has developed its own distinctive concepts to explain the
phenomena which it has investigated and discovered clinically. For example,
interest in the earliest pre-verbal relationships of mother and infant have given
rise to the concepts of maternal reverie and containment. Interest in symbolization, and in investigating states of mind found in individuals who have never
acquired or have lost the capacity for symbol formation, has generated a
typology of mental functions which operate on both sides of the developmental
divide marked by the acquisition of symbolic capacity. In *Learning from
Experience* (1977) Bion distinguishes alpha function — symbolization — from the
function of beta elements — aspects of experience which cannot be thought
about and thus find expression in bodily or somatic states, fused at this

primitive stage with psychic experience. Bion, while in one respect among the most phenomenological of psychoanalytic writers, is also one of the most extreme adherents of scientific and mathematical models of reasoning, as evinced in his attempt to devise a kind of conceptual grid or 'periodic table' on which developmental moments could be plotted.

Interest in psychotic states, located as a developmental moment in infancy as well as in psychic disorders in later life, led to the development of the concept of projective identification to explain a particular kind of unconscious inter-action. This concept names a state of affairs where aspects of the self are projected into another (into mother in infancy, into analyst in therapy, or into a group in certain kinds of social interaction) and pushed, so to speak, outside the self in order to keep mental pain at a distance. The study of babies' modes of attachment to their mothers — both those leading to growth and those signi-fying its arrest — led to the evolution of distinctive concepts — for example, the ideas of 'adhesive identification' and 'second skin' developed by Bick (1968) to describe the 'false' protective self found in autistic defences.

All these concepts are situated in models where causal links are made between different mental functions and phenomena: for example, the links made between the capacities of mother or care-taker in responding to the infant's feeling-states and the infant's inner world and modes of attachment. While these concepts have here been drawn as examples from a particular theoretical school to illustrate the central role of generalizing theories in psychoanalysis (theoretical constructs, that is, which postulate relations at a more than phenomenal or descriptive level) examples could equally be taken from most, if not all, subdivisions of psychoanalysis which trace their filiation from Freud. The Klein-Bion tradition is not distinctive in its postulation of theories and models of mental topography.

These examples also illustrate the continuing and fertile development of new concepts and theories within psychoanalysis. It is no more adequate to base a study of psychoanalysis on the exegesis of its founding texts than it would be for any other contemporary field of investigation.

It is a distinguishing tenet of those committed to the idea that meanings rather than causes are the central point of reference of psychoanalysis that such theoretical concepts have to be apprehended and registered through their manifestations in subjective experience. Particular emphasis is given in the British psychoanalytic tradition at the present time to the process by which concepts are grounded and made concrete by reference to the phenomena of analytic experience. Theoretical reasoning for its own sake seems to have been devalued in this tradition, except where a precise and emotionally resonant embodiment of theoretical concepts in phenomena of experience can be given. These phenomena include observations, verbal communications from the patient, and states of mind in the analyst held to be valid registers, through 'countertransference', of the unconscious feelings and projections of analysands.[3]

There has been a reaction against mere 'theorizing' and model-building unsupported by the evidence of analytic 'experience', and a great deal of attention is given in training to the development of what might be called 'observation skills' to ensure that concepts and theories are as securely and consensually as possible anchored in the perception of psychic events. Even so, it is one thing to seek the firmest observational grounding of a theoretical system, and another to dispense with theory altogether. The proliferation of new explanatory concepts in contemporary psychoanalysis, and the exploration of theoretical and aetiological connections between them, is quite inconsistent with a return to merely descriptive phenomenology. What seems to distinguish psychoanalaysis from other 'talking cures' is its postulation of 'deep structures' of mind unavailable to common-sense observation, and the equipping of its practitioners with concepts and theories which, under specified observational conditions, can grasp hold of this ulterior level of meanings. The hermeneutic approach has enabled the necessarily phenomenological aspects of psychoanalysis to be more clearly conceptualized, and was to this extent an advance on positivist accounts. But the level of subjective meanings should be seen only as one constitutive dimension of psychoanalysis, not as a self-sufficient alternative and rival to realist accounts of it.

Realism and the Relevance of the 'New Sociology of Science'

David Will (1986) has capably argued that the realist model of science developed by Roy Bhaskar (1978, 1979), Rom Harré (1972, 1983) and others accounts for psychoanalysis more adequately than either positivist or hermeneutic approaches. Bhaskar's idea of generative structures, known by inference from their effects but more than the sum of observations, seems exactly to characterize the theoretical conceptions held in mind by psychoanalysts when they postulate 'internal worlds' and states of 'internal relations' as formations constraining and shaping everyday experience. Neurotic symptoms, in Freud's work, seem to be an ideal-typical instance of an 'effect' from which states of structure and relations can be inferred.

In any case, it seems impossible to formulate a coherent model of science based on direct observation alone, as opposed to inference from the observed effects of structures. All perception depends on chains of material and physiological effects emanating from phenomena which are known only through such effects. (Consider, for example, the many physical and mental processes involved in seeing.) The natural sciences routinely depend on the measurement of such 'indirect' effects. These are registered through various forms of instrumentation whose validity depends on extensive secondary constructions of theory, which justify the inferences made from observed data. The idea of a world understood as stratified and differentiated (also central to Bhaskar's realism) also accounts both for the specificity of the domain of the unconscious and for the layering and complex organization of the mental world theorized by psychoanalysis.

Bhaskar's (1979) insistence that meanings can and do function as causes in the human sciences is also highly apposite to the understanding of psychoanalytic theory. While it is necessary to grasp structures of meaning in hermeneutic terms, as systems of 'internal relations', this is not inconsistent with the idea that subjective definitions of the situation — conscious or unconscious, private or socially shared — operate as causal restraints on individuals' understanding and choice. Theories about the world are constitutive of human existence and are always therefore potentially relevant, if not decisive, to its characterization. But this is not to say that observers need be limited in their understanding of situations to the reproduction of agents' own meanings. Such a methodology would restrict social science to the mere report and formalization of actors' existing self-definitions. Descriptive reports of this kind may be illuminating about unfamiliar types of experience,[+] but they fail to penetrate beneath the surfaces of meaning and behaviour. The 'value-added' by social science to common knowledge should on the contrary be found in the *additional* understandings it offers over and above those already possessed by the agents themselves. Bhaskar is right to point out also that it is a distinctive virtue of social science to be able to account for the distortions and partialities of 'agents' knowledge' in the light of the broader or deeper perspectives of the social scientist. Psychoanalysis has always distinctively sought to explain and to re-situate the subjective mind states of its objects of study in its own theoretical terms.

Thus the 'fit' between the 'realist' view of science and psychoanalysis seems in general to be an illuminating one, and I do not wish to elaborate further an account already clearly set out by Will. Instead, I should like to explore the degree to which psychoanalysis in fact, rather than by idealized prescription, succeeds in generating knowledge about human beings. Or, more relativistically, what kinds of knowledge does it generate, compared with other natural and human sciences? How far do the problems of access to its postulated deep-level phenomena and the consequent difficulties of method identified, for example, by empiricist critics such as Grunbaum, impede the development of psychoanalysis as a dependable form of knowledge? What measures in practice are taken within the psychoanalytic community to surmount these undoubted problems? To make progress with these questions we need an empirical approach to psychoanalytic practice, if we are to avoid being as ideological in devising criteria of inclusion in an alternative 'realist' canon as the empiricists have been in composing their anathemas. Realist philosophy needs to be more than a legitimation exercise for psychoanalysis and Marxism, though to be sure it does give a convincing account of the procedures of both.

I want to argue that psychoanalysis, at least in Britain, has in recent years been particularly preoccupied with the interface between its theoretical conceptions and models and the observed phenomena to which these refer. This focus has come about not primarily in defence against empiricist criticism (to which the field has on the whole found it hard to respond effectively) but rather through concern to improve clinical and training methods. Sympathy with the more hermeneutic or 'meaning-orientated' approach described above is one aspect of this shift of interest and attention away from theory and model-building and towards a closer attention to 'raw' mental phenomena. As analysts have sought to extend the range of conditions and subjects which can be treated by psychoanalytic methods (for example in the development of child analysis, the analysis of psychotic states, group analysis, analytic approaches to institutions), so close attention has been given to the kinds of material with which analysts in these different circumstances work.

In effect, this has led to some shift of attention from general theories of development and mental topography to the micro-level of mental phenomena, to the understanding and interpreting of relatively discrete moments and sequences of material. Bion polemically insisted on the overriding importance of attention to the specific moment of analytic experience, remarking that the analyst's mind has to be emptied of 'memory and desire' in order to respond to the particular psychic events of the moment. Psychoanalysis is specifically constructed in fact as a framing and sequencing of discrete events, standardized in setting and timing to facilitate observation and comparison. Understanding what happens by session, or even by fragment of session, is the building block of analytic work, and only from the understanding of such micro-sequences can accounts of the longer-term development of cases — as narratives and theoretical models — be built up.

The priority of understanding the immediate phenomena has also greatly influenced the method of training analysts and analytic therapists, at least within the British school. Characteristically, trainees learn from supervisors by submitting reports for discussion, session by session, in literal detail. Discussion in analytic supervision is typically of detailed fragments, not of a case's general development or background. In supervisory and seminar work within this tradition, if there is no detailed session material (selections of as near as possible verbatim transactions and descriptions) there seems to be nothing of substance to work on. Published case reports in the journals give a very misleading picture of this process to lay readers, since for reasons of space and convention they omit most of the detailed session material on which reflection and inference are based.

Patients' responses to the controlled settings of therapy provide some constants by which their states of mind can be compared. Analytic technique constructs an artificial temporal framework, with beginnings and ends of sessions, holidays and breaks, and final termination as its markers. These patterns of repetition make possible differentiation and comparison between states of mind, both over time and between cases. Responses to feelings of need and loss within the therapeutic frame can be regarded as a metaphor or indicator of earlier developmental patterns evoked by need or loss. The standardization of analytic settings in time, space and technique enables grounded inferences to be made, connecting particular moments and episodes to more holistic accounts and narratives of developments over time — but always dependent on reference to and corroboration by particular fragments or sequences of material.

While analysands' acceptance of interpretations is one important index of their validity, it is also clear that this is by no means the only way in which analysts assess the truthfulness of their conceptualizations of mind states. Indeed, this emphasis (in Grunbaum's 'tally principle', for example) on analysands' response subtly misrepresents the process by which a picture of the patient's state of mind is built up. Analysts have to develop skills in grasping the meaning of analysands' material *before* they interpret it, or the process of interpretation would be nothing but blind trial and error. Analytic supervisors, guiding therapy at a distance, have often to assess material days after its appearance and to make suggestions for lines of interpretation which may not be tried out for days, or even weeks. The activities of understanding material, and of presenting such understanding as clinical interpretations, are distinct in both principle and practice.

Training methods have evolved in recent years in response to this growing concern with accurate observation and 'pre-interpretative' reflection as the precondition of good therapeutic work. A separation has been effected in analytic training between procedures of observation and clinical intervention. In some trainings, learning competence in analytic observation skills over a two-year period is a pre-qualification for training in interventive clinical work. This means that candidates are quite extensively trained in the recognition and classification of analytically relevant phenomena before they begin to practise clinical interpretation. Analysands' response is not the only means by which the applicability of analytic theory is tested against experience.[5]

The principal method of observation training developed in recent years is the programme of infant observation developed by Esther Bick (1964) for the child psychotherapy training at the Tavistock Clinic, and subsequently incorporated in the training of psychoanalysts at the British Institute of Psycho-Analysis and in training programmes elsewhere. By this procedure, observers undertake weekly visits over a two-year period to normal families following the birth of a child. The purpose is to learn to observe child development and mother–baby interactions, especially in their implicit emotional dimensions, through considering the whole range of observed experiences including physical behaviour, conversation and subjectively felt states of mind treated as a possible register of the states of mind of the observed couple. Observation is passive, and observers are expected not to engage in interpretation or other clinical interventions. They are encouraged to behave only as friendly and self-effacing visitors, and asked to observe and record whatever is to be seen.

This method, described in detail in Miller *et al.* (1989), provides a different kind of access to interactions and states of mind (real or imputed) from that provided through clinical interventions. The observations it generates are at least much less influenced by therapists' definitions of the situation than clinical material, since here subjects are given little feedback on what observers think about them. Observers are encouraged to note and record, in the first instance, naturalistically in ordinary-language terms, so material presented for consideration appears in a 'pre-theorized' form. The encoding of material in explicit psychoanalytic terms is deferred to the work of supervision, seminar discussion, and writing-up when observation has been completed. This again focuses attention explicitly on the interface between the 'raw data' of experience and the concepts which illuminate it.

While data obtained and recorded in this way are subject to their own modes of selective perception and report, this method of passive observation and record is closer in technique than clinical analysis to conventional developmental psychology, and lends itself more easily than clinical work to public scrutiny and replication. (For a review of the current field of child development which compares the perspectives of psychoanalysis with those of developmental psychology, see Stern, 1985.) The method develops the capacity to observe and form judgements in the mind before giving voice to them. Later in training, clinical supervision teaches the different skill of when and how to make interpretations. This involves not only interpretations of the meaning of material but also judgements about the relevance and likely effects of interpreting or not, or in one way rather than another. This also requires prolonged and careful attention to the micro-detail of the analytic process.

Barry Barnes (1982) has argued that procedures of 'ostensive definition' — Wittgenstein's term for the process of fixing the meaning of a concept or the terms of a language game by pointing to instances of it — are found at the core of all scientific activities. All sciences have to deal with an interface between their abstract conceptualizations and the world of experience which these order and describe. Professional training in science consists in developing consensually agreed procedures which enable reliable 'pattern recognition' and classification of data to take place. These are usually far from commonsensical in character, as a recent reported example of a search for subatomic particles in a salt mine 2,000 feet beneath the earth can remind us.[6] Psychoanalysis is no different from other fields of inquiry in having to develop and reproduce reliable observing and classifying procedures as a precondition for rational communication within its own field. Empiricist critics of psychoanalysis hardly seem aware that analysts attend to these issues seriously, and have put them at the centre of their training programmes.

The idea of ostensive definition is helpful in understanding the emphasis on observation skills in recent psychoanalytic practice and training. The basic building block of psychoanalytic technique is the act of giving meaning to feelings expressed or revealed by patients at the particular moment, or within a specific session. It is the immediate sense of being heard and understood that gives the patient relief from pain and releases the further flow of feelings, thoughts and communications which can in their turn be taken in and responded to in analysis. If an analyst cannot provide this, analysis will fail, even before it properly starts. The initial task faced by an analytic therapist with a new patient is how to say something that is meaningful enough for the patient to want to stay in the room, and get involved in this protracted and necessarily frustrating kind of conversation.

Psychoanalysis teaches modes of ostensive definition to its analysands, perhaps as its primary therapeutic function. Effective analysis enhances the capacity in analysands to recognize and think about different states of mind and feeling. It enlarges the usable emotional vocabulary of those who experience it. But this is learned as the capacity to hold in mind and think about particular states of feeling, not to have theories about them. Personal development comes about not through abstract knowledge but from the concrete apprehension of, and capacity to reflect on, aspects of oneself hitherto unrecognized, hidden, or intolerable. (It is particularly clear in analytic work with children that personal development cannot come from patients' theoretical knowledge about themselves, but only through forms of self-understanding achieved through the resources of ordinary language.) Analysis, as Bion has put it, is concerned with 'knowing', not 'knowing about'. What distinguishes mutative (or, in a different idiom, liberatory or emancipatory) knowledge in psychoanalysis is that it is knowledge anchored to a specific moment of experience or to a specific emotional referent. Psychoanalytic concepts are more or less useless except where they are linked closely to the experience and recognition of actual states of mind.

The 'deep structure' of psychoanalytic theory is a precondition of this process of self-understanding. The idea of unconscious states of mind, systematically and 'intentionally' hidden from the patient's conscious awareness, is the crucial hypothesis which prises open the possibility of bringing the patient fresh insight about him- or herself. The essential theoretical hypothesis is that there *is* an ulterior structure. Without this the analyst would have little to offer beyond sympathy and common sense, resources which many patients will already have tried to the point of exhaustion among their friends and relatives before seeking professional help.

It is clear too that the process of naming and classification within psychoanalysis, as in all sciences, is deeply impregnated by theoretical ideas. The concepts of, for example, psychic mechanisms, an internal world, metaphoric communication, and unconscious phantasy are used to map the presenting phenomena of the patient's mind in ways which depart considerably from common-sense descriptions. The concepts of feeling (envy, jealousy, desire, depression) used in this process of classification and recognition are more elaborate and systematic in their implications than their everyday versions, though as usual in the social sciences there is an area of overlap with common-sense meanings. The distinctive value of analytic descriptions of states of mind depends on this available theoretical structure or mapping system. But theories function more, I suggest, as a discursive resource for most analysts than as a set of deductively applicable models. Emphasis in the analytic process is given more to the interface between specific naming-concepts and their referents in experience, and to their more local relationships with one another,[7] than to elaboration of larger theoretical models and their application. It is both more practicable, and more meaningful to patients, to establish that *this* is the reality and meaning of a state of mind or feeling in this session, or these few sessions, or in this period of analysis, than to discuss more generalizing theories of mental structure or aetiology. The point is that except where concepts are anchored in relation to specific states of mind, they offer no relief from pain. While theoretical reasoning is a crucial background resource for analysts, theory has to have very particular reference before it is helpful in analytic dialogue. There are invaluable theoretical maps to the psychic terrains encountered in the consulting room, but the way nevertheless has to be found each time on the ground.

For related reasons, I think analysts undertaking normal clinical work use a very restricted range of the possible theorizations that might be relevant to a case, selecting from the large potential field only that which seems most immediately relevant. In practice analytic therapists often struggle to achieve and communicate understanding of a patient's material through the use of a small number of core concepts which seem most apposite. Case literature — for example in the *Journal of Child Psychotherapy* — often reports years of rich, detailed work which has revolved around the application and realization in understanding of only a few illuminating theoretical ideas. While these pre-suppose and connect with a much larger theoretical structure, it is usually found possible to think critically about only a small part of this at any one time. Often, with training cases undertaken under experienced teachers' supervision, the concepts may be drawn from current analytic discoveries and constitute an extension of the research programme of supervisors. (See, for example, the work presented in Meltzer, 1975, 1986.) The fact that analytic concepts are useful only in specific application also tends to lead analysts to work within distinct schools or schemes of ideas, sub-branches of the broader analytic field. This is not because a wider range of concepts might not in principle be relevant to their cases, but because it is too costly in time and effort to master the disciplines of application of several schemes of thought at once.

There is in effect a division of labour. Most analytic therapists remain pre-occupied with the demanding task of bringing new individual cases within the explanatory frame of existing theories, with an overriding therapeutic aim. The 'fit' between theory and instance within this field is particularly difficult to accomplish, given that this is an interactive and therapeutic as well as an explanatory task. Most day-to-day analytic work therefore takes place on this 'ostensive' interface (that is, in the task of finding a fit between concepts and phenomena) using theory as a resource rather than considering it, as the ethnomethodologists would say, as a topic.

Nevertheless, the body of analytic ideas has undergone dramatic revision and enlargement over its history, and continues to do so. It seems that a number of experienced analysts, sometimes working collaboratively with colleagues, are able to hold in mind, put in question, and revise a significant part of their theoretical system at the same time as working with particular cases. In many important instances (child analysis and work with psychotic and autistic states of mind, for example, as in Tustin, 1981, 1986) such theoretical advance has followed therapeutic work with new categories of patient, previously deemed intractable to analytic treatment. A conflict of priority between the goal of advancing knowledge and that of helping individual patients is sometimes observable in this work. The claims of therapeutic need and those of intellec-tual interest do not always pull in the same direction in the human sciences, psychoanalysis included.

I have emphasized the observational core of analytic procedure, locating this in the process and in the more recent development of specific observational techniques. This seems to be a distinctive emphasis of the 'British School', perhaps an effect of the influence of a generally empiricist climate in British culture.[8] But psychoanalysis has been sustained as a credible form of knowledge in many other ways. The social sciences are reflexive in nature — that is to say, their conceptions interact with and become part of the self-understanding of the cultures they study. Psychoanalytic ideas too have percolated into the general field of understanding and become subject to test not only by technical methods but also by ordinary observation and self-observation. The spread of psychoanalytic understanding in the modern world seems to result from the fact that it is found, in everyday life and culture, to 'fit' many people's experi-ence. It is clear that in some cultures (in the United States most clearly) a capacity for self-analysis which makes day-to-day use of psychoanalytic assumptions has become a common resource of character. The application of analytic theories to literature and art, to group processes, and to the under-standing of social institutions and their practices are other examples of the widespread extension and social application of this form of understanding.

There has been some convergence between the findings of psychoanalysis on the early development of relationships in infancy and the work of ethologists such as Bowlby (1969, 1973, 1980) and developmental psychologists, though with characteristically different emphases on behavioural rather than 'internal' forms of explanation. On this convergence, see Boston, 1975, Murray, 1989, Shuttleworth, 1989, Stern, 1985 and Urwin, 1986. The effects of separation, loss, and institutional care on children are other areas of convergent understanding between psychoanalysis and neighbouring fields. While psychoanalytic insights derive originally from self- and personal analysis, and continue to depend on the clinical method, analysis has also been supported as a plausible form of knowledge by these other kinds of experience. There is no single counter-factual test on which this whole system of knowledge depends, any more than there has been for any other major scientific paradigm.

The clinical method remains psychoanalysis's primary source of new knowledge. Whatever the problems of publicly testing inferences about uncon-scious mental structures developed through analysis, there is no doubt about analysts' intense conviction of the truthfulness of their insights. There is equal conviction of the revelatory clarity with which patients and analysts sometimes share this sense of realized truth, which analysts compare to the revelations of art. The standardization of clinical procedures and training, and the elaborate mechanisms for reporting and subjecting to professional scrutiny the findings of analysis, also give analysts confidence that their procedures can be no less scrupulous and rigorous in their standards than those of other scientists.

The demonstration by the 'new sociology of science' of the degree to which all science depends on consensual procedures and on acceptance of the expertise of qualified observers should make one wary of an idealized view of natural scientific method conceived as commonsensical in its method of obser-vation, open and democratic in its access to findings, and freely competitive in its modes of selection between competing hypotheses. There is no point in judging psychoanalysis by a normative standard to which virtually no scientific work conforms. Observations in X-ray crystallography, palaeontology and neutrino experiments in salt mines depend no less than psychoanalysis on the consensus of trained experts.

The distinctive features of the psychoanalytic field may be a function not of its methodological failures but of the particular dimensions and attributes of the slice of the world which it investigates. A theory of stratified and differentiated reality suggests that modes of investigation will necessarily vary with the nature and levels of phenomena being studied. Not all these, in the human world, may be equally transparent, or equally separable from the life world and subjective experiences of observers. It may well be that deep knowledge of human minds and emotions can be obtained *only* through reflection on interactions in depth between one person and another. The aim of psychoanalysis has been to establish techniques which can enable this to be done consistently and reliably.

The Limits of Psychoanalysis as a Science

Finally, I wish to address some limits and possible methodological weaknesses of psychoanalysis as a science. These reflections are prompted by the ways in which theory seems to function as a discursive resource rather than as a coherent and cumulative system, and by the plurality of partially overlapping concepts and theories to be found coexisting or competing within this intellectual field.

Some of these limits may be those of all human sciences. As Bhaskar puts it, human science takes place in 'open', and not 'closed' systems. (Or to use another idiom — paradoxically, considering analysis takes place in consulting rooms — it is an 'outdoor' rather than 'indoor' science.) This imposes constraints on the formal and deductive applicability of its models, since there is little possibility of finding exemplars of its theoretical constructs in the world in a pure state. Psychoanalysts study a mental life which is subject to social and cultural changes: some of the patterns of symptom studied by Freud (for example, hysteria) no longer seem to be so common and have been replaced in their frequency by others. Because psychoanalytic ideas — like most concepts of the social sciences — become available as resources to actors, they reflexively interact with their own object of study, reducing the probable temporal and social scope of application of given theoretical models.

Thus psychoanalysis influences the culture of which it is a part, so that its findings, as with other human sciences, serve to transform over time its own object of study. This is another reason for the social relativity and historical specificity of psychoanalytic models and descriptions. We might reasonably expect some, if not all, the relational patterns they describe and explain to be subject to cultural mutation. The theoretical knowledge achieved within psychoanalysis and other social sciences seems both more historically relative and less deductively applicable to phenomena known in experience than those of many of the natural sciences. The use of the natural sciences as a prescriptive model for psychoanalysis, the usual implicit critical weapon of empiricist philosophers, seems therefore to have only a limited point.

But it seems too that psychoanalysis is more than usually particularistic (compared with some other social sciences) in its transmission of ideas and its institutional self-reproduction. Its theories are, as I have argued, usable only when they can be linked to specific observation procedures, which have to be learned in an unusually self-referential and introspective way. This learning process depends on one-to-one or small-group interactions in which someone deeply versed in consensual modes of mapping mental states transmits these skills to novices through supervised trial and error. This mode of transmission is also the basis for the reproduction of the profession and for the dissemination of new theories, concepts and methods, through training analysis and supervision. This is highly labour-intensive, and a single analyst can have the necessary degree of intense pedagogic contact with only a very restricted number of pupils and colleagues. Sociologists of science have pointed out that such implicit and personal modes of knowledge-transfer are also significant in the natural sciences, which by no means rely wholly on the formal system of published papers for communication. But I suggest that psychoanalysis is rather different from most other fields in its balance between formalized, impersonal means of communication, through published report, and personally mediated transmission of knowledge. Because of the peculiar constraints of its distinctive mode of observation, psychoanalysis remains largely dependent on a form of craft apprenticeship for the transmission of its ideas.

We might add that this is a field — unlike many hard sciences — in which there are no technological factors to impose economies of scale and a consequent concentration of power in the hands of controllers of scarce material resources. The work is done in single rooms, not large laboratories, and needs little specialized equipment. High-tech science seems naturally to lean towards intellectual oligopoly and the concentration of intellectual resources in elites. While dominant psychoanalytic groups can and do seek to use organizational means (and even the professional licensing authority of the state) to uphold their own power and to marginalize their opponents, the technical conditions of analytic work do not of themselves support monopolistic practices. Appeals can be made — as in the example of R.D. Laing and David Cooper in the 1960s — over the heads of the established professional community to new publics, which may offer alternative support to dissenters. Or, if the state of demand for therapy will bear it, institutional splits can occur and different factions can take their chance in the client market.

These factors have encouraged a characteristic fragmentation of analytic knowledge and the analytic community, despite its own sometimes frantic efforts to resist this (on these tendencies see also Dyne, 1985, and Hinshelwood, 1986). Knowledge obtained by one-to-one interactions, requiring extensive personal training but few other resources, is inherently democratic in institutional potentiality, even though its organizations have favoured (for good and bad reasons, to protect standards of knowledge and service as well as professional privilege) internal hierarchy and closure. This creates conditions in which it has been difficult for analytic knowledge to become systematically codified and unified by consensus, even within its own scientific community. It is liable to become differentiated and bounded by schools and tendencies whose scope of influence is limited by the feasible extent of analytic training and referral networks.

Of course there is contact and often theoretical convergence between these tendencies, whose members may find themselves working at a particular time on closely related problems. These may be generated by commonly perceived theoretical gaps and anomalies, or by new clinical phenomena which reflect changes in the real world: the recent psychoanalytic interest in 'narcissism' may be an example of the latter kind (Kohut, 1971, 1977; Lasch, 1979, 1985). But as is often the case in the social sciences, the institutional mechanisms for decisively settling intellectual disputes between contending factions are weak. There are no multimillion-dollar linear accelerators, disused salt mines, or any other technical resources vital for knowledge generation to which only one or two research teams can have privileged access. The organizational resources and powers of state-funded clinics and professional training programmes are perhaps the nearest equivalent means of unification and concentration.

It also appears that the highly personal mode of intellectual transmission characteristic of psychoanalysis is subject to particular interruption and sway by personal passion and interest. While personal loyalties to teachers, referral networks centring on the powerful, and the resentments of the excluded affect the development of knowledge in all professions, there seems reason to believe that psychoanalysis is more than usually exposed to these perils, given the highly reflexive and personal nature of its object and mode of study and the affectively intense relationships through which this has to be accomplished. All this may also impede the orderly and consensual accumulation of knowledge.

As I have pointed out in Chapter 4 above, psychoanalytic institutions devote considerable efforts to trying to limit the damage caused by these factors.

Another possible obstacle to orderly development and reputation is a naturally occurring imbalance between the numbers of competent practitioners available and potential therapeutic demand. One might almost expect this from psychoanalysis's own assumptions concerning the inherent human obstacles to rational self-knowledge. It seems that the reflexive, intellectual and emotional skills required to practise psychoanalysis effectively are simply scarce, and are hard to reproduce to a sufficient and reliable standard. If this is so, one would expect, given the abundant demand in modern societies for psychological help and comfort, that many not very capable practitioners would enter the field. Any such unreliability of standard will unavoidably sow confusion and discredit, though given a democratic and compassionate attitude towards the relief of mental suffering and the facilitating of personal development, it seems likely to be an insoluble and continuing problem at almost any imaginable level of expanded provision.

I would nevertheless claim, with these qualifications, that psychoanalysis undoubtedly has a real object for scientific study and has organized itself in such a way as to produce rational and consensual means of generating knowledge. The evidence of scrupulous attention to reliable method in analytic training, and for the advance of analytic knowledge in the face of perceived anomalies and therapeutic failures, seems to me to exist for inspection. Critics of analysis argue that its ideas are infinitely elastic, inviting the barren method of reclassifying phenomena to fit a dogmatic system of ideas instead of the harder discipline of modifying theory in the light of fresh evidence. Certainly ideas of metaphoric communication, protean and reversible meanings and unconscious resistance can legitimate an 'anything goes' approach in analytic explanation, but this is not how the analytic community actually behaves. Observation of the routine work of analytic therapy in Britain suggests, on the contrary, a strenuous commitment to understand individuals as they are and to tolerate extreme uncertainty in the process of finding out what ideas might best explain psychic phenomena. Perhaps the strongest motive supporting this responsiveness to fact is the concern to help patients in considerable mental pain. Judgements about whether a field shares the various attributes of 'scientificity' with others can be based only on empirical knowledge and comparison.

The final issue I want to consider is the relationship between psychoanalysis and value-commitments. Do the arguments presented above for a 'realist' concept of psychoanalysis also support the view that psychoanalysis provides objective grounds for defining and choosing human ends, as some notions of scientific realism prescribe (Bhaskar, 1979)? Or does the construction of the psychoanalytic field of investigation already presuppose a moral standpoint, a definition of human needs and purposes which precedes and gives shape to this whole frame of thinking? On this latter conventionalist or pragmatist premiss a different view of man would generate an alternative psychology, the choices between psychologies being as much a choice between desired end-states or life worlds as of ontological realities. In the nature of the case, such choices cannot be settled by scientific means alone. This view is compatible with a weaker version of realism: it posits a real object of knowledge (the world is not merely what we wish it to be), but attributes to it an indeterminacy related to human consciousness and choice. While we can experience the world in different ways, we cannot escape the constraints of material and human nature, which will be made evident in our knowledge of the world through whatever category-system we employ.

Consistent with this modified realism, I argue that psychoanalysis as a discursive practice both embodies and depends on specific values and human purposes, and seeks to furnish experiential grounds to sustain them. In its broadest terms, the psychoanalytic world-view is constituted by a commitment to rational understanding of the self and to such freedom of choice as can be furthered by this. More specifically, it is evident that the various traditions and subschools of psychoanalysis differ from each other in part by virtue of divergent underlying views of the human life world and its purposes.

Within the field of psychoanalysis, different accounts have been given of the dominant structures of the mind and feeling. National cultural traditions have clearly played their part in this differentiation. Ego-psychology in the United States, to take an often-discussed case, has absorbed from American culture a certain meliorism — the assumption that rational adjustment to a competitive environment may be readily attained without undue attention to psychic depths. But in a later American development in reaction to this, in the more radical climate of the late 1960s, Kohut (1971, 1977) gave emphasis to the importance of difficult-to-treat character disorders and borderline states. This had the effect of problematizing these somewhat egoistic values, and of calling in question not only the 'narcissism' of certain kinds of patient but also, by extension, the narcissism of a whole social climate. (On this see Lasch, 1979.)

Also reacting against the perceived compromises of 'ego-psychology' was the contribution to psychoanalytic thought in France of Jacques Lacan. This, shaped by and in its turn influencing a French cultural tradition which emphasized the primacy of language and culture in human development, also had implications for values. These were to stress the deep and unconscious roots of social repression, much as Freud had done, and led in Britain to an important 'feminist' rereading of psychoanalytic ideas, as explaining the oppressions of gender. On these developments see Mitchell (1975), Mitchell and Rose (1982), Benvenuto and Kennedy (1986), and most recently Forrester (1990); also further discussion in Chapter 7 below, and in Rustin (1985b).

Kleinian theories in Britain gave a still different moral inflection to psycho-analytic thought. These, in postulating a 'death instinct', an innate disposition to envy and jealousy, and an 'epistemophilic instinct' (this concept later developed in Bion's work), advanced a more intransigent and conservative view of human nature, but also gave reason for placing greater hope on familial and other forms of intense intimate relationship as means of further development. Differences between the Kleinian and 'Middle Groups' in the British School of psychoanalysis, explored further in Rustin (1988b), focused on this more and less 'benign' view of human nature. Clearly the connections between psycho-analytic ideas as these develop in their clinical and professional settings, and wider social contexts, are complex and difficult to establish with certainty. (For some attempts to make such connections, see, for example, Turkle, 1978; Richards, 1985, 1989a, and arguments developed elsewhere in this book.) But there seems no doubt that psychoanalysis is a discursive resource for a number of different views of human possibility, within the fundamental postulate that developmental potentialities are shaped and constrained by the emotional events of infancy and can be liberated by analytic understanding. In a static social system, in which analysts could function only to reproduce existing values, a closure of the field around some single ontological and ethical commitment might be imaginable, if highly undesirable.

We do not, however, live in a conflict-free or static social system, and there are reasons inherent in human nature and society why we are never likely to do so. While attempts at ideological closure around a single world-view have been made in different social sciences in both East and West, their success has been short-lived and their dissolution sometimes dramatic. The self-defining and symbolic capacities of human actors which are the key resource of psycho-analytic understanding are also the cause of the 'open-endedness' and plasticity of human societies and their individual members. According to various socio-logical accounts, such indeterminacy and scope of choice are liable to increase in the long term, as the overcoming of scarcity and social differentiation proceeds by means of industrialization and post-industrialization. This is a vision of a more pluralist future society.

One attribute of the open-endedness of such systems as ours is that discursive resources may be used to ground and justify many different values and ways of life. Theories can point to hitherto unknown states of affairs, or extrapolate new possibilities from existing states of things, viewed as potentialities. The rather demanding specification given by both Klein and Winnicott of the kinds of infant care most conducive to emotional development were grounded in observation and experience, yet differed from what both knew to be common practice in their time, or even in their own personal experience. They were implicitly assertions of possibility as well as descriptions of a known empirical reality.

Thus psychoanalysis does not ground its account of human possibility and value on nothing, as pure prescription, since it distinctively offers factual description, causal hypotheses, and theories of human nature to support its view(s) of human life and development. On the other hand, in a world in which there are continuing differences between lifeworlds and points of view, and personal and political choices to be made, there is no reason to think that psychoanalysis will provide support only for one ethical, ontological or aesthetic standpoint. One could demonstrate what range of commitments is in fact held to be consistent, at a given time, with the corpus of analytic ideas; at present this range would be finite and would exclude at least certain anti-rationalist and anti-libertarian positions. But that would be a description of an actual or imagined consensus, not a logical deduction. Any complex system of ideas is capable of an almost infinite reselection and interpretation of derivative assertions. There is no logical 'essence' of this or any other system of thought (see Barnes, 1982), only a set of cultural affiliations which predispose practically and tendentially to a particular direction of development.

The relation between psychoanalytic knowledge and human interests therefore consists in the fact that psychoanalysis is a ground, a legitimation and a consequence of certain definitions of purposes, in what might be thought of as a virtuous circle of reasoning. It begins from a point (or points) of view regarding human nature and possibility, but then provides evidence and justification of its plausibility and claims. The density and richness of psychoanalytic accounts of human motivation have made it, in fact, into an exemplary form of moral reasoning.[9]

Notes

1. Lakatos (1970) distinguished scientific programmes in which theories were modified in the light of fresh findings from theories whose terms were merely stretched and redefined to accommodate anomalies. This latter process he termed 'degenerative problem shifts'. Psychoanalysis has been subjected to much criticism for its alleged evasions of counter-factual tests by elastic reinterpretation of the meaning of evidence.

2. For readings of Freud's work which emphasize his development in a more 'mentalistic' direction, see R. Wollheim (1971) and D. Meltzer (1978). See also, for a more comprehensive review of theoretical developments from Freud's work, J. Greenberg and J.A. Mitchell (1983).

Incidentally, the shift towards hermeneutic approaches as a self-description of psychoanalytic work was contemporary with a similar evolution in other social sciences, for example sociology. The 'micro' focus on the immediacy of the analytic session found in work influenced by Bion also has its parallels in sociology. These developments seem variously to be part of a broader 'culturalist' trend in the human sciences from the 1960s onwards.

3. The concept of countertransference was first used by Freud to describe distortions of understanding brought about by the analyst's unconscious feelings towards the patient. Subsequently the idea was developed, by analysts influenced by Klein (notably Paula Heimann, 1950), that the countertransference could be used as a positive analytic resource. It was held that feelings evoked in analysts by patients could, if they were subjected to analysis, provide useful insight into patients' states of mind. The validity of this depends on the idea that painful states of mind are sometimes dealt with by being projected outside the self and then experienced, so to speak, through others.

4. Much of the value of ethnographic sociology, from the pre-war Chicago School to later developments of symbolic interactionism, has consisted in the quality of its descriptive reports of little-known, deviant or officially disregarded areas of social life (Becker, 1970).

5. There are similarities between the task confronted by psychoanalytic observers in seeking to relate data to their conceptual resources and that faced by field researchers in social science. On this see Clifford Geertz's (1983) reflections on the relations of concepts and field experience in anthropology. Analytic supervisors also insist on the provision from their students of observation reports of sufficient 'thickness' to make conceptualization worthwhile.

6. The Science Section of the *New York Times*, 26 February 1985 ('Strange Subatomic Particles Herald a New Astronomy') reported a series of experiments intended to locate the cosmic source of the high-energy subatomic particles known as neutrinos. Neutrinos are exceptionally penetrative; therefore the experimental detector (a tank containing 10,000 gallons of highly purified water in which the path and direction of particles could be tracked) was sited in a disused salt mine below Lake Erie, under a thickness of rock sufficient to screen out other unwanted kinds of particles. The decay of a proton or neutron believed to yield neutrinos is thought to be an extremely rare occurrence, 'and in five years of operation the detector has recorded none with certainty'. High-energy muons, however, which are generated when a neutrino strikes an atomic particle and were believed in this case to originate from Cygnus, were detected. There were more than predicted, however, and the finding was thus regarded as either 'an important discovery' or 'a cause for concern about the validity of the analysis'.

I quote this report only to show that the relationship between theoretical conjecture and observation procedures is not a problem only for psychoanalysis. The phenomena of outer and inner space are both known through their effects; in each case, the attainment of knowledge depends on the consensus of qualified observers and interpreters of the phenomena. The *NYT* report refers to 'the bizarre object known as SS 433 that is ejecting jets of matter in opposite directions at almost the speed of light'. ('Bizarre objects' also feature in Bion's description of psychotic states of mind.) Incidentally, one of the scientists engaged in the salt-mine experiment was named Dr Learned.

7. I suggest that the use of psychoanalytic theory for purposes of prediction and explanation in analytic work is accomplished most often in terms of 'local' connections made in relation to specific phenomena. Analysts are quite often able to anticipate the direction of patients' development and mental preoccupations, in terms of theoretical concepts which by no means coincide with common-sense expectations or even hopes. But these are most likely to be applications of 'middle-range theory' to the immediate case, not comprehensive models of mental structure or development. Such larger-scale generalizations rapidly lose all empirical referent, useful as they may be as theoretical scaffolding. Their prevalence in the analytic literature accounts for much of its aridity.

8. Comparisons might be drawn between the distinctive strengths of British work in the Marxist and psychoanalytic traditions. Perhaps the foremost area of British Marxist scholarship has been in history, which in the writings of Christopher Hill, Edward Thompson and the large school which they have influenced has been distinctively attentive to the life experience of ordinary citizens and to their own attempts to give meaning and shape to their world in the face of subordination and suffering. Those around the journal *History Workshop* have given even greater emphasis to everyday experience, widening the definition of the 'political' in response to contemporary preoccupations with gender, family, childhood and leisure, for example. The 'clinical' emphasis of the British psychoanalytic school (so much in contrast with the philosophical and linguistic concerns of much psychoanalytic writing in France) seems to have something in common with this commitment to recording personal experience in its own terms. Perhaps both these adaptations of highly theoretical ways of thinking result from the influence of the British intellectual climate's empiricism, and especially of a British literary tradition which values the representation of common experience.

9. This is not least because of the central importance which Melanie Klein's work especially gave to the development of moral capacities in the child.

6

Post-Kleinian* Psychoanalysis
and the Post-Modern

In a number of papers written in the early 1980s, I attempted to explore the social and political affiliations of Kleinian psychoanalysis in Britain.[1] I characterized some of the leading themes, both implicit and explicit, of Kleinian work, and suggested some connections between these and the social preoccupations of the post-war welfare state in Britain. The purpose was partly to explore these connections as matter of fact and explanation, but also to establish the positive values of these psychoanalytic ideas for a democratic socialist vision. These papers, it is now clear, were already historical in their reference when they were written, since the age of Thatcher had begun, and the dismantling of the post-war consensus and settlement of the welfare state was in its first stages. However, in 1981 it seemed reasonable to hope otherwise — for an early resumption of the admittedly uneven progress towards full social citizenship which had been initiated during the Second World War. It was not obvious at the time that the social programme to which one's arguments sought to relate psychoanalytic practice, especially in the public health field, had

---

*The term 'Post-Kleinian' refers here in the first instance to work within the Kleinian tradition by members of the subsequent generation of Kleinian analysts, most of whom were pupils of Melanie Klein herself. The nature and extent of the departures of thinking in this second generation from the assumptions of Klein's own work is one of the issues explored in this chapter, together with the possible affinities of this thinking with a 'post-modernist' climate of ideas. Whilst important developments have taken place in Kleinian thinking in this later period, the emphasis of the argument that follows is ultimately on the continuity of the Kleinian and post-Kleinian tradition and of its fundamental assumptions. 'Post-Kleinian' thus differs as a term from 'post-modern' or 'Post-Marxist' in not intending to imply, to the same extent, that a revolutionary intellectual break has taken place.

stopped in its tracks or, still worse, been put into reverse.

Now, in the early 1990s, the radical change in political climate is unmistakable. It is hardly possible at this point to see the evolution of welfare institutions supportive of personal development as a thriving cause, or to see ideas of caring and inclusive social membership as particularly central to mainstream British society's view of itself. Integrative conceptions of British society, binding both within and to some degree between social classes, have for the time being at least weakened, first under the pressure of intensified social conflicts in the 1960s and 1970s, as different class and social movements mobilized and evoked counter-mobilizations from the right, and then in a pervasive process of privatization and atomization of social interests. British society has become both more pluralistic, in the diversity of social identities which have emerged, and also more individualistic, as the Thatcherites have rewarded and legitimized the priority of self-interest over ideas of the social good which they now define as coercive, but which at an earlier moment seemed to be widely consensual.

Significant changes are also taking place on the plane of intellectual and cultural life. I have in mind less the revival of militant neo-conservative ideologies (which are often similar in their *form* of thinking and practice to the ideologies of the left, even if opposite in values and content) than the disintegration of established systems of theory and belief. On one view (which has interesting echoes of Nietzsche) we live on after the death of ideology, in a period of 'post-Marxism', 'post-modernism', 'post-structuralism', post-whatever. Unfortunately, the 'end of ideology', when it came, didn't usher in an era of consensual, ethically based harmony, as Daniel Bell and liberal functionalists like him had hoped, but instead one of anomic disintegration, self-seeking, and confusion. The links between the art and ideas of post-modernism, and the economic and social infrastructure of post-industrialism or post-Fordism, have been explored in interesting ways by a number of writers.[2] What I want to do here is to characterize the development of a 'post-Kleinian' body of psychoanalytic ideas, suggest some affinities this shares with the wider postmodernist climate of thought, and to raise some questions about its potential political and cultural linkages, these being still to a degree undetermined and dependent on choices yet to be made.

The Kleinian Paradigm and its Political Affinities

In order to clarify what is distinctive about the concerns of 'post-Kleinian' psychoanalysis, it may be helpful to give a brief sketch of the main themes of classical Kleinian ideas, and their social affinities, following the accounts attempted in earlier work.[3] I argued in Chapter 1 that Melanie Klein's investigations of the mental states of infancy gave rise to an intensely *social* view of the origins of the self. The baby, she saw, depended on the mother (or other primary care-taker) not only for its physical well-being, or even its sense of emotional comfort, but also for the development of its sense of identity and its powers of mental functioning. Klein saw the infant's fragmented, diffused, and often violent states of mind and feeling becoming integrated into a coherent awareness of self and others only through an intimate relationship with parenting adults. Unconscious communication links mother and infant in a symbiotic unit in the early stages of life, without which the infant is no more psychologically viable than he or she is physically viable if abandoned when young. This emphasis on infantile relatedness and dependency, especially in the earliest months of life and in the primary relationship with the mother, leads to a perspective on human nature distinct from the robust individualism of Freud, though it is a development of his own discoveries.

There is some consistency between this theory of infantile development and Bowlby's attachment theory, which stressed the dependence of infants on primary maternal care, and argued that emotional and mental capacities were damaged by its absence. Bowlby grounded his theory on biological considerations of species survival, and made relevant use of ethological evidence from the behaviour of primates. There is, however, an important difference between these theories. Attachment theory is environmentalist in its main emphasis, holding (like the early Freud on infantile sexual experience) that it is actual contact with parents which makes possible (or its absence impossible) normal development. Separations and interruptions of care, and their consequences for bonding, are therefore of most account, and the most important modes of intervention are designed to prevent such breakdowns. For the child analysts, these infant-parent transactions take place in unconscious phantasy as well as in external practice. There is an inner-world dimension of development, not necessarily directly corresponding to the intentions or external manifestations of parental care. Because of the role of innate disposition in infants and parents, and the importance of phantasy in the development of an internal world and the perceptions and expectations it shapes, outcomes of parental care are both less predictable and more alterable from the perspective of child analysts than from that of attachment theorists. The development of child analysis, especially in its attempts to treat extreme cases of developmental failure such as autism or schizophrenia in children, arises from its view of the importance of these unconscious dimensions. Bowlby and his colleagues have been more sceptical than the Kleinians about the effectiveness of analytic therapeutic methods, once emotional damage has been done.

A second characteristic of Kleinian analysis was its emphasis on the ethical. Kleinian theory makes the development of moral capacities in the infant a criterion of normal personality development. Moral feelings are held to be innate, arising from the primary intensity of feelings of both love and hate for the object. The infant recognizes that the kinds of well-being and pain that it experiences are also experienced by the mother, and can be given to or withheld from her by its own agency. The discrimination between good and bad in this primary relationship, and the recognition of responsibility for these states, are the roots of moral discriminations of a more general kind. The Kleinian model in which development takes place from paranoid-schizoid to depressive positions (as recurring constellations of feeling, not merely as chronological phases) incudes moral capacities in the definition of these positions. This is pictured as a transition from states dominated by persecutory, split-off, projected bad feelings (lodged in the phantasied other through projective identification) to the recognition of the vulnerability of the loved object, and a state of mind where there is capacity to bear pain and loss within the self. The ideas of gratitude and reparation held to emerge with the depressive position are terms which belong to a complex ethical language, as well as to psycho-logical description. In these ways Kleinian analysis provided a resource for enriching a somewhat depleted discourse of English moral philosophy, though not one which has been widely taken up.[4]

A third aspect of Kleinian thinking which, I shall argue, had significant social affinities was its teleological dimension. There is inherent in Kleinian theory the idea of a 'normal' pathway of development, given both explanatory and evaluative significance. The 'depressive position' defined a state of affairs that was normative, what one should want for human beings, which was held in some way to correspond to the potential of human nature. This theory offers a complex account of the developmental needs of the moral individual. From its presuppositions one could point out favourable and unfavourable conditions for such development, and practices and institutions (for example kinds of childcare, therapeutic and remedial intervention, understanding and support for families) which might further these. It seemed reasonable to link this normative account of the development of the individual to a 'progressive' view of social development, in which society or governments gave greater priority to such developmental goals and their desired moral outcomes.

One central theme of Kleinian theory, however, was contrary to the meliorist climate of post-war Britain, and was difficult to assimilate into its social thought. This was its emphasis on destructiveness and aggression — the concept of an innate 'death instinct' which was so important in the conflict between the Kleinians and the two other rival groups in the British Psycho-Analytical Society in the 1940s. The 'Middle Group', or Independents, who mostly rejected this negative emphasis in Klein's theory, remained closer to the prevailing temper of British liberal thought, being less committed to theoretical consistency and less intransigent in outlook than the Kleinians. This darker current in Klein's thought contributed in large measure to its remaining a minority, oppositional tendency, marginal to British intellectual life, though it nevertheless proved capable, within its own field, of a long period of creative development. Considering the experience of war and mass murder at the time, it is odd that the Kleinian view of innate human potential should have been regarded as extreme and alien. It seems to relate to this experience of surrounding catastrophe in the same way that Freud's own pessimistic writings did to the events of the First World War, though for the most part (in Klein's own work, at least) without explicit reference to this public context. It is not, I think, coincidental that Kleinian analysts have subsequently been amongst those most prominent in the campaign among British psychoanalysts against nuclear war, given the central place of unconscious destructiveness in their theory, and the imperative need to bring this within the field of conscious understanding.

These psychoanalytic ideas connected to several of the central preoccupations of social thought in post-war Britain. The ethical cast of Kleinian thinking paralleled a moral emphasis in social-democratic political thought evident, for example, in Titmuss's forceful contrast of altruism with individualism and sectional class interests. The idea of human nature and its potentials, as a moral benchmark against which social progress could be measured, figured also in the most vigorous area of post-war cultural criticism, notably in that of Leavis and his circle. Leavis defined the main tradition of English literature as a field of moral inquiry and reflection, generative of values higher than those of utility and business ('Benthamite–utilitarian civilization'). The Kleinian, or perhaps more broadly the object-relations theory of development, could be seen as the systematic theory of human nature and its potential emotional and moral capacities that Leavisism lacked. In the late 1950s, with the emergence of the New Left, the idea of human potentiality was given a socialist and indeed Marxist form, with the rediscovery of Marx's early manuscripts and the revival of humanist Marxism. There was some continuity between a liberal idea of fulfilment through self-expression and a socialist view of a democratic culture, a development which Raymond Williams's work did most to make possible. A teleological vision was the common background assumption of a wide variety of more-or-less humanist theories, from the Kleinian view of individual development, to both liberal and socialist ideas of social improvement. Liberal, social-democratic, and neo-Marxist theories of progress in each case incorporated ideas of individual self-expression into their moral foundation, at least until structuralist and post-structuralist critiques put all this implicit or explicit liberal humanism in question. Education and the personal social services became fields in which psychoanalytically informed conceptions of individual development achieved a limited practical influence. This occurred, for example, in the recognition of the emotional needs of children in hospital, in critiques of impersonal institutional care, in the growth of school counselling, and in the development of psychotherapeutic treatment for children and families.

A 'Facilitating Environment'

The organicism of Kleinian and other object-relations thinking is another point of affinity with post-war social concerns. The idea of the integration of the self in what Winnicott termed a 'facilitating environment' corresponded with a broader ideological concern for social reintegration, following the disorganization and disruption of war and the fresh memories of class antagonism and polarization, clearly central to the pre-war crisis and the onset of fascism. Bowlby's initial work was concerned with the ill-effects of evacuation on children, and led him to a broader concern with experiences of separation and loss. Titmuss's work was manifestly preoccupied with the idea of an integrated social order, unified as a moral community. The figuring of the child as an emblem of hope was central to post-war progressivism, not only reflecting a demographic primacy but also expressing the hopes of an adult generation scarred by war, and wanting to build a different future for the next generation. In the 1960s it became possible to acknowledge more extreme and disturbing memories and experiences in symbolic terms, and Kleinian thinking (and psychoanalytic ideas more generally) became an occasional resource in attempts to encompass or recognize greater depths of destructiveness in art and literature. Whether readily absorbed into British cultural discourse or not, there is no doubt that Kleinian concerns with psychotic, paranoid, and suicidal states of mind connected with prominent themes in post-war culture, once writers began to explore these. R.D. Laing's early works, *The Divided Self* and *The Self and Others*, were influential in introducing these ideas — though they were barely acknowledged as Klein's — to a wide audience.

Within Kleinian analytic practice, these background ethical and humanist conceptions were also evident. Classical Kleinian analysis not only used developmental concepts which had a central moral dimension but sometimes applied them judgementally, invoking guilt and blame to the detriment of analytic understanding. The Kleinians were characterized by their possession of a strong background theory, by their commitment to strict analytic technique, and by membership of a strongly defined group, sectarian at least in respect of its liability to defection and split. Some Kleinians remained most committed to maintaining the standards and purity of psychoanalysis, accepting as a concomitant of this goal its necessary confinement within the marginal though elite institution of the British Psycho-Analytical Society. Others developed a more proselytizing and socially committed conception of analytic practice and consultation, through institutions such as the Tavistock Clinic. But what was taken for granted in both circles was the commitment to a definite form of knowledge, its connection to central human values, and its demanding claims as a vocation. These qualities it shared with other secular but nevertheless transcendental humanisms of the period, including Leavisism and humanist Marxism. The distinctiveness and vulnerability of these moralized ways of looking at the world has become fully evident only as they have begun to be challenged by the outlooks of the 'post-philosophies'. While they are radically different in their content and their specific ontological and ethical claims, they turn out to be quite similar in the humanist certainty of their perspectives on human nature and purpose.

Liberal humanism, Marxism, even orthodox psychoanalysis, have in recent years come under attack, from within and without their own traditions, as absolutisms, for demanding improper 'guarantees' (of truth or virtue) in a world deemed to be one of contingency, relativity and pluralism.[5] Even those (like me) committed to the defence of absolutist positions have to take account of these critiques and the new orders of phenomena they address. This change of cultural perspective has its reflections within the Kleinian analytic tradition too. It is now possible to characterize a 'post-Kleinian' psychoanalysis, and to explore its relationship to the current cultural climate.

Post-Kleinian Analysis

The central figure in the development of 'post-Kleinian' psychoanalysis was Wilfred Bion, though his work forms part of a broader evolution to which many other analysts have contributed.[6] There has been no repudiation of Klein's ideas by these analysts — on the contrary, a deep engagement with and development of them, parallel to Klein's own reading and reworking of Freud. Yet the effect has been to achieve a deep shift of interest and focus, identifying phenomena for investigation distinct from those which were central for Klein and her earlier followers.

The impetus for this development came primarily from the attempt to analyse patients with more extreme disturbances of mind than those previously thought amenable to analytic treatment. In the brilliant papers collected in *Second Thoughts*, Bion describes how he tried to understand the mental states of psychotic patients who were either unable to communicate verbally during most of their analytic sessions, or whose communications seemed to represent states of hallucination or delusion. Bion was led to rely on the counter-transference as a major analytic resource, but he also focused on the processes by which sensation and emotion became capable of symbolic representation, and what happened to the mind when they did not, or when the capacity to distinguish symbols (especially words) and their objects was not achieved. In these conditions, the intense passions and anxieties aroused in infancy by bodily sensations, desires, and terrors would literally disintegrate the mind. The processes of thought which normally clarify boundaries between phenomena, and thus reduce the anxiety attached to them, could be experienced in these circumstances as threatening conjunctions. Bion understood that in extreme psychotic states, the process of thinking itself, the very idea of language, could be experienced as a mortal threat. Freud thought that (for patients deemed not too ill for analysis to be possible) *particular* infantile experiences and phantasies would be fraught with anxiety and subject to repression, while some generally rational thinking capacity could be used as the platform, so to speak, from which the irrational depths could be investigated. The function of analytic method was to uncover specifically repressed meanings (from dreams, dream associations, etc.) while assuming that analyst and analysand shared a linguistic medium which could to some extent be relied upon for this communication.

This assumption was made by Klein also, for the most part. Though she extended analytic interest to mechanisms of denial, splitting and projective identification, which she thought of as more primitive processes, her analytic work with children nevertheless proceeded on the assumption that there was a rational as well as an irrational part of the child patient's mind, functioning well enough to sustain analytic dialogue. But for Bion, and those like him who have attempted to analyse schizophrenic and autistic patients, this assumption could no longer be made, since the absence of a capacity for ordinary mental function was the central issue. Attention shifted from what was supposed to be contained (in whatever repressed or distorted form) by the mental apparatus to the properties of the container itself, to use two of Bion's most influential terms.

This implicit paradigm shift within the Kleinian tradition was not achieved without psychoanalysts being willing to expose themselves to an experience of extreme disturbance and disorientation. This is especially clear in Bion's description of his work with psychotic patients, but it is also reported in the writings of other contemporary analysts of such extreme states of mind, such as Frances Tustin (whose work is with autistic children), Herbert Rosenfeld (the other major Kleinian writer on psychotic states) and Donald Meltzer (who has been one of the main interpreters of Bion's ideas).[7] Bion came to feel that in order to make any progress with analysis of psychotic disturbance it was necessary to empty the mind of theoretical preconceptions, which became in these conditions merely defences against what had to be experienced in feeling before it could be thought about, known before it could be known about. Bion urged this technical requirement of a wholly receptive mind, working without preconceptions very graphically, when he called on analysts to empty their minds of memory and desire during analytic sessions, as a positive discipline: 'Memory and desire are "illuminations" that destroy the analyst's capacity for observation as a leakage of light into a camera might destroy the value of the film being exposed.'[8]

This ideal of total receptivity (which was compared to the aesthetic idea of 'negative capability') was received in part of the analytic community as a kind of renewal of the pure spirit of analysis, felt to have become somewhat routinized in the hands of some orthodox Kleinians. It is perhaps parallel in this respect to movements for internal renewal in modernism (for example, the phase of the 'new brutalism' in architecture), where a return to fundamentals was called for by a new generation against the institutional compromises of elder practitioners.

Thus there is a move in post-Kleinian analysis towards an extreme phenom-enology. The here-and-now transactions of the analytic session itself are given an ontological priority over established theoretical models. It is as if post-Kleinian analysis makes a shift from the mode of 'normal science' — often fairly standard applications of established conceptions and techniques to recognizable conditions — to a 'revolutionary' mode, in which every theoretical belief, at least in principle, has to be suspended for the moment. It seems that even the theories and models held to be basically correct by analysts like Bion and Meltzer were found an obstacle, in actual analytic work, to thinking about psychotic patients whose communications were barely verbal and had to be intuited largely through the countertransference. The moment of discovering a meaning in a fleeting experience, of tentatively putting together the fragments of a language through which analyst and patient could talk, became the key task. These patients, it must be recalled, were extremely disturbed — the issue is not the usual repressions and misrepresentations of self and others found in neurotic symptoms, but the absence in such patients of almost any undisturbed communicative capacity.

Similar experiences arose in an equally dramatic way in therapeutic work with schizophrenic and autistic children. The problem was to find a language, sometimes in relationship with a virtually mute child, or with a child whose language seemed completely deluded. The templates of established theories and procedures had to be to some degree held in suspension to achieve this. Furthermore, establishing some capacity for thinking in the patient — that is, helping the child in some way to bear and deal with the overwhelming or terrifying feelings which *prevented* thinking — clearly had a priority, if anything was to happen, over worries about where the patient was located in relation to the developmental stages and implicit norms defined by Klein. These were patients whose development had hardly started, or had been so arrested that the achievement of 'emotional maturity' in Kleinian terms was not going to become an issue until years of psychotherapy had taken place, if ever.

This shift of attention was also driven by a new interest in problems of technique, especially represented in the work of Betty Joseph (1990), whose papers have been published together as *Psychic Equilibrium and Psychic Change*. She recognized that the possession of a good theory by the analyst was itself of little use unless this could be put to clinical use in work with patients. Joseph's view is that effective contact with the patient requires above all addressing the ongoing emotional transactions of the analytic session.

Process and Product

In the context of this work, priority came to be given to the process of making sense of chaotic mental and emotional phenomena, over its product in or reference to ordered theories and models. Kleinian theory had brilliantly postulated a theory of development, identifying in temporal — and, more important, teleological — order a set of psychic and relational capacities on which individual development could be mapped. This could also be seen as a developmental journey which individuals could be helped, through psychotherapy, to undertake. In the post-Kleinian work discussed here, the idea of a 'known model' is pushed somewhat into the background, though not entirely repudiated. Whereas the main task of analytic observation in the earlier work was one of recognition — identifying a familiar or precedented pattern in new particulars (specific analytic sessions or cases) — the emphasis in the more recent work is on the process of discovering patterns which may have no precedent, and diverge from established models. Process has priority over product, the making of sense over the normative or standard sense which is supposed to be made.

One can identify other dimensions of this paradigm shift. In thinking about methodology, we find a shift (described and defended in Meltzer's account of the Kleinian tradition) from earlier aspirations to scientificity and a causal model of the psyche, first to a hermeneutic view of psychoanalysis, as concerned with meanings, and then on to the properly phenomenological concern with the process of meaning-construction or coming-into-being.[9] The view of psychoanalysis as an orderly evolution of ideas (the normal science model) is disturbed by the discontinuist ideas of 'catastrophic change', enunciated by Bion and followed also by Meltzer. Catastrophic change, tolerance of extreme disorder in order to discover new orders of truth, is deemed to be the source of real creativity. The idea of catastrophic change — creativity which breaks the boundaries of established thinking — is seen as the generative source of authentic development. This leads to a different and more negative valuation of institutions dedicated to the reproduction and propagation of psychoanalysis than that which followed from the 'normal science' paradigm (once the early battles over Kleinian ideas had been fought to a standstill). The ordered compromises and hierarchies of the Institute of Psycho-Analysis were implicitly or explicitly attacked by both Bion and Meltzer, in their different ways. The exemplary figure of the prophet whose creativity cannot be tolerated by any institution, in Bion's work, implies a deep hostility to what are regarded as the stultifying effects of any routinized institutional practice. ('An easily seen example of this is the group's promotion of the individual to a position in the Establishment where his energies are deflected from his creative-destructive role and absorbed in administrative functions. His epitaph might be "he was loaded with honours and sank without a trace".'[10]) Bion's valuation of the experience of knowing — as a process of containment through thought of ineffable experience — amounts almost to a mystical valuation of contemplation as the highest human experience.

The stretching of the frontiers of analytic knowledge to encompass very early, extreme and primitive states unavoidably leads to some dismantlement of the idea of the individual as a coherent mental entity. Bion describes thought as transcending the thinker, as an immersion in or glimpse of some order of being beyond individuality. Conversely, anti-thought, 'attacks on linking', and what Bion and Meltzer term *lies*, come to be seen as the major enemies of the good, more insidious than destructive hate. Meltzer speculates on the state of mind of the unborn baby in the womb, and suggests that human beings have an innate sense of beauty, evoked by the perfection of the breast as it is experienced by the infant, and by the discovery of the other wondrous features of the world as it makes itself known. Bion's work was built on a development of Klein's notion of an epistemophilic instinct, an innate appetite for knowledge; he models his views of consciousness on the alimentary process, seeing it as a process of conversion or transformation of materials into an ordered symbolic form. Somatic expression through bodily illness or symptom is seen as an alternative mode of discharge for anxieties where the thinking apparatus has itself been damaged by internal attack, or has failed to develop.[11] Meltzer's so-far underdeveloped concept of the aesthetic might be understood to refer to the elemental pleasure obtained from recognition of order, from the containment of experience in symbolic form. This may also make possible a psychoanalytic account of the aesthetic functions of the mind described by Kant in the *Critique of Judgement*. On these issues, see Chapter 8 below.

The main Kleinian contribution to the theory of art stressed its functions of integration and reparation.[12] The symbolizations of art were deemed to be powerful in proportion to the conflicts which they were able to resolve, and the degree to which they were able to give external representation to objects therefore saved or restored from the ravages of internal attack. The achievements of art were thus closely linked to the attainment of the depressive position, and hence with a morally informed vision of development. The post-Kleinian theory of art is as yet less developed, but the indications are that its concerns are less with conflict between love and hate than with the surmounting of disintegration and catastrophe. Truth, not love, becomes the primary issue, and the greatest artists are those with the capacity to withstand internal threats to mental function and to create new symbolic order from 'catastrophic change'.

A more gradualist reading than the above can be given of the shift in concerns represented by the work of 'second-generation' Kleinians, who include not only Bion and Meltzer but also Herbert Rosenfeld, Hanna Segal, Betty Joseph, and their pupils. Such an account is provided in Elizabeth Spillius's valuable two-volume collection *Melanie Klein Today* (1988) and by her introductory contributions in the two volumes. This account demonstrates how the challenges to Kleinian orthodoxy represented by Bion's work in particular (and sometimes carried to further extremes in Meltzer's) have been assimilated within the mainstream Kleinian tradition located in the British Institute of Psycho-Analysis. Whilst the important developments in Kleinian thinking during this period are set out in this presentation, the emphasis is on development of themes and interests already broached by Klein herself, and on the continuity of the newer contributions with the Kleinian tradition understood as a whole.

Among the key developments described in this collection are advances in analytic technique by analysts including in particular Betty Joseph; a major interest in symbol formation and thinking, beginning with Hanna Segal's work but developed in its most original way by Bion; a major development of the concept of projective identification (especially by Bion, Meltzer, Rosenfeld and Joseph); and a new interest in 'pathological organizations' of the personality, including in particular those described as 'borderline states' and an exploration of 'destructive narcissism', a term first developed by Rosenfeld.

Links can be seen between each of these areas of relatively recent development in Kleinian thinking, and parallel developments in the preoccupations of the neighbouring human sciences. The principal insight of post-Kleinian work on psychoanalytic technique, for example, concerned what one might think of as the 'performative functions' rather than the informational content of analytic communications. Freud initially tended to think in terms of the reference of analysands' communications to unconscious states of mind evoked by their infantile or childhood experience. The major innovation of Kleinian work was (and remains) to focus on the meaning (and reference) of communication within the transference, and to see the transference relationship as the immediate focus of analytic attention. But attention to questions of technique became necessary because transference interpretations were sometimes found too crude or persecutory to be effective, assuming a therapeutic alliance which did not reliably exist between analyst and patient. Gradually it was realized that there were many levels on which analysands' communications (or non-communications) could be interpreted, and that understanding the unconscious intention of the communication (possibly to defend against emotional contact with the analyst, rather than bring it about) might be more crucial than interpreting its apparently more obvious references.

The greater complexity of the model of the mind being evolved at this time, and understanding of the mechanisms of projective identification in particular, also had important implications for analytic technique, as earlier discussions of the therapeutic use of the 'countertransference' has already indicated. Similarly, the problematizing of 'thinking' itself, as a process not to be taken for granted but deeply shaped by unconscious emotions in its process as well as its objects, also made a difference to issues of technique. Spillius describes a tendency to make interpretations less in the literal part-object terms of breasts, penises, etc., and

> more in terms of psychological function (seeing, hearing, thinking, evacuating, etc.). Together with this emphasis on function, concentration on the patient's immediate experience in the transference often leads to discovery of deeper layers of meaning, some of which may be seen to be based on infantile bodily experience. Talking about unconscious phantasy in bodily and part-object terms too soon is likely to lead to analyst and patient talking about the patient as if he were a third person. (Spillius, *Melanie Klein Today*, vol. 2, p. 9)

This is an instance of a shift towards more mentalistic approaches. Changes of technique of this kind may also be brought about to some degree by patients themselves becoming overfamiliar with a particular set of conventions, and the need for analysts, like writers, continually to find forms of expression not unduly blunted by overfamiliarity.

In effect, Kleinian analysts in this period have devised their own version of the 'speech act' theory (Searle, 1969) being evolved contemporaneously in analytic philosophy, though as usual with little explicit reference to this debate in another discipline. The precedence given to the 'performative functions' of speech over its factual reference is a common feature of both philosophical argument and the development of psychoanalytic technique. The displacement of reference by intention, of truth by meaning, is an indication of the move away from 'modernist', truth-dependent modes of thought in both cases, though in the post-Kleinian tradition this move proceeds only so far.

The centrality to late-Kleinian work of modes of thinking and thinking capacity as a distinct sphere of mental function also links these ideas with the wider shift in the cultural climate towards essentially idealist approaches. The human sciences become dominated by perspectives which emphasize the roots of social organization in the mind, in the individual lifeworld of actors precariously maintaining some shared common universe of meanings, in discourses, or in ideological structures of meaning. This even has its analogue in the development of positivism, in Popper's later work on the world of created meanings of 'World 3'. The preoccupations of psychoanalysis with this ideational dimension is therefore perhaps unsurprising.

The concept of projective identification has already been discussed as one of the central ideas in Bion's work. Its relevance to the wider climate consists in its consequences for the idea of personal identity as a bounded and relatively stable entity. Of course, the undermining of a 'centred' concept of the self was always seen as the contribution of psychoanalysis most subversive of classical humanism and realism. Contemporary post-modernism in cultural theory, influenced by Lacanian versions of Freud, frequently reaffirmed Freud's importance to the deconstruction of these received liberal rationalist ideas. The idea of the literal displacement of aspects of the personality into surrounding persons, visible in the process of psychoanalysis but through this also understood as a familiar feature of both intimate and even institutional life, undermined still further any unproblematic idea of 'the individual' as the indivisible subject of his or her intentions and actions. On this account, the personality is not only split up internally, between conscious and unconscious parts of the mind or various parts of the inner world, but is liable to be lodged by identification in surrounding 'objects' – sometimes merely in phantasy, without effect on the external persons concerned, but sometimes in more dynamic interactions where the internal scripts of some individuals find themselves being inscribed in the minds of others. One valuable consequence of these ideas has been for the understanding of emotional and cognitive processes in institutions, in particular in the idea of the deployment of defences against anxiety, developed especially in the work of Jaques (1977) and Menzies Lyth (1988). But whilst these accounts descriptively identify states of dispersed identity and boundary-confusion within the process of analytic therapy, in childcare, and in institutions, it must be stressed that the commitment of analysts working within this tradition is strenuously towards reintegration, towards the idea of 'containing' explosive impulses and aspects of the self within a personality, or a shared dialogic space, capable of functioning approximately in the mode of Klein's 'depressive position'.

A fourth major preoccupation of second-stage Kleinian analytic writing is with 'narcissistic' and 'borderline' states of pathological organization. These latter are defined as structures of precarious equilibrium, somewhere midway between paranoid-schizoid and depressive organization, in which defences are mounted which are strong enough to fend off the psychotic confusions of the paranoid-schizoid position, but also defend against the pain of depressive anxiety — that is, the pain attendant on loss and guilt. The Kleinians' interest in 'narcissistic' forms of personality overlaps with the concerns of American psychoanalysts, in particular Kohut, with similarly named narcissistic personality disorders, though their understanding of these is quite different. Christopher Lasch's *The Culture of Narcissism* (1979) has developed this psychological model into a major term of contemporary cultural criticism, identifying 'narcissism' as a typical character pathology of a society which has overthrown the internalized authority structures of the traditional family and pursues the hedonistic satisfactions of consumption and competitive status-seeking as its principal values.

There are important and representative differences between these different definitions. The Kohutian definition takes as its starting point the orthodox Freudian view of a primary narcissistic stage in personality development, thus positing what we might think of as a primordial individualism, always congenial to American cultural assumptions. Rosenfeld, the first major theorist of narcissistic states in the Kleinian tradition, instead takes Klein's starting point of an initial relatedness of the infant, and views the narcissistic organization of character as a defence against the perceived (which need not be the actual) insufficiencies of the object. Narcissism is closely linked in this account to envy and the death instinct, destructive attacks on the goodness of the external object being, so to speak, compensated in a somewhat pathological psychic equilibrium by idealization of the self. Among the attributes of the self idealized may be the most envious and destructive components, 'bad' aspects becoming engaged in a terrorizing relationship to more vulnerable, trusting and tender impulses. Meltzer[13] has pointed out the ways in which this internal character structure can find its representation and reinforcement in social relationships. These pathological forms of character organization — resistant to change in part because of their stability and their success in suppressing those more intense states of feeling which might lead towards hope and despair, but thus also to a desire for change — are somewhat similar in phenomenological content to those described by Kohut and Lasch, but different in their explanation.

What is nevertheless of our times in the post-Kleinian discovery of these

Table 2

dimension	Kleinian	Post-Kleinian*
conception of theory	realist	more phenomenological
pattern of development	teleological	discontinuous/ catastrophic change
stages of development	paranoid-schizoid/ depressive	delineation of borderline states
main psychic mechanism	idealization/splitting	projective identification
analytic technique	transference interpretations	increased attention to countertransference
reference of interpretations to	body part–objects	mental functions
implied ethics	reparative morality	truth as prime value
implied aesthetics	reparation through art	generative of cognitive order
view of organization	hierarchical/ institutionalized	anti-organizational/ charismatic

* Most present-day Kleinian concerns are reflected in the 'Post-Kleinian' column above, but there are internal differences among members of this group, particularly in regard to organizational and institutional issues, and in the priority given to aesthetic questions, with Donald Meltzer now holding a rather extreme position.

intractable states of mind is the realization that there is a greater diversity of apparently viable character-formations than the Kleinian schema might once have suggested. The emphasis of this schema is on the potency of envy and destructiveness as underlying forces. The link of these emotions with the negative processes of thought elaborated in later Kleinian writing, and the scope these linkages provide for self-deception, perverse idealization of the bad, and resistance to truth, enlarge the Kleinian understanding of the natural resistances to development. The broader consequence for the analytic culture of these painful discoveries, made chiefly through the treatment of analytically intractable but more-or-less functioning adult patients, is probably to scale down somewhat the social hopefulness and transformative aspirations of psychoanalysis, and to legitimize a more conservative view of its broader potential. Whereas the initial discovery that psychotic or autistic patients may be amenable to analytic treatment lends itself to rather idealistic and heroic task definitions by child analysts and psychotherapists, especially in their first passion for psychoanalytic work, the longer-term drudgery of work with 'borderline' adult patients who do not always respond deeply to analysis may generate a more cautious outlook.

One might summarize this paradigm shift in Table 2, at risk of considerable oversimplification.

This seems to have its institutional correlate in the rather cautious approach of the British Institute of Psycho-Analysis to the development of the psycho-analytic field, at a time when there is evidence of considerably increased interest in psychotherapies of all kinds. Whilst the Institute has recently sought to have a more public profile — by means of publishing, public lecture programmes and the like (in part prodded by its competitors) — there is little evidence of serious efforts to extend its activities much beyond its tiny enclave in North London. This contrasts with a significant development of analytic child psychotherapy now taking place in five or six cities in England and Scotland, often with the support of the Tavistock Clinic, and with the develop-ment of a number of private- or voluntary-sector quasi-analytic trainings.

The Cultural Affinities

This development of analytic thought in Britain has some unexpected affinities with 'post-modernism' as a broader cultural tendency. What in particular links current developments in psychoanalysis with the post-modern climate is the questioning of central paradigms of 'modernist' thinking, of which psycho-analysis is a prototypical instance. Post-Kleinian analysis reflects this context of fragmentation, but in providing a powerful means of analysing fragmented states of mind in their most extreme and private form it may also point to means of overcoming this condition.

Classic modernism presupposed hitherto unrecognized transcendental truths to which new symbolic forms might give access. These domains of truth were sometimes rationalist in conception — for example, the commitment of modernists in architecture to ideas of rational form and function. In other domains (for example, modernist writing), hitherto unrecognized domains of the irrational were posited, which called for new literary techniques. While the methods of Lawrence or Woolf were not 'realist' in the earlier social-realist sense, these writers were undoubtedly committed to an idea of external reference, even though their new referents were hitherto unrepresented states of feeling or consciousness. Freud was a 'modern' in this sense, committed to the investigation of a distinctive order of truth, as was Klein. So, at an earlier historical moment, was Marx. Modernism — one can include the constitution of the classical sociology of Simmel, Durkheim and Weber, and the structural linguistics of Saussure — posited new domains of reality and new kinds of causal determination. While these theorists undermined and supplanted the conventional assumptions of the dominant culture, they did so in the name not of indeterminacy, relativism or subjectivity, but of new orders of transcendental truth. Even the rediscovery or reinvention of tradition (by T.S. Eliot, for instance) was presented as a transcendental truth, conceived as a renewed relationship to the religious and cultural meanings of the past. Modernism announced new 'deep structures' which determined or situated the existing surfaces of culture. Advocates of modernism proclaimed a privileged access to new forms of knowledge and experience, variably grounding these in the rationalities of class, science, the expertise of professionals, or the intuitive capacities of artists. They proposed evolutionary schema or 'meta-narratives' to explain the superiority of the 'modern' over the pre-existing, and its inexorable historical advance. It is these claims to *truth* which 'post-modernism' has repudiated in its various ways, as indefensible forms of intellectual and cultural closure.

'Post-modern' thought has set out to undermine all such transcendental certainties, from theories of history (such as Marxism) to normative theories of the subject, in liberal humanism. Normative concepts — ideals — formerly thought of as critical means of emancipation, to be set against the given, are now viewed as themselves forms of closure. The process of cognitive and cultural production takes precedence over its product — the constitution of identities or texts over the substantive identities and states of reality that they represent. Radical politics is defined as the construction of collective identities by the self-definition of actors, not as a disclosure of communities of interest or value which are objectively given. The micro-sociology of the day describes how the world is constructed, moment by moment, from scripts used as rhetorical resources to rationalize interests, rather than viewed as the constituting meanings of social groups. Post-modern macro-sociology, on the other hand, has sought to replace 'grand narratives' of societal transformation with more episodic, pluralist and subjectivist accounts of historical change.

This situation is in part the cultural concomitant of consumer society, a way of rationalizing (and celebrating) the experience of an overload of meanings, cut off from their integral location in historical time and social space. As a free play of differences impacts on the citizen, unavoidably relativizing the values, meanings, procedures and skills learned in a particular place, what could be more tempting than to make a virtue of the capacity to negotiate disorder, and even enjoy it? Identity is both fragmented by the multiplicity of choices and also depleted in its sense of depth by discontinuities, by the seemingly untenable and provincial quality of any definite cultural affiliation. Fragmentation thus becomes a state of authenticity, discontinuity the means by which authentic desire can make itself known in the interstices, between the lines of necessarily repressive scripts. Lacanian psychoanalysis has been one of the major legitimations of this outlook, defining language and culture as inherently agents of repression, advancing a metaphysic of unavoidable contradiction between an authentic self banished to the unconscious, and the symbolic forms which violate this even as they are necessary to give it existence. As the utopian hopes of the late 1960s were unfulfilled, so the idea of authentic possibility was fragmented into textual traces, or repressed into an inner realm of the unknowable. The 'impossible' (the inevitable mismatch of desire and language) becomes elevated into a general view of the human condition.

Some parallels can be drawn between these 'post-modernist' preoccupations and ways of thinking, and the evolution of post-Kleinian ideas. The post-Kleinians have moved their attention away from the posited metaphysical structures of Freud (his topographical model of the psyche) and adopted instead a phenomenological approach to the mind. They have become interested in the forms of language and expression — indeed, the very possibility of these — as alternative registers or means of processing primitive sensations and feelings. Bion's idea of 'transformations' refers to the migration of meanings across various levels of mental process, and through various means of interpersonal communication. It would be a further step (though one that Bion and the post-Kleinians do not take) to abandon the framework of posited mental structures and a constituted internal world altogether, and to attend only to the transformations of meanings at their surface. This would turn analysis into an infinite regress, and from a post-Kleinian point of view would be near to entering a world of madness. A constituted world of internal objects is the precondition of sanity, and to abolish deep emotional structure is to abolish the possibility of reason.

There is an unexpected affinity also between the post-Kleinian commitment to the authenticity of the analytic process and the priority given to exposure to the experience of the unconscious, and the Lacanian hostility to the routinization of psychoanalysis. Both Bion and Lacan are capable of writing in startlingly elliptical ways. In each case, the pressure to do this arises in part from a sense of the inexpressibility of the phenomena of the consulting room, and the need to expose oneself to the disturbing reality of this — to the experience of *not knowing*. Each seeks, from his very distinct theoretical position, a renewal of the primary task of psychoanalysis, attention to its distinctive levels of phenomena (or in Bion's terms vertices) against the grain of superficial theorizing. It seems to me a strength of post-Kleinian work, in contrast to the orthodox Freudian limitations of Lacanianism, that it has also succeeded in extending its theoretical system to encompass the new depths of phenomena that it disclosed. The Lacanians, by contrast, have been constrained (by their combination of Freudian orthodoxy and post-structural linguistics) to regard the primitive unconscious mainly as a negative anti-space, what can*not* be known fully through the resources of language.

The move from ethical to aesthetic concerns, from the dynamics of love and hate to interest in how feelings are processed as thoughts, or in other ways, also has its parallels in post-modern thinking. The problem with ethical judgements from the post-structuralist point of view is that they depend on criteria of some kind, grounded in a priori or absolute ideas. Like the idea of the humanist subject, they are deemed to be inherently ideological, conceptual vehicles of power, not the rational principles or grounds of moral sense from which power relations can be judged. The concept of *jouissance* is more aesthetic than moral, signifying moments of authenticity and of escape, glimpses of the imaginary (and moments of discharge of its affects) in the interstices of the symbolic.

The Cultural Context

There seem, therefore, to be some interesting parallels between recent developments of post-Kleinian analysis and wider post-modernist/post-structuralist cultural tendencies. Even though these conjunctions are by no means simple or symmetrical, and even though there has been little or no direct dialogue between these perspectives, each seems to represent a move away from the ethical, humanist, and progressivist certainties of the earlier post-war period. Why should this be? In particular, how did the clinically preoccupied and professionally secluded world of Kleinian psychoanalysis come to respond to these broader changes in the cultural and social climate?

Of course, there have never been simple connnections between broad visions of social improvement and the world-view of psychoanalysis. (Avant-garde psychoanalytic work, first by Klein and then by Bion, anticipated in each case by some years the cultural context with which it was subsequently to seem most consonant.) The social agenda implicit in the Kleinian perspective on human development was never of primary interest to a majority of analysts, whose main concern remained the work of psychoanalysis itself. Even so, the crisis of the welfare state, from the late 1960s onwards, may have had its effects on analytic preoccupations, driving these further inwards into the individual essence of analytic work and away from its institutional applications.

For example, the profession of social work, initially the most receptive to analytic ideas after the war, turned firmly against this tradition and against work with individuals generally, as separate subprofessions (like psychiatric social work and childcare) and departments were amalgamated into a unified professional, training, and departmental structure (as Social Services Depart-ments). In psychiatry, new developments in pharmacology became the domi-nant factor in making community-based treatment of mental illnesses possible. Whilst child and adolescent psychotherapy has succeeded in establishing itself as a profession recognized within the National Health Service, analytic psychotherapy for adults has so far failed to do so to any major extent. The main competing profession, clinical psychology, adopted behaviourist, cog-nitive and family therapy techniques as its dominant expertise, their aspirations to scientificity also serving to exclude analytic orientations. In education as in social services, large-scale comprehensive reorganization initially tended to set a managerial rather than a professional agenda, and the contesting of this in collectivist ways (in part to realize the egalitarian aims of comprehensive education in terms of class, gender and race) also left little space for the individual orientation of psycho-analytic ideas. (Relationship to the experiences of race and gender remains a politically sensitive issue for psychoanalysis.) The consensual space on which psychoanalytically orientated work with individuals in the public sector depended was eroded first by institutional reform and politicization, and then by Thatcherism.

The marginal position of psychoanalysis within British society has always, in truth, limited its impact on social institutions. Its relation to mainstream British life has been more like that of the fine arts, existing in a state of licensed toleration or opposition, only occasionally having some wider resonance with public concerns. But although psychoanalysis in Britain has been concerned with individual development, its dominant values have not been individualist in a mainly material sense. Whilst psychoanalysts in private have often been able to achieve a comfortable professional position (in part because of their restricted recruitment and numbers), the overall scale of opportunities has not been large, and has not provided a powerful incentive for entry into the profession by comparison with many fields of medical practice. The British Psycho-Analytical Society has chosen throughout its history to function as a small enclave, even to this day training only just enough analysts each year to ensure its reproduction. The maintenance of pure analytic standards, an elite position *vis-à-vis* other psychotherapies, and a respected cultural position have been the dominant goals, and there has been little or no attempt to 'market' analysis more widely and profitably. Parallel to this, as already stated, has been a commitment to extending the work of analysis within the national health and welfare systems, but to no great material advantage. The significant contrast is with the much larger-scale private proliferation of psychoanalysis in the United States, where there are many psychoanalytic institutes rather than the single national society in Britain.

The increasingly materialist climate of Thatcherism does not seem to have brought an avaricious response from the analytic world. The distinctive Kleinian insight into greed and envy and their interrelationships has an obvious critical purchase on a climate of values in which greed is encouraged and envy provoked. The post-Kleinian concern with the overriding value of truth, and corresponding focus on what one might term the moral pathologies of thought — such as lies and the positive hatred of reality — also have applications beyond the narrowly clinical. The negative passion of the Thatcherites towards enemies within and without, their projected envy and violence, and their frequent subordination of truth to interest must have set many psychoanalytic teeth on edge, given the analytic commitment to very different forms of communication between persons.

A particular object of Thatcherite envy is perhaps the capacity for thought: one sees this in the demagogic populism of the New Right, and in the anxiety about uncontrolled thought shown in relation to education, a malign component of the concern about 'standards'. It must be admitted, however, that psychoanalytic sensitivities are liable to be upset by any dogmatic political ideology, left or right, given analytic commitments to 'space for thinking' and intimate human communication. A psychoanalytic response is liable to be made to the emotional form as much as to the rational content of public communication.

The idea of the individual has several dimensions, as Abercrombie, Hill and

Turner have usefully clarified in *Sovereign Individuals of Capitalism* (1986). They distinguish between *individualism* as the conception of 'economic man' (the dominant ideology of Thatcherism), *individuality* as a romantic expressive conception of the individual (the high cultural version of individual value, advanced against utilitarian ideas by J.S. Mill and a considerably literary and artistic tradition), and *individuation*, the bureaucratic categorization and surveillance of subjects, theorized most importantly by Foucault. Those who have seen psychotherapies of various sorts as new forms of 'soft' social control make use of this last definition. It is the idea of the individual as 'individuality' — that is to say, implying an expressive and 'self-realized' version of self — which has the strongest affinity with recent psychoanalytic thinking in Britain, and indeed with the psychoanalytic tradition as a whole. This core of Romantic individualism has been further developed in the post-Kleinian tradition, which asserts the priority of 'inner space' and individual development both against the claims of politics and institutions (especially when these turn hostile) and against merely instrumental materialism. Psychoanalysis thus retains its affiliation to the world-view of the most artistically minded and humanist segment of the bourgeoisie, whose values have also been subjected to attack by the entrepreneurial ethos of Thatcherism.

New Directions

What has occurred is a re-emphasis in post-Kleinian thinking on pure psycho-analytic ideals and techniques. At a time when wider applications and pros-elytization of psychoanalysis seem to have become blocked, new ideas and techniques have evolved within the primary analytic setting, through work with hitherto untreatable kinds of patients. This choice to work with the apparently most intractable kinds of mental illness — psychosis, narcissistic states, and autism — may have been partially forced by the competitive developments of pharmacology, family therapy and other non-analytic treatments for more remediable conditions, but it has also reflected the inner logic of psychoanalytic thought, always most concerned with the infantile origins of adult states of mind. The inevitable imperfections and compromises of public-service psychotherapy, in both practice and training, are put up with by many because of the urgency of the needs that this practice is designed to meet. Progress in the development of analytic psychotherapy supported by the NHS and by some local councils has in fact continued to be made in this period. But to some, an unfavourable climate induces a different response: public institutions themselves come to seem intolerable as settings, and private space for analytic work is valued more. This is a tension inherent in psychoanalytic work. Donald Meltzer has argued for the priority of private, intimate relationships over all other kinds of social relation, in terms of their consequences for emotional growth and learning. It is a natural and precedented response for those committed to versions of expressive culture to retreat to the purest locations of the cultural, faced with the pressures of an aggressive and cynical materialism. The semi-mystical preoccupations of Bion's later writing, and the idealization of artistic genius among some of his followers, arise from this commitment to intrinsic analytic ends. Both Bion and Meltzer were notably hostile at different times in their careers even to the professional institutions of psychoanalysis, holding them to be inimical to creative work. The positive claims made for the aesthetic sense, as a hitherto neglected dimension of human experience, which emerged from the Kleinian and post-Kleinian interest in symbol formation may seem to generalize less readily to society at large than do ideas of ethical responsibility, even if the sense of beauty is held in principle to be innate to all human beings, and is inferred in the first place from the observation of normal infants. However, this analytic purism, and its emphasis on authentic individual experience, also represents a form of distance from, and implicit protest against, the dominant climate of material individualism; it is not a conformist adaptation to it. An analogy might be drawn with Adorno's view of high art as a domain of negation of the given, and thus of alternative possibility.

The post-Kleinian development has some features which link it with a wider climate of post-modernism, sceptical of previous absolutist claims of many kinds. More important, however, are the continuities that remain between post-Kleinian analysis and the earlier Kleinian tradition. These continuities are insisted on by the major analysts of the later generation, who believe themselves to be a development of, not a break in, the earlier tradition. This contrasts with the emergence of a 'post-Marxism', which in some forms has repudiated many fundamental propositions of the Marxist paradigm. For all its interest in the experience of discontinuity, and its commitment to what one might describe (by analogy with post-Marxism) as a psychoanalytic experience 'without guarantees', the post-Kleinians have not rejected their own heritage in Freud's and Klein's work, and continue to depend on its foundations. This has a bearing on the continued potential of post-Kleinian analysis as a social vision.

At a theoretical level, the post-Kleinian attention to the conditions of possibility of mental function aims to extend the Kleinian theory of the inner world, not to impose a closure or a priori limit upon its understanding. The purpose of post-Kleinian theory is to integrate the frameworks of Freud (models of libidinal energy, topographical structures) and Klein (internal objects, mechanisms of splitting and projective identification, a dualism of instincts) with Bion's insights into the modes of mental functioning. What Bion and other post-Kleinians have done (the analogy of the post-modernism debate in architecture might suggest 'late Kleinians' as a more accurate term) is to explore the mental processes whereby love and hate, good and bad objects, are internalized in the mind. Where Freud dwelt on the objects of these feelings, and their bodily location, and Klein on the introjection of these as 'internal objects', Bion and others explored their transformations into thoughts, bodily sensations, projections into others, the proto-mental stages prior to the constitution of a stable self.

Whilst these discoveries were made in the course of work by Bion, Rosenfeld, Meltzer and others with psychotically ill patients, they have nevertheless informed and inflected all analytic work in the Kleinian tradition, and beyond. The ideas of projective identification and containment have proved fertile in analytic work with many kinds of patient, as has attention to the range of verbal and non-verbal communications studied initially among non-verbal patients. Just as Klein's work made it possible to 'look for the infant' (or infantile part of the self) in child patients who were chronologically and in their normal behaviour well beyond infancy, so these later researches into psychotic parts of the self turn out to have application to many patients who are, in general terms, far from psychotic. As Freud's work established the normality of 'infantile sexuality', so later work in the psychoanalytic tradition has brought to visibility the traces and residues of even earlier mental states, and their continued influence on child and adult states of mind. Each development of analytic understanding in this tradition has illuminated and added to earlier models of understanding, absorbing them into a more comprehensive theory of development and mental function.

This later work has not severed links with the earlier interest of Kleinian analysis in pathology and healthy development in infancy. Later analysts in this tradition have developed Klein's understanding of the introjection by the infant of an internal image of the parents and their creative interaction. They have explored the states of frustration, jealousy, envy and pain inseparable from the infant's recognition of its dependence and relative weakness. Bion and other post-Kleinians investigated, in particular, what happens in and to the mind where these processes of internalization and integration are aborted or blocked.

What happens when there is no containing boundary, no responsive adults to take in and share with the infant the intense feelings and sensations of its inner world? What defences are set up; how does the mind (conceived as a psyche-soma, experiencing pain through bodily sensation as well as in thought) work when it does not work? What mental work (conscious and unconscious) do care-takers have to do to enable the infant's mind to grow? What parallels does the activity of psychoanalysis have with these vital mental aspects of the work of parenting? This is not, in fact, a retreat from either the theoretical or practical understanding of human development (though it may have seemed heuristically or tactically necessary to treat it as such) but a remarkable extension of the scope of psychoanalytic theory, to encompass previously untheorized states of mind.

A Symbolic Space

Nor need this be a retreat from the ethical or latent social programme of Kleinian psychoanalysis, and that of the British School more generally. The developmental agenda of Kleinian analysis is enlarged by the concerns of post-Kleinian analysis with processes of thought and symbolization. The idea of a contained symbolic space within which — and only within which — thought and development can take place links this idea of psychic process to a fuller conception of human development and its preconditions. In earlier Kleinian work, mother-infant relationships constituted a kind of template from which broader kinds of social relationship could be conjectured. The early version laid greatest stress on the emotional responsiveness in parenting figures needed to sustain development. The idea that early relationships are also essential to the development of mental function extends this argument. They are the pre-conditions for the achievement of attachment to objects in imagined and symbolic terms, as well as in the intimate personal modes of love and gratitude. The experience of creating shared meaning, in mother-infant interactions, can thus also be seen as the model for a variety of later aesthetic and cognitive experiences, which depend on the experience of and response to emotions for their possibility. Winnicott's ideas concerning the relationship between creativity and play are also consistent with this view of human life as inherently concerned with symbolic forms.

To add cognitive and aesthetic capacities to the moral as specifications of human identity extends psychoanalytic thought, in ways which are both more intensely individual and more culturally differentiated than classical Kleinian ideas. The importance given to space for thinking — whether in institutions, families, or treatment settings — as a condition of development follows the classical psychoanalytic valuing of conscious reflection as a means of liberation from compulsions of all kinds.

One might see the evolution of psychoanalysis in this tradition as a movement from the scientific (Freud's lifelong aspiration) to the ethical (Klein's idea of the depressive position, whose defining criterion was capacity for concern for the other) to the aesthetic; that is, to the post-Kleinian valuation of understanding itself, a disinterested and wondering relation to the objects of experience. (These categories are those identified by Kant as the three distinct modes of human understanding, though the aesthetic ideas developed in *The Critique of Judgement* have been given less attention than the forms of scientific and ethical understanding.) Conceived as a social project, what this implies is the importance of symbolic capacities and their human and material resources, as the precondition for complex and challenging human lives. Even those committed to the defence of the institutions of the welfare state must surely see that its earlier values, defined in terms of caring, mutual dependency, and an idea of material sufficiency and improvement, no longer carry the appeal of a utopian social idea. Some enlargement of political vocabulary and vision is called for if socialists are to recover a capacity to define a new shape for the future. As advanced capitalist societies become more differentiated, and as more citizens gain the time, resources, and cultural space in which to define their own goals, the issue of *what* goals and meanings becomes central. To this extent the 'aesthetic' capacities and objects identified within post-Kleinian psychoanalysis acquire a potential political resonance, as an enlargement of, not a decadent substitute for, earlier ethical imperatives of altruism and mutual responsibility. The capacity for disinterested contemplation and admiration of objects outside the self (whether these be human creations, or aspects of nature) becomes a defining aspect of good lives, which are otherwise impoverished. The imperative to nurture the capacities for expression, task-solving, and engagement with the new, follows from this, as do the institutions, roles and skills which make this possible. Post-Kleinian psychoanalysis has contributed an understanding of the roots of these capacities in infancy, and of the states of feeling and relationship which are their precondition. This is to define socialism as in part a cultural project. But doesn't any remotely appealing socialist vision of society now need, to a large extent, to have something to say about the sphere of culture, in its broadest terms? Even after thirty years of argument by the New Left (and a lifetime's work by Raymond Williams, its greatest figure, to establish its foundations), this insight still remains disappointingly marginal to British politics.

Notes

1. See chapters 1 and 2 above; Rustin and Rustin (1985).

2. E.g., Fredric Jameson, 'Postmodernism, or the Cultural Logic of Late Capitalism', *New Left Review* 146, July-August 1984; Scott Lash and John Urry, *The End of Organized Capitalism*, London 1987, ch. 9; Peter Dews, *Logics of Disintegration*, Verso, London 1987; David Harvey, 'Flexible Accumulation through Urbanization: Reflections on "Post-Modernism" in the American City', *Antipode*, vol.19, no.3, 1987; David Harvey, *The Condition of Postmodernity*, Oxford 1989.

3. For introductions to Klein's work see J. Mitchell, ed., *The Selected Melanie Klein*, Penguin, Harmondsworth 1986; H. Segal, *An Introduction to the Work of Melanie Klein*, London 1975.

4. But for a text which does attempt this investigation, see Richard Wollheim, *The Thread of Life*, Cambridge 1984.

5. For a critique of one influential version of 'post-Marxism', that of Laclau and Mouffe, see M.J. Rustin, 'Absolute Voluntarism', *New German Critique*, no.42, Winter 1988, as well as recent debates between Norman Geras and these authors in *New Left Review.*

6. See especially W.R. Bion, *Learning from Experience* (1962); *Attention and Interpretation* (1970), both Maresfield Reprints, 1984; *Second Thoughts*, Heinemann, 1978. An account of Bion's development is given by Donald Meltzer in *The Kleinian Development*, Part 3, Clunie 1978. Elizabeth Spillius, ed., *Melanie Klein Today*, vols 1 and 2, Institute of Psycho-Analysis/Routledge, 1988, contains many valuable articles reflecting recent Kleinian developments.

7. F. Tustin, *Autism and Childhood Psychosis*, Hogarth, 1972; *Autistic States in Children*, Routledge & Kegan Paul, 1981; *Austistic Barriers in Neurotic Patients*, Karnac, 1986; H. Rosenfeld, *Psychotic States* (1965), Maresfield Reprints, 1982; *Impasse and Interpretation*, Tavistock Institute of Psycho-Analysis, 1987; D. Meltzer, *Sexual States of Mind*, 1973; *Dream Life*, 1984; *Studies in Extended Metapsychology*, 1986; Meltzer *et al.*, *Explorations in Autism*, 1975 (all Clunie).

8. *Attention and Interpretation*, ch. 6, but see also chs 3–5.

9. These issues are explored further in Chapter 5 above.

10. *Attention and Interpretation*, p. 78.

11. Bion's insights concerning the somatic expression of unbearable states of feeling have been further developed in Joyce McDougall's *Theatres of the Mind: Illusion and Truth on the Psychoanalytic Stage*, Free Association Books, 1986.

12. See Hanna Segal, 'A Psychoanalytic Approach to Aesthetics' (1952), reprinted in *The Work of Hanna Segal*, Free Association Books/Maresfield Library, 1986. For Meltzer's recent views, see D. Meltzer and M. Harris Williams, *The Apprehension of Beauty*, Clunie, 1988.

13. For example, in D. Meltzer, (1986), 'A One-Year-Old goes to a Day Nursery – a Parable of Confusing Times', and 'Family Patterns and Cultural Educability' (with M. Harris), in *Studies in Extended Metapsychology.*

PART III

Psychoanalysis and Culture

7

Kleinian Psychoanalysis and Cultural Theory*

The purpose of this chapter is to explore the relevance of Kleinian and other object-relations theories in psychoanalysis to the understanding of culture. In particular, it will be argued that this psychoanalytic tradition can contribute to a socialist and humanist view of culture, and to its much-needed remaking after some years of fashionable theoreticist attack.[1]

In seeking to explore the relevance of psychoanalysis for cultural studies, one enters a field already densely populated by impenetrable thickets of Lacanian interpretations of Freud, and their application to the theory of culture. One had hoped it would be possible to set out some clear comparison between absorption of Freud's work within this semiotic and post-structuralist debate, and work undertaken in recent years within the 'British School' of object-relations psychoanalysis, which has also given some attention to aesthetic matters. This, however, turned out to be easier said than done. There are many difficulties in understanding the work that is being done in cultural studies under the influence of Lacan, and while it may be useful to make some observations about it from my different perspective, it would be presumptuous to pretend that this is a thorough or rigorous critique. The fundamental difficulties stem from divergences in theoretical and philosophical presuppositions between the Lacanian reading of Freud and most psychoanalytic work undertaken in Britain. But since, in general, the opening of cultural theory in Britain to influence stemming from continental sources — structural linguistics, semiotic

---

*I would like to thank Ian Craib and Margot Waddell for their written comments on this chapter.

analysis, discourse theory — has been fruitful in exposing new terrains to theoretical investigation, there is every reason to give close and receptive attention to the interpretation of psychoanalytic theory offered within this framework.

This is especially the case given that this 'reading' of Freud appears to fill a number of important gaps within the theoretical debate. The problem Freud's work seems to address in such a richly textured way is the construction of the individual subject through cultural discourse. It offers the promise of doing this in terms which can escape an unwelcome polarity: on the one hand the reduction of the individual to a point of intersection of social roles, a mere bearer of social forces. Such a sociologically determinist view of the individual is particular difficult to sustain in the field of cultural studies, where so much emphasis is traditionally given to the individual particularity of experience, sensibility, etc., though this has not impeded valiant efforts by Marxist structuralists to attempt just this reduction. On the other hand, the Lacanian reading of Freud also appears to escape the problems of positing a 'human nature', whose fixity and universality would then contradict the whole programme of demonstrating the historical and social construction of culture, and of the subject itself. In this reading of Freud, both the 'subject' and 'culture', both the individual *and* society, are problematized. The subject is seen, following Freud, as a script in continuous process of articulation, a point of contact between an unconscious nature and the only partially definitive constraints of culture and language. And while in this reading some elements of 'culture' can be seen as repressive and ideological representations of a supposedly 'natural' subjectivity, other kinds of cultural work can be seen to reflect upon cultural codes themselves, to disrupt them through contradiction and polyvalency, and to make unconscious desire available to reflection and thus, perhaps, to political action.

It is the convergence discovered between Freud's account of the transformations of unconscious thought through 'condensation' and 'displacement' in *The Interpretation of Dreams* (Hogarth, 1953) and the structuralist account of the basic figurative elements in language and literature, defined by Jakobson as metaphor and metonymy, which has made possible this programme of a parallel analysis of subject and culture, since the same mechanisms appear to be involved in the formation of both. Lacan's formulation 'the unconscious is structured like a language' asserts this dependence of inmost subjectivity on the cultural process, just as the converse programme of psychoanalytic investigation of culture asserts its unconscious (or desire-rooted) dimensions. The earlier concerns of 'Marxist psychoanalysis' are absorbed into this new discourse in the sense that there is still, beneath the texture of cultural analysis, an idea of infinite desire blocked and repressed by social arrangements, while the Oedipus complex is seen in this new account particularly as a mechanism of reproduction of patriarchy.

One problem in relating Lacanian work to the object-relations tradition is their different philosophical presuppositions. One of Lacan's main tasks was the naturalization of Freud's work within a predominantly Hegelian and post-Hegelian philosophical tradition. Since Freud's work was not originally conceived in these terms, there is a double problem of translation: first that undertaken by Lacan, and second that undertaken by those seeking to understand Lacan's work from a British cultural setting largely shaped by empiricism. Desire is an example of a concept which in the orthodox psychoanalytic tradition has rather concrete empirical referents (signifying states of feeling or instinct, and their imagined or real objects), but which, as Lacan's Hegelian version of the id, becomes a more abstract disposition. It did not need the particular indulgences and difficulties of Lacan's personal style to make this philosophical recoding of psychoanalysis a daunting task.

There is, however, something rather extraordinary about an attempt made to incorporate Freud's work into cultural theory in Britain which almost exclusively relies on this double transformation, while largely avoiding direct acquaintance with psychoanalytic work undertaken in Britain in the same fifty-year period. Even more odd is the fact that this British 'object-relations' work has had some influence on Lacan and his associates, and that there are some convergent elements in their approaches to the psychoanalytic tradition. There is a strange xenophilia involved in this pattern of intellectual transmission, and there cannot be much doubt that it is not helping the cause of psychoanalytic influence in British culture.

One major cost of this routing of all messages via Paris has been the disconnection of psychoanalytic discussion in cultural theory from its proper base in clinical work. This disconnection is also probably a doubly amplified one, in that one has the impression that in his last years Lacan, like Laing in England, had tended to cut himself off from the psychoanalytic community and orientate himself instead towards a broader cultural circle not professionally engaged in psychoanalysis. So those whose psychoanalysis is learned mainly from Lacan, and from Freud's classic texts, are removed not only from current psychoanalytic work in their own culture, but even from the greater part of psychoanalytic work in France. A small knowledge of the work by those influenced by Lacan — such as Laplanche, Pontalis, and Maud and Octave Mannoni — suggests that the loss is serious, and that the two fields of British and

Lacanian-influenced French psychoanalytic discourse are less distant from one another than a reading of Lacan alone would lead one to think. A parallel comes to mind in the field of Marxist theory and history. Here, writers such as E.P. Thompson have forcefully urged the importance of empirical historical work to any living Marxism, and while his arguments have called in question the value of 'theory' *per se*, it has been a source of strength to Marxist studies in Britain that there has been a continuing practice of historical research. The analogue of empirical research in the psychoanalytic field is the clinical practice of psychoanalysis. Psychoanalytic theories have not developed mainly through textual elaboration, but have been formulated and tested in relation to experience of analytic cases. This was Freud's own procedure (together with his self-analysis which, however, appears to be even less attractive as a model to his modern interpreters) and has been the basis of the development of psychoanalytic understanding ever since.

The costs to any proper understanding of psychoanalysis of this divorce from case material are so great as to threaten to doom into sterility the whole project attempted by Lacanian cultural theorists in Britain. It seems also that the efforts to relate Freud's ideas to the various problematics of linguistics and semiotics have taken precedence over the detailed study of the development of his own work. A rather small number of Freud's texts are repeatedly cited to make some key points, but one has the sense that it is a reading of Lacan's reading of Freud, not a reading of Freud, that is the decisive source. Althusser's 'reading' of Marx led many others to read Marx for themselves; there is less evidence that this has been happening in the instance of Freud. This lack of interest in the internal development of Freud's work (a development which is very helpfully set out in, for example, Richard Wollheim's *Freud* [London 1971] and donald Meltzer's *The Kleinian Development* [Clunie, Perthshire 1978] may go some way to explaining the lack of curiosity about the evolution of his ideas in the last forty years.

A second major problem with this Lacanian interpretation of psychoanalysis is its classical orthodoxy, a consequence of its dependence on certain texts of Freud. This orthodox model excludes from study many important unconscious phenomena, with serious consequences for the analysis of culture, and also with serious moral and political implications. What in effect has happened is that the empiricist individualism of Freud's own early account (Freud's 'pleasure principle', and instinct theory) has been translated into a quasi-Hegelian vocabulary of desire (for recognition by the other), but with an unchanged core of tragic contradiction between desire and its impossibility of social fulfilment. Antony Wilden has pointed out in his translation of Lacan's *The Language of the Self* (New York 1968) the implicit connections between Lacan's early work and Sartre's. In this model, it seems impossible to conceive of subjects who are related to others without inevitably being part of some relationship of mutual imprisonment. The emphasis in the reading of Lacan on the 'mirror-stage' brings out a related connection with this Sartrean perspective. The 'me' fixed in the definitions of the other by the forms of language and culture is in inevitable contradiction to the 'I' of unconscious and repressed desire, in close parallel to the contradiction of 'being-in-itself' and 'being-for-others' expounded in Sartre's work. Such models — they are also to be found in the 'I' and the 'me' of symbolic interactionism in the work of Cooley and Mead in the United States — have the effect of contrasting an inauthentic 'social self' with a potentially real (even if unknowable) inner self. This model provides only for oscillation between the imprisonment of human beings by social and cultural structures, and the temporary lifting of these structures, either in revolution or in the necessarily ungeneralizable practice of avant-garde art. Some more inherently social concept of man is essential to any socialist vision.

There are in fact two crucial developments from Freud's own later work which need to be central to the assimilation of psychoanalysis into cultural theory. The first is the shift from a 'bioenergetic' and topographical model of the mind, conceived in terms of instinctual energies and more or less mechanical structures, towards a more phenomenological account. What is meant by 'phenomenological' is that the model of the subject's mind held by the analyst attempts to map the mental constructions experienced by the subject. While theoretical models are used by object-relations theorists (in this there can be agreement about the unconscious being the key theoretical object of psychoanalytic science), these models attempt to represent, in a generalizing and systematic way, the phenomenology of the subject, more closely than is the case with Freud's topographical accounts. This does not displace explanations in terms of flows of energy and its discharge, or of mental structure, but complements them in order to map the subject's own inner experience. A number of important developments in the substantive theory of the mind, and in analytic method, are associated with this shift towards a more phenomenological approach.

The second development is the evolution of substantive theory involved in the concepts of 'object relations'. What is involved here is the idea of an internalization by the subject of mental images of the parental figures, and the foundation of the personality on a persisting phantasy relationship to internal and thus unconscious 'internal objects'. Klein found that the earliest experiences were of 'part-objects' — phantasies of the breast and nipple, for example — which were continuously split and fragmented by the operation of violent feelings of love and hate. A mental picture of the mother as a whole person was only gradually put together in the infant's mind, through the mother's capacity to contain the anxieties of the infant and to mitigate its frustrations through both physical care and emotional understanding.

The model of the internal world which results from this account is one composed of different 'parts of the self' related to different internal objects. These 'objects' will be associated with different bodily functions, will have different dispositions towards the infant (persecuting, caring, abandoning, etc.) and will be phantasied in relation to each other, the infant's phantasies of its parents' sexual relations being a very early feature of development according to Melanie Klein. The anxieties involved in these experiences of 'parts of the self' are dealt with in this account by a variety of mechanisms, of which the classical process of 'repression' described by Freud is only one. Whereas Freud's mechanism of repression describes the censorship and inhibition of forbidden feelings, Klein developed additional concepts of 'splitting' and 'projective identification' by which unwanted feelings were displaced into other persons and objects, which were then invested with qualities which derive from unconscious phantasy. This was a process not only of phantasy attribution but also of the actual pushing of feelings on to others, making them experience aspects of the self in order to relieve the self of mental pain. This idea of parts of the self, and its internal objects, being projected into others leads to a heightened concept of the unconscious dynamics of family interaction, and of the role of phantasied internal worlds in the making of marital and parental relationships.

The containment of projected parts of the infant self by the mother is held in this account to be crucial to the infant's development, and to its capacity to reintroject and integrate its conflicting feelings and internal objects. This concept of projective identification has been one of the most important in the Kleinian development, and has especially furthered the understanding of primitive psychotic states of mind, in which fragmentation of the self and its internal objects is a crucial phenomenon. Particular attention has been given to the experience of the countertransference, whereby analysts are able to study the mechanisms of projective identification through understanding of feelings evoked in them by the transference. The underlying model of the self employed in this view is not merely one of desires bound to certain categories of object, or narcissistically bound up in the self, but of a mental structure understood as an unconscious representation of the self related in phantasy to others. These others are conceived primitively as part-objects but also, in more developed states of mind, as persons.

The Oedipus complex is of course one such product of unconscious phantasy, and one ground for asserting that the 'object-relations' model is a development of Freud's own work. But Klein revised Freud's view, discovering 'oedipal' preoccupations with parental intercourse at a much earlier stage of development than Freud assumed. These were linked in her view to the development of the 'depressive position' and to the recognition of the other as a whole and separate person. Oedipal anxieties therefore occur in conjunction with intense and sometimes violent phantasies about the mother's body, and are dealt with not only by means of repression (so central to the Lacanian account) but also through the mechanisms of splitting and projective identification. The Kleinian model generally draws attention to earlier stages of development, through which the differences between self and other are constructed, notably in the theory of the paranoid-schizoid and depressive positions. These, together with the early oedipal anxieties associated with the depressive position, are located initially in the first few months of life — not, as in the case of Freud's Oedipus complex, in the third and fourth year. This suggests that a capacity for phantasy and thought is developed in the infant prior to the development of language, and is therefore inconsistent with Lacan's view of language as the precondition for the development of the differentiated self.

These Kleinian models describe the integration of the sense of self as a reciprocal of the development of awareness of the mother (or mother-figure) as a whole being. The initial fragmentation of experience as a series of physical sensations and powerful emotions (love, hatred, terror and anxiety) is resolved, through the 'containment' of these experiences by the mother, into a continuing sense of self and other which can survive these extremes and discontinuities of feeling. The infant's sense of its own body is formed through its mother's handling of it, and its transmuting of potentially catastrophic sensations and boundaries into ones through which a continuing sense of self can survive. (The significance from this standpoint of the Leboyer approach to childbirth is that it seeks to initiate from birth this tender approach to the experience of 'difference'.) The infant's sense of the benignness and reliability of the world is dependent on its care-taker's ability to attend to and mitigate its frustrations. Its sense of the meaning of love and hate, and of the possibility that the former feelings will in the end take precedence in its infant scheme of things over the latter, depends on the containment both of its own and of its parents' negative feelings in their mode of caring for the baby. Klein describes how in the first few months (and later in recurring relivings of this developmental 'position' throughout life) the infant comes to perceive the mother as a 'whole object' combining good *and* bad qualities, vulnerable to its attacks, and needed and loved even in its apartness and difference from the infant. Following this, the infant must encounter the reality of two parents, and of other babies made or potentially made by them, and of many other kinds of 'otherness' in its parents' lives. Many kinds of identification of the self with these parents, and as possible objects of these parents' love or hatred, are possible as an outcome of these stages of development.

What are formative, in this account, are the phantasied internal objects which represent the parent-figures in the mind of the child. These internal objects may be cruel or kind, strong or weak, fragmented or whole, related to each other in love or hatred, and the self will be phantasied in different identifications to and relationships with them. This account does not imply that the mental stages of the infant's life are a direct precipitate or imprinting of the real-life behaviour of its parents. On the contrary, the inner world of the child has its own structure and dynamics, and constitutional factors in the infant as well as part-experiences of the parents will interact in its development.

It is important to stress that in the object-relations account, the elaboration of phantasy about the parents in the inner world of the child precedes the development of what Freud called 'repression', and involves other means than unconscious censorship of dealing with anxiety. In order to deal with mental pain, arising from bad qualities in the self and its objects and also from vulnerability and dependence, the self will organize its experience through unconscious phantasy, redistributing dangerous or unwanted parts of its self and its objects in accordance with the demands of its inner world. Psychoanalysis provides a scene for these transferences (the operations of envy, greed, idealization, projective identification) as well as the oedipal jealousies and identifications with which orthodox Freudians remain preoccupied. The work of psychoanalysis consists of seeking to make conscious the internal world of the analysand, and above all to make conscious and thus relieve the anxiety and mental pain inseparable from it. Clearly, in the Kleinian account, negative emotions, especially of envy and jealousy, are given great emphasis, and are often perceived as the primary source of resistance to analytic understanding. There are important differences between Kleinian and the large group of 'Middle Group' analysts ('Middle Group' signifying a non-aligned tendency influenced to some degree by Klein but not committed to all her ideas, especially those concerning the importance of envy: Winnicott is perhaps the most representative figure). But from the point of view of considering the work of the 'British School' of psychoanalysis, the large measure of agreement on these early phenomena of object relations experienced in phantasy is most significant, and contrasts with the continuing dominant emphasis on the later Oedipus complex by the Lacanians and other orthodox Freudians.

These differences of view can be clearly grasped by comparing Lacan's much-cited paper on 'The Mirror-Stage' (1977) — one of the main foundations of Lacanian cultural theory — and Donald Winnicott's (1967) paper 'The Mirror-Role of Mother and Family in Child Development', which incidentally acknowledges the influence of Lacan's paper. Lacan's account of the mirror-stage[2] is based on Freud's idea of primitive narcissism, and seeks to explain how the idea of a unified self is first constructed, in anticipation of the infant's full mastery of bodily co-ordination. He seeks to explain the constitution of the 'imaginary' ego, proposing that between six months and eighteen months, when it begins to recognize itself with jubilation in the mirror, the infant develops a (mis) conception of itself as a 'whole' being. This self-recognition through an external, apparently complete image becomes the basis for an alienated conception of the self as the object both of reflected self-regard, and of the regard of the mother and others. It appears from Lacan's account that the infant's sight of its own reflection is an important moment in its development, though the 'mirror-stage' seems no less a founding myth of primary narcissism for Lacan than was the original Greek myth of Narcissus. It would have been necessary to conjecture the role of the mirror, even if mirrors were in fact rarities or relatively unimportant in infant life. The idea of an alienated, falsely unified self, seen as an object of regard by self and others, is a primary foundation of the essential division in Lacan's work between the 'real' — conceived as a process always eluding understanding or 'naming' by self or others — and the imaginary and symbolic realms through which it is (mis) represented. Lacan's acceptance of Freud's stage of primary narcissism differentiates his position in a fundamental way from the object-relations tradition, though his account of the 'gap' between the real of what we might describe as mental process, and its representation or description in thought and language, does properly identify psychoanalysis's main terrain of investigation.

Lacan begins from the fundamental opposition in Hegel and Sartre's work between the self-as-held-in-the-regard-of-others, and the inner being (a contrast also developed in symbolic interactionist thought in America, where a social 'me' is counterposed to a primary 'I'). But he vehemently rejected the self-sufficiency and omnipotence of Sartre's ideal of a wholly transparent and 'free' self, and is here consistent with the way the whole tradition of psycho-analysis has problematized the unified individual subject, questioning the idea that it could ever be free, least of all by act of will, from unconscious desire and conflict.

Winnicott (1967), by contrast, starts not from the individual infant regarding itself in the mirror, but from the infant barely separated in conscious-ness from its mother. Not primary narcissism, but the primary unity or symbiosis of the mother-baby couple is the starting point of human identity in Klein's and Winnicott's view, though Winnicott rejected much of Klein's emphasis on innate destructiveness. He proposes that the face in which the baby first begins to gain a sense of itself is its mother's: 'What does the baby see when he or she looks at the mother's face? I am suggesting that what the baby sees is his or herself. In other words, the mother is looking at the baby and *what she looks like is related to what she sees there*.' The infant learns about itself as capable of being loved, or causing fear, distress, or repugnance through observing its 'reflection' in the face and mind of another. Winnicott suggests that we sub-sequently interpret what we see in the actual mirror in the light of how we have learned to see ourselves in this 'human mirror', and in the regard of those others who are significant to us. The literal mirror is not a primary experience of the constituting of the self, and when it becomes so ('mirror, mirror, on the wall', etc., as Winnicott puts it) it is because something has gone wrong with our sense of ourselves in our inner dependence on the love of others.[3]

If the mother reflects back not the infant's actual state of being but merely her own defences, problems begin, and the infant's sense of self will not be able to grow. Winnicott thus distinguished between a benign process of 'reflection' and a pathogenic process. In the former, recognition of the qualities of self, and exploration of the qualities of the other, are gradually differentiated in 'a two-way process in which self-enrichment alternates with the discovery of meaning in the world of seen things'. In the latter, where mother or other intimate carer is not able to respond to the infant's being, the baby will not learn to trust in the other's gaze or response, and will deal with the danger to it by withdrawal or by merely learning how to interpret others' reactions, without exposing itself to risk. Whilst actual mirrors play some part in the process of self-recognition as development proceeds, the sense of self is mainly built up in childhood through reflection in the faces of family members: 'The actual mirror has significance mainly in the figurative sense.'

Lacan views the act of self-recognition as the primary source of selfhood, and sees this as leading to a necessarily false and idealized self-conception. The gaze of others, and the categorizations of self in language, add further layers of constraint and illusion to this imaginary or idealized image of a 'completed' self. Authenticity has to be sought against these reflected definitions, both inner and outer, and is attainable only in fragments and moments, through the disruptions of the symbolic and imaginary realms. For Winnicott and the object–relations tradition, by contrast, the mutual recognitions of mother and infant give meaning and form to the being of each, providing in normal conditions ('good enough mothering') a basis for development of capacities for feeling, understanding, and relationship with others. What is represented as an ontological condition of psychic alienation in Lacan's account might be viewed merely as one end of a developmental continuum in Kleinian theory. To explore this, however, one would need to examine the fruitful recent development of the Klein–Bion theory of thinking.

In later Kleinian work, much has been added to the understanding of how the infant is able to integrate its various experiences into a coherent process of perception of others and its own relation to them. The infant does not arrive at this capacity merely through innate cognitive virtuosity, as Lacan characteristically supposes, but as a result of a relationship in which the infant's experiences of emotion and thought have been communicated with and absorbed by the mother (J. Shuttleworth, 1989). In more technical language, there needs to be a process of containment of the infant's more extreme states of mind as these are conveyed by projective identification, if the infant's mental climate is to be predisposed to development. Just as the physical needs of the infant must be attended to by its carers, so must its mental needs, from its earliest days.

Narcissism, in Klein's view, is not a primary condition from which the idea of the self emerges, but a defence against envious attacks on good internal objects. Narcissism is a consequence of intense splitting, in which the self preserves an omnipotent sense of its own worth to defend itself against the loss and pain arising from damage to its object, on which it of course in reality depends. Klein's work, in contrast to Lacan's, begins from an idea of a self intensely related to others, but torn by conflicting feelings of love and hate aroused by the object's not satisfying its every desire. Symbolization and thought arise not in an inevitable process of idealization and misrepresentation (though these occur) but as separation and loss become capable of being borne. Symbolized objects, or Winnicott's pre-symbolic 'transitional objects', are means of giving form to internal objects, not inherently misrepresentations or misrecognitions of the self or other.

Klein (1923, 1930, 1931) postulated an 'epistemophilic instinct', believing that a relation to truth and reality was inherent in the human being. There seem to be good evolutionary reasons for believing this to be so. Later work in this tradition — for example by Bion (1977) and Meltzer (1986) — has further investigated processes of thought, and their susceptibility to unconscious distortion or perversion under the pressure of envy or hatred.[4] From this perspective, thought may be truthful or its opposite, and there will be unconscious reasons, sometimes susceptible to analytic understanding and change, why mental process may or may not take place, or may take negative or self-destructive forms. Whilst any idea or representation can become a falsehood, or means of resistance to thought or feeling, the theory which holds that thought and language are inherently and inevitably sources of misrepresentation and alienation is not supported by the Klein/Bion view of development. The trust in the Kleinian tradition that knowledge of mental processes *can* be advanced (which may depend on a good internal relation within this tradition to analytic parent figures) seems to have been a positive support to its continued intellectual development. There is a 'metascepticism' in Lacan's work about the unavoidable deception of language itself which seems to have inhibited its own theoretical development, as it undermines and disturbs Lacan's own writing. At his best, however, Lacan seems to have inspired his followers with the belief that he had a unique courage and talent for facing up to the doubts and confusions inherent in thinking psychoanalytically. In this respect, his impact and example were not dissimilar to Bion's, in a different context.

Lacanians argue that it is precisely the 'fixing' of the perception of the self by the other (and its categorization in language) which creates a tragic space between the inner self's plasticity of desire and its thinkable forms of expression. In this sense, the 'mirror-stage' can be taken as a metaphor for the positioning of the self in culture and its inevitable self-recognition as such, as a self-for-others. The contribution of structuralist theory to this model is that this self-for-others does not merely become the contingent product of specific social interactions, as in Sartre's work, but reproduces the categories and roles of a definite social structure (for example, its categories of gender).

Both object-relations and Lacanian accounts agree that the self is constituted by a process of interaction, and both would also agree on the inevitable sacrifices of possibility and repressions of desire inherent in this process. But the object-relations tradition stresses also the potentially creative elements of this interaction, the realizing of potential through mutual recognition (for example, of mother and baby), as well as its loss through denial. The utopia of infinite desire is on this view a pointless projection of primary narcissism on to the world, and cannot constitute a conceivable standard of what might be. The self cannot be constituted except through others — this is not a metaphysical catastrophe, but man's social nature — and our concern should be to understand the more and less benign and creative forms which this social process can take.

It must be said that a very large amount of cultural theory seems to have been misconstructed on the premises of Lacan's 'mirror-stage'. Christian Metz's influential 'Psychoanalysis and Cinema', for example (*Screen*, vol.16, no.2, 1975), which has the merit of being an unpretentious and intelligible piece of writing, depends on this largely erroneous premise. On the strength of 'mirror-stage', the cinema is attributed the functions of the subject-constituting mirror. The theory of the child's relation to the Oedipus complex leads to the equating of cinema-viewing with voyeuristic observation of the parental couple. The theory of castration anxiety and its displacement into fetishism leads to Metz's view of excessive attachment to the techniques of the cinema as a kind of fetishism. Well, no doubt identifications of a narcissistic type, voyeurism and fetishism can all be found as important phenomena in regard to the cinema, but as a whole account of the relation of the cinema to the unconscious this displays all the marks of its disastrously narrow and schematic origins. There are many different forms of identification with whole and part-objects, besides narcissistic ones. Many other interests and identifications can be expressed by looking at others, besides voyeurism focused on the parental couple. Symbol formation is about many things, other than fetishistic displacements of the lost phallus. A psychoanalytic account of film or of other arts needs to take account of many more unconscious processes and states of mind than these — and, indeed, of a rather different range of symbolic activities than fetishism — if it is not to be reductionist and denigrative of art in its effects.

Kleinian psychoanalysts, like the Lacanians, have given great importance to the development of symbolism and the capacity for thought in recent years. Kleinians agree with Lacan in locating the origins of symbol formation in the experience of what they call 'the absent object' (which seems to translate as the 'imaginary Other' in Lacan). But because of the way in which Kleinian approaches have developed through the psychoanalysis of children, and are based on hypotheses about the mental state of clearly pre-verbal children in the first months of life, the emphasis is not primarily on language *per se*, but on symbolic representations of the internal world which are most commonly interpreted through the child's play and through visual symbols as well as language. (Indeed, the provision of a set of toys, including invariably different sizes of human figure, and of drawing materials, is a basic technique of child analysis.) Hanna Segal argued in 'Notes on Symbol Formation' (in Segal, 1986) that the development of a capacity for symbol formation was related to the attainment of the depressive position — that is, the capacity to internalize the mother as a 'whole object' in her absence, and to achieve the integration of conflicting feelings in the mind. W.R. Bion has subsequently discussed, in the series of papers published as *Second Thoughts* (London, 1978), the phenomenology of more primitive mental states, in which thoughts are (as Freud earlier put it) indistinguishable from the objects which they represent, and are projected and exploded in phantasy rather than being used as the materials for 'linking' experiences and objects with one another.

This combination of attention to the phenomenology of infantile experience and to the importance of the mother's role in thinking, and retaining and modulating feelings for the child, has given rise to a key concept in later Kleinian work (influenced especially by Bion and Meltzer) — that of containment.[5] The parent-figures need to be actual containers, in emotional experience, for the angry, greedy and frightened feelings of their child. Most commonly, Meltzer has pointed out, the mother's role is to contain the anxieties of the baby and the father's is to contain the anxieties of the mother, but there are many possible divisions of labour. The internalization in phantasy of the parent-figures will give prominence to their capacity to be satisfactory or unsatisfactory containers, of which mother's body is a powerful and basic image, and a house is a common symbolic transformation in play. The role of symbolism and of language itself is also to contain and to bind feelings. The failure to achieve a primary level of integration — the capacity to experience both the self and others as persisting, whole, and related beings — will be reflected, so these analysts have discovered, in failure in the capacity to symbolize, in schizophrenic and autistic states.

The development of symbolic capacity is seen in this tradition not merely as an aspect of repression, as the means by which the subject is inscribed in society through the cultural definitions of the other and especially of patriarchy. It is, on the contrary, through symbolization that the infant learns to achieve a continuity of experience, both of his own existence and of the mother's. Winnicott's paper 'Transitional Objects and Transitional Phenomena' describes[6] an early stage in the development of symbolic capacity in which the baby's illusion of mother or the breast, not clearly differentiated from itself, is transferred to a bit of blanket or cuddly toy which is then able to represent something comforting for the infant. This might be described as a primitive symbol, developed before the capacity clearly to discriminate symbols from what they stand for (through language, for example) has evolved, and used with special intensity at moments (such as going to sleep) when the child needs an illusion of not-being-separated from mother. This early symbolization is not of the phallus (though Winnicott uses the term 'maternal phallus'), or of a fetish, least of all of a 'subject' defined by culture, but of aspects of the primary figure of attachment in the child's life.

The role of symbolization in achieving both differentiation and relationship (linking) of the experiences of the self and others makes it a crucial element in development. The relationship of symbolism to the containment of anxiety (separation, disintegration, disappearance, destruction, abandonment, jealousy, envy, and greed are sources of anxiety for the infant and therefore reasons for symbolic activity) gives symbolic capacity a critical importance in the development of the subject, but of a rather different kind than that proposed in the Lacanian tradition. Bion develops Klein's idea of an epistemophilic instinct — a primitive desire for understanding — parallel to the primitive emotions of love and hate. It is through understanding (symbolic representation, linking, containment) that the self is able to contain and resolve anxieties, and to achieve progressively greater capacities for differentiation. The internal objects that will shape the forms of symbolization will depend on the transactions between the internal and external worlds of self and caring figures. The mental world can be composed of punitive, feeling-less, ravaged internal objects as well as relatively benign phantasies of parents and babies. (Sometimes infants attribute the natures and relations of parents and babies to every animate and inanimate object in sight, almost as soon as they can speak.) No doubt the *forms* of symbolization will vary too, in ways which correspond with definite states of the internal world. Bick, Bion, Tustin, Meltzer and others, as well as Winnicott in somewhat different terms, have already undertaken some of this exploration in relation to psychotic and autistic states of mind among children. The point is that to understand symbolization, from the findings of psychoanalysis, as the primary instrument of growth and development, leads to a very different approach to culture from that which interprets symbolization and language mainly as the instrument of repression; of the imposition on to the desiring subject of categories which necessarily misrepresent and distort its unconscious wishes. That is a metaphysic of inevitable alienation, however little these anti-humanists may own the term, a psychoanalytic and linguistic reassertion of a world of almost universal Being-for-Others or Bad Faith. From this (in this world-view) only the avant-garde (and perhaps the psychotic) can escape, in the few cracks that can be opened in the hermetic structure of 'realist', or mirror-like cultural representation.

Interestingly, one of the passages most frequently cited by Lacan and the Lacanians, the *Fort! Da!* (Gone! Here!) section in *Beyond the Pleasure Principle*, where Freud describes a fifteen-month-old child's game with a cotton-reel in which he throws it away from his cot and pulls it back within sight, is also important in the genesis of the object-relations approach to symbol formation. Freud, in his delightful and memorable piece of observation, is led to think about the child's game as an instance of repetition compulsion which he regards as not explicable by the pleasure principle, and later relates to a sort of law of entropy or regression to a state of stasis which he called the death instinct.

The cotton-reel game is important to Winnicott and the Kleinians, however, as an instance of early symbolization of the absent mother, through play. The cotton-reel's disappearance and reappearance (under his own control) provides reassurance to the infant. This space — neither the real mother nor hallucination, but illusion or symbol — is crucial to growth and development in Winnicott's view, and is parallel to his idea of the transitional object. For Klein, the cotton-reel is a symbolization of an internal object, and she suggests that there is an element of depressive anxiety (evoked by the child's fear that he has harmed the mother and caused her absence) which is being overcome through this game. The child's subsequent discovery, in Freud's account, that his own image too can be made to appear and disappear in a mirror, and his excitement in conveying this to the mother, shows the child learning to generalize his idea of absence as something temporary, seeing himself as absent and returned in his mother's eyes, as he has just observed the cotton-reel gone and come back with his own. It is interesting in this example, in relation to our earlier discussion of the 'mirror-stage', to see that the mirror probably has its strongest meaning as a representation of mother's regard, baby gone and returning being a way of showing mother that baby has gone and returned for her. We see in this example the infant self learning to hold on to a feeling of the internal reality of its loved others, and of itself, even when they are not physically present.

Freud's example has been significant in this tradition in a number of ways. It demonstrated the fertility of direct observation of babies which has since become a major element in analytic training. It suggested the relation of the development of symbol formation to the absence of the mother, and to the child's capacity, depending on its state of emotional development and actual experience, to cope with the anxieties arising from this. It indicated the role of play and non-verbal symbolization, as well as words, for children, which subsequently became a central insight in the development of the 'play technique' in psychoanalysing children. It also showed the importance of symbol formation (and, as Freud said, repetition compulsion) as a means of dealing with anxiety. The child is able to hold on to a reality that is symbolized in a form of play with which he would be in danger of losing contact without such a representation: his anxiety is thus contained by his game. It is for this same reason that a child analyst might draw charts to represent analytic holiday periods, and help a child to visualize its break with a sequence of coloured squares.

The *Fort! Da!* game is also very important in Lacan's work. There is some convergence in the sense that the example also illustrated for Lacan the relation of symbol formation to absence of the mother, before the experience of the Oedipus complex. But whereas in the object-relations tradition one can point to the cotton-reel example as just one early empirical observation followed by innumerable others from the analysis and observation of children, in Lacan's work it appears to be the canonical case, from which much theory is then constructed. Wilden comments that 'if Freud had not reported the *Fort! Da!* it would have been necessary to invent it, since it plays the role of necessary "myth of origins" in Lacan's theory', and he points out how much weight Lacan rests on this single instance in the development of his concepts of the Imaginary and the Symbolic. Lacan appears to use the example for purposes of a philosophical recoding of Freud's work, not to suggest any new empirical investigation. The contrast between the various discussions of this observation (including Freud's own) not least in their relative clarity and intelligibility, seems to me a powerful testimony to the perverseness of the choice of Lacan as a major point of entry to psychoanalysis, at least for those with easy access to writings in the British psychoanalytic tradition.

It remains for me to summarize the most important differences between Lacanian and object-relations theory in their implications for cultural studies, and also to indicate what their respective political implications might be. These will be stated briefly.

Lacanian cultural theory seems to me pessimistic and elitist in its political implications, as well as academic in its practice. Culture and society are conceived as inherently repressive (rather than, in their essence, as both repressive *and* as the only positive means of self-realization that is conceivable). Emphasis is given to this metaphysical state of being and to the restricted possibilities for particular individuals — through psychoanalysis or in other ways — to transcend these limits in more-or-less momentary ways, rather than to the historical and particular conditions of repression. The emphasis in

Lacanian-influenced cultural theory is on the generally ideological character of cultural forms, as bearers of imposed social categories, illusory ideas of subjective agency, and mirror-like identifications of the self with imposed definitions. To this is contrasted a practice of deconstruction in criticism and in art, for which only the most highly educated and informed (and perhaps some marginal individuals) have the capability.

The social vantage point from which this theory is advanced is mainly that of academics, educated and privileged out of any broader relationship to their wider society. One might say that the elitist pessimism of the Frankfurt School is echoed in these modern writings, but without that intellectual generation's historical tragedy as a justification. There have of course been positive features in the exposure of British cultural studies to more theoretical traditions evolved on the Continent, and the attention to ideology in modern cultural theory reflects the real power of the communications industries in late capitalism. But the creation of these various theoretical discourses has served other purposes than the advancement of a more comprehensive and sophisticated Marxist theory of culture. What from one point of view can be seen as a sustained attempt to extend serious consideration to popular cultural forms, from another can be seen as their academicization, as a process of incorporation into quite traditional and hierarchical academic procedures of cultural forms and their audiences to which intellectuals should have a different kind of relationship.

Leavis's influence led to a more positive and committed cultural practice — notably in education — than Lacanian cultural theory. One reason for this is that the *Scrutiny* group maintained, especially in its earlier years, the view that a particular English literary tradition carried a discourse of moral dissent from dominant social values, and also that it gave an imaginative possibility to potential life forms different from those which were actually realized for the majority. Limited, nonconformist, humanist and 'untheorized' as this vision might have been, it at least provided some positive grounds for a cultural commitment against that of the then dominant classes and their cultural representatives, whereas a theory of ideology and demystification, especially in the context of vanishing beliefs in the socialist potential of the working class, leads to a Frankfurt School style of pessimism, or even to a Nietzschean recourse, in desperation, to negative understanding as the only defensible standpoint and pleasure. The attack on 'humanism' and 'moralism' as ideologies, even though initially presented as the implication of a scientific materialism, also has echoes of Nietzsche's own attack on the ethical as a form of illusion.[7] The fact is that the intellectual difficulty and frenetic fashion changes of this discourse are related both to its theoretical presuppositions (which require a ceaseless critique of unreflective ideology) and to the social location of its practitioners. In a highly competitive and stratified intellectual environment (competition is between both individuals and coteries) theoretical sophistication and cosmopolitanism constitute a distinct competitive resource.

Work in the object-relations tradition, on the other hand, remains mainly confined to the field of psychoanalytic clinical work. Lacanians have attacked the 'biologism' of Klein, and this is an aspect of a more general rejection in these quarters of positions held to be essentialist or humanist. I argued in Chapter 1 that attention to the biological substructures of human life, and the limits and preoccupations which they necessarily impose on cultures, should be no more exceptionable for socialists than Marx's attention to the material preconditions of life, which in any case derive from biological needs. The distinctive contribution of object-relations theory has been its attention to the preconditions of development in human infancy, providing understanding of a formative stage of life neglected in most socialist discussion. This account depends on the interrelationship of conditions which are biologically given with those which are social and cultural in origin; neither aspect of this interaction can be neglected in the study of socialization without serious confusion.

A second fundamental difference from the Lacanian perspective lies in the emphasis in the object-relations tradition on the containing (Bion) and facilitating (Winnicott) properties of cultural and social forms, including those of the family, as well as their repressive and alienating properties. For anyone trained in the psychoanalytic tradition, this must be a matter of emphasis and not of contradiction, since both dimensions are central to its account of development. But the distinctive value of the object-relations tradition is its attempt to discriminate between conditions favourable to growth and development and those inimical to it.

One may as well grasp the nettle at this point and say that Kleinian and related approaches to psychoanalysis can contribute vitally to the reconstitution of humanism on a theoretically coherent basis. The 'subject' is described in this account as only gradually individuated, and as continually enmeshed in unconscious projections and projective identifications with others, into adult life. There is no prior postulation of a given individual, and the internal and external others in the individual's experience are also constitutive of his or her identity. Nevertheless, there is a concept of the differentiated and individual subject as a goal of development, with capacities for thought and feeling as primary attributes of successful growth. In Chapter 1, I maintained that the postulation of an inherently social human being, nurtured by others and with the capacity to create and nurture actual and symbolic others as its 'normal' fulfilment, is a potential foundation for a socialist universalism, which cannot be said for the juxtaposing of abstract desire to inevitable cultural alienation.

Symbolic processes are central, in the object-relations as in the Lacanian accounts of the formation of the self. In both, it is mental pain and loss which provoke and necessitate thought and symbolic representation. For object-relations theory (both Winnicott's and in the Kleinian tradition) this symbolic activity, shared and supported by others, is seen as the precondition for growth, not necessarily as an imposed and alienative misrepresentation and displacement of unconscious desire. Cultural forms are one mode of containment and facilitation for this growth, throughout life, and their availability to all as living forms is therefore central to the possibility of a good society.

Critical life experiences will recur and need to be surmounted in most, if not all, individual lives, over generations — loss and mourning, for example — and such mental and emotional experience must be symbolized and given its due human value in literature and art. Cultural artefacts can therefore properly be understood in terms of the central human experiences to which they give representative form. Some element of human commemoration and celebration (and not only of class struggle) cannot therefore be missing from any socialist view of culture. The understanding achieved in relationship with another represented through psychoanalysis is one valuable contemporary model of cultural process, combining as it does the experience and toleration of intense mutual feeling with the attempt to think about and represent these states of feeling and mind in words.

Object-relations theory is at this point better adapted to the recognition of the dynamics of individual life crises, and their representation in literature and art, than to the understanding of more broadly social or historical phenomena. The main immediate resource that a psychoanalytic approach can provide for cultural studies is its capacity to disclose meanings derived from states of object relations in the individual's inner world, in cultural forms which may have a different manifest meaning. Our experience in responding to cultural forms (as well as that of making them) derives from inner unconscious experience and its symbolization. Inappropriate and reductive 'psychobiography' sometimes arises from psychoanalytic 'readings', but it is what is represented in the work, not its author, which should be their subject. An educational conclusion which can be drawn from the relevance of psychoanalysis is that it is necessary to create learning settings which give space to the experience of feeling as a primary element of understanding. Psychoanalysis here gives a more explicit and theoretical form to a familiar precept of Leavisian criticism, whilst this emphasis on feeling is a dimension which much recent critical discourse seems to have rejected.

There is, however, a more difficult but also necessary task: to relate these 'unconscious' perspectives to the specifically social and historical aspects of cultural forms. How, that is, are the experiences of the inner world differently formed and represented in different 'sociological' or class contexts? A psycho-analytically informed cultural theory will have to address these problems, but it must be admitted at this point that its derivation from contemporary clinical practice provides few resources for this. Indeed, the historical differentiation and placing of psychoanalytic ideas has not proceeded far within its own principal clinical domain, let alone in such wider applications. What is perhaps needed to begin this work are analyses which connect the representation of unconscious experiences (inevitably mainly of the inner world of individuals) with their wider social determinations and representational forms. This may be best attempted at this stage through the consideration of particular works.

Notes

1. This chapter develops an argument already attempted for a broader area of social theory in Chapter 1.

2. Lacan's paper 'The Mirror-Stage as Formative of the Function of the *I*' was published in English with a helpful introduction by Jean Roussel in *New Left Review 51*, September–October 1968, as well as in Lacan (1977). This paper was first delivered by Lacan in 1949; he had first intro-duced these ideas in 1936.

In addition to Lacan's own text, J. Laplanche and J.-B. Pontalis (1973), A. Lemaire (1970) and B. Benvenuto and R. Kennedy (1986) are useful. The last is a particularly clear introduction to Lacan's work. More wide-ranging reflections on lacan's work can be found in J. Rose (1986), and J. Forrester (1990).

3. Margaret Rustin has pointed out to me how in a girl of ten she has observed that the 'mirror' in which the child continues to prepare herself for the world (in getting ready for school, for example) remains her mother's gaze, not an actual mirror. And later, adolescents will provide this 'mirroring' for each other, in a *social* process of preparing a presentable appearance for them-selves. Actual mirrors may be something we learn to use rather late, *faute de mieux*, in an indi-vidualist culture.

4. The entries in Hinshelwood (1989) under 'thinking' and 'epistemophilia' provide a useful guide to this topic.

5. This emphasis in later Kleinian theory on the concept of containment can be taken as an index of the wider process of feminization of psychoanalytic theory which I think that this tradition has accomplished.

6. In D.W. Winnicott (1975), *Through Paediatrics to Psychoanalysis.*

7. A further hidden affinity of post-structuralist theory with Nietzsche arises from the consequences of a thoroughgoing relativism. If all values are historically constructed, and ethical or philosophical justifications (of the kind Marx attempted through his concept of 'species being') are in principle rejected, then differences can be resolved only by arbitrary fiat (existential choice), by mechanical materialism, or by recognition of the overriding imperatives of power. A related point about Nietzschean influence is developed by Peter Dews in his admirable *Logics of Disintegration* (1987).

8

Psychoanalysis, and Aesthetic Experience*

In Chapter 6, I suggest a characterization of the major stages of thought in the Kleinian psychoanalytic tradition as giving primary emphasis respectively to a scientific, to an ethical, and to an aesthetic perspective. Freud is interpreted there as primarily scientific in outlook, concerned to develop an account of the mind which provided causal explanations of mental states — at first as transformations of an initial 'input' of instinctual drives. But even when it became more fully psychological (presupposing object-related desires as primitive terms) this account nevertheless remained committed to a framework of causality. Melanie Klein — whilst retaining all Freud's commitment to explanatory models of the mind, and with a remarkable theoretical inventiveness and ambitiousness of her own — was distinctively interested in the origins and primary role of moral capacities. Her teleological model of human development, based on the oscillating shift between the paranoid-schizoid and depressive positions, provided an explanation of the early role of the moral sense (concern for others, recognition of the self's capacity to cause damage to others). This framework then gave to Kleinian analytic practice in its classic period a morally centred outlook, according to which patients' states of mind were liable to be judged in relation to criteria of developmental benignness. The greater involvement of psychoanalysts in this period (the 1940s and 1950s)

---

*Earlier versions of this chapter were given as papers at the Psychoanalysis and the Public Sphere Conference at the Polytechnic of East London in 1988, and in a seminar series on the history of psychoanalysis in the Department of the History and Philosophy of Science at Cambridge University in 1990.

in more public concerns for child and family welfare provided external reasons for formulating an ethical or ameliorative approach to development.

More recent developments in the Kleinian tradition, I argue, have shifted attention away from prescriptive ethical concerns (which had been felt by some to lead towards somewhat dogmatic attitudes, reinforced by the institutional-ization of psychoanalytic practice). Linked interests in the origins of the capacity for thinking and its relation to early emotional experience, and in the qualities of thinking within the analytic process (especially influenced by the work of Wilfred Bion), have markedly influenced Kleinian and related analytic practice.[1] There has been a renewed interest in the essence or pure spirit of psychoanalysis, and a valuing above all of authentic discovery and insight within the analytic context, contrasted with a somewhat routinized mapping of theoretical orthodoxies on to each successive patient. This might be understood as an attempt to recover the atmosphere of 'revolutionary' as opposed to 'normal' science, even though there has been no fundamental break with Kleinian ideas at a theoretical level. As usual in such cases, this renewal has been accompanied by impatience with institutional conventions and constraints on the part of those identified with the idea of reformation or a 'return to essentials'. The ensuing unorthodoxies are then open to be interpreted either as merely irresponsible and arrogant rule-breaking, or alternatively as expressing a refreshing preference for the essentials of analytic practice over mere surface conformity to the rules.

The 'aesthetic' preoccupations of late Kleinian analysis are evident in the reverence shown for the qualities of the analytic experience, over and above the relation of practice to established theoretical models, or to considerations of 'cure' or development according to conventional moral or emotional norms. There is something of a return here to Freud's own attitude of tolerance and disinterested curiosity towards his patients and their ways of coping with their individual configuration of desires and defences. The analytic experience is seen to exemplify a capacity to apprehend 'truth', understood not as a rational scientific correspondence with some objective interpersonal structure already established in theoretical terms, but as something more like the meaning of a shared emotional experience apprehended within a relationship. This state of 'knowledge' has a mystical or religious quality more than a scientific one, though it seems that Bion at one stage thought, in a somewhat Platonistic way, that abstract mathematical formulations could also represent truths about mental functioning and development. Bion's development, following Klein's postulation of a primary epistemophilic instinct, of a 'vertex' of knowledge to accompany the earlier primary motivating drives of love and hate, attempted to give a theoretical articulation to this cognitive dimension of experience. The processes of knowing and thinking are promoted in this development from a given presupposition of psychoanalytic theory and practice, interesting mainly in so far as they are liable to be distorted by unconscious mental processes, to a key and problematic aspect of development. Knowledge in its different forms thus becomes a topic and value in its own right.

The detachment of this perspective of 'knowledge' from both pre-existing frameworks of scientific validity and judgement, and from ethical valuations of this or that state of mind against developmental criteria, is what marks it out as distinctively 'aesthetic'. Kant, in *The Critique of Judgement*, characterizes aesthetic judgement as distinct from scientific and ethical understanding in having to do with disinterested contemplation of objects of experience, related neither to the goal of interpersonal knowledge of causes nor to issues of conformity with moral law. Habermas, in his writings on the subject of modernity,[2] defends Kant's threefold differentiation of modes of thought as an advance in human consciousness and culture, freeing each of the related spheres of action (scientific and technical discovery, moral and social improvement, and human self-discovery and self-expression) from the constraints of a unified world-view. It is interesting to see that this differentiation is reflected not only in the very different rules governing major fields or disciplines of human thought, but also as emphases *within* the highly specialized discourse of psychoanalysis. This possibility arises because of the position of psychoanalysis at a point of inter-section of various different ways of thinking about human beings — the scientific, the ameliorative or curative, and the expressive. These can therefore give rise to different preoccupations within psychoanalytic thought, whilst all nevertheless remain important elements within it, and there is no necessary inconsistency or incompatibility between them.

Recently, writers within this late Kleinian or Bionian tradition have begun to give more explicit consideration to aesthetic issues in themselves. Meltzer (1988) has postulated a 'sense of beauty' as a primary, innate human capacity. 'Knowledge' in one of its most formative and important forms is understood as 'knowledge of the beautiful' (linked by these writers with knowledge of the good), and this is seen to begin with the infant's earliest apprehensions of the beauty of its mother. Clinical writing, especially about analytic work with children, has given a more detailed and vivid texture to this insight. Poignant moments in the recovery or emotional development of seriously damaged children or adolescents sometimes figure as turning points in clinical reports, when a patient first demonstrates in a graphic way that he or she can recognize the beauty of some aspect of the world around them. So far, however, the significance of the apprehension of beauty within psychoanalytic thought has been more persuasively demonstrated in these descriptive, clinical kinds of writing than more abstract conceptual or theoretical terms. In theoretical terms, the 'aesthetic sense' or the sense of beauty remains more or less a postulate or blank hypothesis — a 'preconception', in Bion's terms — which still needs its binding concepts.

Psychoanalytically inspired writing about works of art, especially literature, has been another way in which this emerging preoccupation has been given shape. In such writing, for example by Meg Harris Williams (1982, 1987, 1988), the poet or dramatist is seen to represent the capacity to learn and change; the inspired process of finding poetic form for experiences of inner conflict and disorder exemplifying this essential human capacity. Some of the writing about literature from this viewpoint is proving of great value in clarifying and developing the psychoanalytic view of the 'aesthetic sense', in parallel to the insights of clinical practice. This work, however, has not so far contributed much in the way of new theoretical ideas with which to think about these issues. The 'phenomenological turn' of some late Kleinian analytic writing, especially that of Donald Meltzer, has also led to a partial repudiation of the idea of theory as such, on the grounds that it is inseparably linked to aspirations to scientificity and causal explanation which are for various reasons rejected.

Psychoanalytic Approaches to Aesthetics: Freud and Klein

Freud's interest in art as a psychoanalyst was concerned with the dimension of repressed and unconscious meanings. He saw the work of art (in the paintings and sculptures of Leonardo and Michelangelo, for example) as providing a kind of sublimated expression for forbidden desires. Desires and impulses which would not be permitted more direct representation can be expressed in the indirect symbolic form of a work of art. Like dreams or jokes, therefore, they provide a means of expressing, recognizing, and working through repressed feelings, both for creative artists and for audiences who in part relive and share the artists' experience through their work. Freud admitted that he was not very interested in the formal issues or problems involved in making art-works, but mainly in the specific dimension of latent 'content' in which he had a scientific interest. This approach was for many years found powerful but also somewhat one-dimensional and crude in its application to works of art. Whilst something important could certainly be learned, for example, about *Hamlet* from recognition of the strength of oedipal feeling in the hero – morbidly preoccupied, for instance, with what is going on in his mother's bed, and paralysingly ambivalent in his identification with his dead father — this approach suffers from its apparent elision of a play or painting with a case history. Only works where some such repressed state of mind is a central theme or preoccupation seem likely to be much illuminated, as a whole, by this approach.

An advance in the psychoanalytic understanding of art was brought about by Kleinian work. Klein's typology of paranoid–schizoid and depressive positions, and her account of the link between depressive anxiety and the capacity for symbol formation, provided a new framework in which to think about art.[3] The development of symbolic capacity was linked with the capacity to hold in mind the absent other — Winnicott's (1958, 1971) idea of transitional space and transitional objects captures a similar moment of development. Recognition of the separate existence of the other, as the recipient of both loving and hating impulses from the self, also created space for the idea of reparation — that is, of being conscious of damage that could be done to the maternal object, and wanting to protect it.

Hanna Segal developed these ideas into a valuable theory concerning the functions of artistic creation.[4] The artist lived his or her relations to objects in symbolic terms, through the construction of a world of symbols or artefacts corresponding to internalized objects. It is just in this way that a child in its play may represent the figures of its internal world — that is to say, of its inner experience of its relations with parental figures or parts of itself. The distinctive capacity of the artist is to find an elaborate 'language' or set of equivalents for these inner states, which are otherwise, in most people, relatively unarticulated — but also, Segal argued, to face up to greater mental pain than most people in his or her capacity to recognize inner emotional experiences: for example of loss, or of damage wrought to inner objects.

Segal suggested that good works of art were primarily integrative and reparative in their effects. She cited as a prime instance the works of Proust, which she saw as holding and preserving in mind an experience lost not so much to destructiveness or hatred as to the ravages of time itself. There is an obvious link between this celebration of Proust and the values of psychoanalysis, which is also dedicated to a detailed practice of remembering, to holding in mind, and to giving meaning to past or unacknowledged experience. Segal suggests that creative capacity depends on an inner identification with sexual parents, and gives several clinical examples of the blocking of creativity as a result of failed identifications. Her essay on William Golding's novel *The Spire*[5] explores these issues further, treating the story as an allegory of imaginative creation and its conditions of possibility. The story describes how Jocelyn, a medieval builder, tries to construct a spire on the weak and putrefying foundations of a cathedral. Jocelyn is unconsciously driven (or overdetermined, we might say), since these unsound foundations equate in his internal world to the two sexual couples in the story on whom the building project depends. Jocelyn is unable to tolerate the existence of sexual parent-figures, and sets out to corrupt and destroy them. The spire, an obvious enough symbol in itself, is thus built on false foundations, of envy and omnipotence, and collapses. The novel itself, on the other hand, is able to encompass and represent the truth of this narrative; Golding succeeds in making a creative work of fiction out of the recognition of how a creative work in another medium can be internally flawed, and fail. This work, and her commentary on it, certainly constitute a powerful fictional and critical illustration of Segal's thesis. However, the novel has much too didactic and allegorical a structure to serve as an exemplary instance for a psychoanalytic interpretation of literature. The formal pattern and symbolic equivalences of the story (as in a different way in Golding's *Lord of the Flies*) drive it in too predetermined a way.

In her work on aesthetics, Segal takes pains to be as sensitive as possible to issues of form, explicitly recognizing as she does Freud's own weaknesses in this respect. She recognizes the importance of the artist's respect for his materials and techniques, and sees this as an indispensable aspect of the true artist's necessary and superior tolerance of reality. Only where the artist is able both to face up to conflicting forces in his own nature, and to achieve the necessary mastery over external means of expression, is good work (rather than sentimental or merely decorative work) likely to result. There is still, however, a strong affinity in this writing between the idea of emotional and moral maturity (equated with the depressive position) and creative capacity. Formal capabilities in the service of reparation seem to constitute Hanna Segal's essential definition of good art.

Kleinian writers on art and literature (or those influenced by this approach) have been able to offer interpretations of works enriched by the idea of a complex inner world, preoccupied not only with repressed sexual desires but also with feelings of destructiveness and loss. The work of art was seen not — as in Freud's earlier writings — as a form of covert release of a repressed desire, but as representation of a complex state of mind or relation to the inner world. Ella Freeman Sharpe's writings on Shakespeare, for example,[6] were extremely perceptive about states of mind — such as mourning and melancholia in *Hamlet* — which, although drawn from Freud's analytic work, had not been employed by him in his analysis of art-works. In the field of painting, sculpture and architecture, Adrian Stokes's delicate and suggestive writing[7] (very different from the deductive method of Freud) tried to capture the moment of experience of a work of art and its characteristic qualities of feeling. Stokes saw the artist and architect as exploring at the same time both hostile and reparative feelings towards symbolic equivalents of mother's body. The apertures, entrances, hollow spaces, smooth or rough surfaces of a building expressed relationships to the primary source of maternal containment and shelter. The rhythm and harmony of classical buildings represented the reconciliation of conflicting impulses and anxieties, shared between architect and public. Architecture succeeded when it represented a particular and authentic relation to this inner space, as a symbolization of the working-through process necessary in every life.

Similar arguments have been developed by a later writer influenced by Klein's and also Winnicott's ideas: Peter Fuller (1980). His work on the Venus de Milo sought to explain the appeal of this work in part through its embodying the physical *reality* of loss and damage. The defect and mutilation of the work was, he suggested, one explanation for its particular fascination. More recently Richard Wollheim has developed an extremely delicate and subtle approach to the question of how paintings relate to their viewers in his *Painting as an Art* (1987), where he continues the explorations begun earlier by Stokes.

Kleinian ideas have thus had a powerful, if partial, explanatory purchase on works of art and literature. There is a constant danger of reductionism in psychoanalytic readings of art-works, not always avoided in the Kleinian tradition. One problem is that the concerns with the development of the emotions and the personality which preoccupy psychoanalysis are only one of many different subject matters explored by the makers of works of art and literature. Whereas certain works seem to lend themselves to interpretation in these terms, many others do not, having quite other themes — for example, of a social or political kind — which may be some distance from concerns with intimate personal emotions. The equating or linking of aesthetic capacity with a certain stage of emotional development or maturity seems to be selective and partisan in its focus, rather than illuminating over the full range of art-works. Understandably, psychoanalysts who value in their work and life a particular version of psychic integration or maturity also value those art-works which are able to realize this state of mind. This is not to say, however, that there are not other forms of consciousness which also find powerful and lasting expression in aesthetic form.

Even the greater sensitivity of Kleinian writers such as Hanna Segal to questions of form fails to give sufficient centrality to these issues in the creation of and response to works of art. In this earlier Kleinian work, emphasis has tended to be given to the representation of certain aspects or stages of development of the inner world, not to the process of giving form and meaning in itself. It seems, therefore, that this classical Kleinian view may still misrepresent the nature of art to some degree, subordinating it unduly to concepts and values of emotional development with which it is perhaps only contingently or partially connected.

It is these limitations in previous psychoanalytic approaches to aesthetics that later work in the Kleinian tradition may now have the potential to overcome.

'Late Kleinian' Psychoanalysis and Art

W.R. Bion and his followers have set out to investigate very early and pre-rational states of mind. Bion's (1967) brilliant early papers enabled him to develop, in clinical experience with psychotic patients. Freud's ideas on concrete 'thing-representations' — the confusion or inability to distinguish between words and their objects, and the states of mind that this produced. Language, for some such patients, was no longer to be regarded either as a transparent or even a distorted medium of communication, lending itself to direct communication or to illuminating interpretation. It could be experienced at various times as a threatening link between separate persons or parts of the self to be feared or attacked, or as a weapon, or as a delusional system. Bion distinguished between the primitive materials of thought — what he called 'beta function' or the raw materials of sensation, desire or feeling - and these materials 'contained' in the mind as thoughts, or 'alpha function'. The violence and extremity of the mental experiences of psychotic patients (or patients who had lacked in infancy a sufficient early containment and modulation of their physical and mental experiences, these states being often causally linked) was such that 'language' could not contain or bind them, and delusional states or (in autism) attempts to block out experiences were adopted as alternatives to 'thinking'.

By problematizing the capacity for thinking itself — that is to say, by distinguishing between the 'content' of thought and the 'form' of thought; between 'thoughts' or sensa and the thinking apparatus needed to 'think' them — Bion introduced a new dimension into psychoanalytic understanding.

It seems probable that the essential core of aesthetic experience lies in the 'containing' or 'binding' of sense experiences, or of mental images or desires, into some 'containing' or symbolic framework. A simple instance of this is the experience of 'naming' — selecting out some recurring and stable set of attributes in the world and 'binding' them under a name or label. This basic use of language is, as Wittgenstein insisted, necessarily a 'public' — that is, an interpersonal — act. Infants learn not only that this is Mummy, or a favoured object, or whatever, but at the same time that this knowledge is shared with someone else, and thus joins them in a confirming and reciprocal world with those near to them. Language is not cognitively dependent only on social exchange, as both Durkheim and Wittgenstein demonstrated, but also, in its initial stages, on the communication and shared experience of feelings.

The net of ideas which comes to be spread over the world of experience is shaped by desires, purposes and feelings, so that coming to use and share with others these words or names for things also confirms the reality and acceptability of the infant's desires. The infant's 'nature' (its interests, preferences and aversions), not merely its picture of the external world, is thus built up in language. As Merleau-Ponty argued,[8] our picture of the world is impregnated and shaped by our desires. The emergence of forms of language which aim for a 'value-free' or non-subjective description of the world, filtering out as far as possible those attributes which reflect our preferences or sentiments, represents a sophisticated and specialized stage in the development of both cultures and individuals. Language provides not a map of the world independent of our relation to it (the positivist model) but a map which embodies our intentions and being-in-the-world.

'Language' should be understood here to mean not only verbal language literally comprehended, but also the prior and accompanying repertoire of sounds and gestures by which an infant's own feelings are expressed, and by which it manages to 'point to' salient features of its world in ways which its parents or others learn to recognize. These processes are of course, in normal circumstances, interactive between infants and parents, and not a merely repressive imposition of prior categories by adults on to infants. Human beings learn distinctive intonations and habits of speech — parents often enjoyably sharing neologisms with their infants in the early stages of language learning — because of the way different parties to the learning process respond to the individuality of their partners.

Human experience, without symbolic containing forms, would be a potential chaos or bombardment of sensations — sights, smells, sounds, pains, bodily awareness of various kinds, hungers, desires and hatreds. Each of these dimensions of experience is given or attains 'forms', or some regular patterning, as development takes place. The range of sounds of the human voice is patterned in the experience of the infant, both wordlessly and in words, and also in music and song. The infant inhabits a visual environment, often carefully modulated for it by its carers to maintain a pleasing but not unduly alarming level of stimulus. For example, an intimate scale of surroundings, with simple patterns and recognizable colours, is provided in an infant's room, or it is placed outdoors where it can enjoy from its pram the sight of gently moving clouds or trees.

Bion argued that the precondition for the attainment of relative cognitive order is a primary experience of maternal 'containment' — the modulation of the most disruptive and disturbing aspects of the infant's physical and mental life to a level which it can tolerate and enjoy. Without this the 'thinking apparatus' would fail to form, being unable to bind the contents being pushed into it. In that case, perhaps, an alternative 'solution' to the problem of sensory and sentient bombardment is found in fragmentation, splitting, or the atomization of experience; or perhaps simply experiencing this mental pain in somatic ways, by being ill. I want to suggest that the primary root of aesthetic experience lies in this basic experience of 'alpha function' or the containing of sensory experience in 'thoughts' — that is to say, in some embryonic symbolic form, whether of verbal language or other symbolization. The *form* or symbolic containment of experience is prior, aesthetically, to its *content*, which may be as various as the experiences of life itself. The 'sense of beauty' in its simplest form, I suggest, is not the apprehension of the quality of any one privileged object — the perception of the beauty of mother, for example, as Meltzer posits it; it is, rather, the recognition of meaning or understanding *per se*. Dreams, as both Rycroft and Meltzer have argued, are best understood as one mode of apprehension or thinking about emotional experience, their strange narrative structures and unities of mood and setting having some (though only some) of the characteristics of works of art.

Meltzer (1988) proposes the 'apprehension of beauty' as a primary human capacity, expressed from the earliest weeks of life. He argues that it has been unrecognized in psychoanalytic thought, which has adopted (under Melanie Klein's influence) too grim a view of the infant's earliest mental states. Meltzer's description seems to me in fact to elide together two distinct attributes or kinds of experience: on the one hand the pleasure of finding meaning or form in *some* object or event, and sharing it with another; on the other, the experience of perfection or bliss in the contemplation or recognition of the other in its earliest and most intensive form — the maternal breast. The latter is primarily a state of emotional well-being or plenitude; the former a perceptual or cognitive process or activity whose 'object' may by no means be simply an experience of the perfectly beautiful or wonderful. Whilst these two aspects of experience can come together — and perhaps it is especially momentous when they do — I want to argue against equating the aesthetic faculty with the experience of 'perfect beauty' in this sense — the experience of the ideal, perfect, or blissful. More fundamental to the aesthetic faculty are the sensations of pleasure found in mental function itself — in moments of recognition or perception; in acts of memory and sharing of meaning. The experience of moments of bliss and contentment may be quite distinct from the state of mental aliveness and connection which I think is constitutive of the aesthetic sense. In psycho-therapy, this sense of mental liveliness may be as important an indicator of emotional development as a sense of the beautiful. 'Do you remember the going-away gypsy?' asked one mainly psychotic adolescent girl patient of her therapist, telling her by this that she remembered their previous conversation, recalled her own perception of her distressingly absent therapist, and in a way could herself make use of metaphor to understand her own state of mind. This rather encouraging moment did not depend on the therapist being perceived at this point as good, but on the fact that her wandering 'gypsy-like' aspects were able to be held in mind at all.[9]

An infant's first experience of a joke with its mother — remembered in the case of one particular infant to have taken place at the age of ten months (in her bath, though the 'subject' of the baby's joke has unfortunately been forgotten) may be nearer to an *aesthetic* pleasure than other and earlier experiences of perfect contentment. This is because the element of independent recognition and perception — not of bliss and plenitude — is what is essential to the aesthetic experience.

For this reason Freud's book on jokes[10] has as much to say about the nature of aesthetics as his work on painting and sculpture — more, in fact. Freud argues that jokes are funny because they allow the expression of illicit emotion or desire in a form of everyday utterance which is made 'safe'. The thought is tamed (in the case of a double meaning, for example) by the fact that from one point of view it is quite innocent, even though from another it is a potent and dangerous breaking of a taboo. The mind oscillates to and fro between alternative 'readings', which allow both a pleasurable discharge or release of feelings and a sense of relief that a boundary after all remains in place. Jokes often play reflexively with such boundaries of propriety or safety, gaining in risk and intensity as they approach closer to the danger line (increasing feelings of both release and relief as they do so) but risking falling over the edge into the catastrophe of balance or control being lost. Embarrassment (closely linked to shame and guilt) seems to come about when 'bad motives' which have sought acceptable disguise in humorous ambiguity (when they are in reality mixed with something else, including a desire to give pleasure) appear in their unwanted, truly negative form.

Jokes which contain an element of hostility or denigration reveal the role of ambiguity, of alternative readings of the same utterance, just as clearly as sexual jokes. Where people are gathered to celebrate retirements or important anniversaries, and the public context and its atmosphere provide a solid ground of reassurance of goodwill, an opportunity is created to make humour out of residual bad will or hostility. Outrageous and discreditable stories against someone, which in other contexts would be taken as offensive and thus embarrassing to utter or listen to, in these settings provide a welcome relief to what might otherwise feel like a banal or insincere ritual, without much emotional authenticity. The skill of such speeches may depend on how subtly the speaker can introduce unexpected or emotionally piquant elements into an otherwise apparently innocuous discourse, can take an audience by surprise with a tang of malice at the very moment when this seems furthest from its conscious thoughts. If the overriding feeling towards the individual in question is positive and affectionate, then this humorous irruption of the negative will only help, adding to the sense of completeness and emotional truth of the occasion without undermining its dominant mood.

Freud well understood the importance of the formal properties of the joke in making the discharge and relief of feeling through humour possible. Jewish jokes (which were probably in his mind when he was writing) are notoriously concerned with ironic self-denigration. A genre of them relives (one might say in a kind of repetition compulsion or 'working through') injuries daily suffered in anti-Semitic communities. But by assuming the authorship of the joke — and also by conferring, through ambiguity of meaning, some autonomy and resource to the apparently ill-regarded central figure — these jokes lightly turn the tables on the oppressors. Jokes can rarely do more than this — seeing the actual in a slightly different way, or allowing some other feelings about it to come into play, rarely changes the actual world. In sexually repressed societies, sexual jokes provide some enjoyable release, but do not much change sexual behaviour. In conditions of political oppression (when it is not so severe as to be beyond even the blackest humour) jokes against a regime do little to change it, but they do embody and celebrate the survival of intelligence and inner autonomy. This can have its meaning outside a situation as well as within it — the reception in the West of Soviet jokes about perestroika, among other things, contributes to the rehumanization of Soviet popular culture in Western eyes.

The central issue in all this from the point of view of aesthetics is that it is the ingenuity of the humorist in using symbolic resources, in making expressions bear more than one relevant meaning, that is crucial to the pleasure he gives. The humour of the television series 'Whose Line is it Anyway?', where comedians improvise performances within certain set formats, depends on the subversion of established performance genres already familiar to the audience. A slapstick comedian who finds a hundred ways of falling, or of threatening to fall but not falling, is doing something similar with *his* symbolic language — arousing fear, anxiety, or sadistic feelings in his audience (who are preoccupied with the physical harm he may come to, or may do to others) whilst then setting this at rest through his virtuoso mastery of bodily skills. The childlike quality of one film comedian in particular — Buster Keaton — suggests an origin of these anxieties and their masteries in very early physical experience. The young Keaton must have experienced both very extreme physical anxieties, and an unusually intense resolution of them by himself and his circus acrobat parents, to have made the representation of this experience into an artistic life work. The 'Whose Line' performers also enable their audience to share the anxiety of improvised performance, and in most cases the pleasure of successfully overcoming it.

One reason why it seems important to stress the element of cognitive ordering or the 'finding of meaning' in aesthetic experience is the manifest complexity of this faculty. States of emotion, or perfect contentment, may be more intensely felt in early life than at any other time, and later experiences of love or passion may echo, recall or repeat these earlier moments in various ways. But the response to form or beauty is not a simple or primary faculty, but on the contrary is learned through experience and from acquired mastery of perceptual, verbal, and other skills. Children's responses to symbolic representations or natural forms — music, pictures, language — are different from those of adults precisely in the child's lack of the adult's developed cognitive capacities. The idea that children have an aesthetic sense just as adults do, as part of their primitive mental equipment, does not seem to square with the usually wide gulf between the symbolic capacities and pleasures of adults and those of children. In particular circumstances — for example, in the conversations with children which take place in psychoanalytic treatment, in some intimate exchanges between parents and children, or in responses to high-quality writing for children — complex 'language games' may be shared between adults and children. But even here, the range is necessarily circumscribed by what a child's experience, memory, and cognitive capacities enable him or her to handle. The 'thinking apparatus' that Bion deemed it necessary to develop before thoughts could be thought goes on evolving throughout life. Because aesthetic sensations depend on the enjoyment of these functions, above all others, they are associated almost more than any other with the development of the mind.

Hanna Segal explains the phenomena of art as resulting from an experience of separation and loss. The processes of art, whether as an act of making or appreciation, depend on the ability to relate to symbolic representations of an absent object. In order for the experience of art to be possible, the mind has to be separate from its primary objects and able to relate to them in its imagination. The intensity of loss of an object, or its felt incompleteness or insufficiency, may be a more important stimulus to its re-creation in art than its actual or remembered perfection. Freud argued that art was the product of unfulfilled (or unfulfillable, impossible) desires, and an alternative to primary satisfaction. In the Kleinian view works of art seek to repair or restore what may have been irretrievably damaged or lost in life. For these reasons the re-evocation of a primary appreciation of the beauty of the earliest love-object seems to be only one constituting element of aesthetic experience, a memory of the good or harmonious which remains in later life as a remembered ideal. Without some such primary memory, however fragmentary, there would be no impulse to create or re-create, just as without some secure internal object there is no possibility of finding real love-objects (or later, through parental identification, children) to whose 'preconception' they can correspond in the world.

The incompleteness of the life world of the artist, rather than its plenitude, seems crucial to his or her struggles to achieve completeness, harmony or integration in symbolic forms. It is the virtuosity of the artist in struggling with the techniques which confer meanings and order, against an unusually powerful sense of loss, inner conflict, or deadness, which seems to produce powerful works. Average or everyday levels of skill in using symbolic languages (whether these involve verbal or other bodily and manual skills) will not usually be sufficient to find registers for unexplored areas of experience. The ability to use and test out the powers of symbolic forms becomes a vital means to expression — a kind of 'play' with expressive forms which is necessary for certain kinds of serious work. This remarkable capacity is represented in a 'real-life' form in the accounts by Oliver Sacks (1976, 1986) of the achievements of patients suffering from various kinds of cerebral damage in nevertheless making sense of what remains of their mental world.

The member of the audience for the art-work also participates by identification with this process, gaining more from the work (at least in certain respects) the more he or she can recognize the problems the artist has had to face and solve through it. Gombrich and others have pointed out that good works of art require an active response of mind from their audiences, parallel in some ways to the mental work the artist has already done in making them. Unless the experience of 'making sense' or finding harmony is won through some effort, there can be no new experience for the mind to digest. The work of art otherwise leaves its viewer unmoved or unaffected, since whatever feelings or sensations there may be floating about and potentially available to symbolic structuring will remain untouched by the work.

This is why any valuable genre or work of art must entail some level of unfamiliarity and difficulty for its audiences, otherwise it fails to stimulate the mental work and satisfaction which are central to art. Attempts to create a merely academic, wholly precedented art, or to return to a valued art-form of the past, are thus misguided, especially since the conditions of the original cultural response to a genre are unlikely to be capable of exact reproduction or restoration. This is not to deny that most works are composed from an interactive relationship with past works and traditions, just as new generations can come into existence only through a dense matrix of identifications and interactions with parents. Copying, however, or literal modelling on the examples of the past, is seldom, if ever, a viable option — either for individuals in their lives or for artists in their works.

There is, however, some tendency to idealization of infancy, and of the mother–infant couple (in part a corrective to the more turbulent picture represented by Melanie Klein) in the postulation of an innate sense of beauty as a foundation of early experience.

A Critical Example

The evolution of ways of thinking about art and culture in the tradition of Freud/Klein/Bion can be exemplified by psychoanalytic writing about *Hamlet*. Ernest Jones (1949), in his classic monograph of psychoanalytic criticism, *Hamlet and Oedipus*, sees Hamlet as subject to intense unconscious conflict, rendering him incapable of the action to which he continually reaffirms his commitment. Hamlet is identified with Claudius, who has done what he has himself unconsciously wished to do — murdered his father and slept with his mother. Revenge is therefore impossible, since the more he urges himself to his duty, the more his repressed memories and impulses arise, and the less capable of action he becomes:

> We might summarize the internal conflict of which he is the victim as consisting in a struggle of the 'repressed' mental processes to become conscious. The call of duty, which automatically arouses to activity these unconscious processes, conflicts with the necessity of 'repressing' them still more strongly; for the more urgent is the need for external action, the greater is the effort demanded of the 'repressing' forces. It is his moral duty, to which his father exhorts him, to put an end to the incestuous activities of his mother (by killing Claudius), but his unconscious does not want to put an end to them (he being identified with Claudius in the situation) and so he cannot. His lashings of self-reproach and remorse are ultimately because of this very failure, i.e. the refusal of his guilty wishes to undo the sin. By refusing to abandon his own incestuous wishes he perpetuates the sin and so must endure the stings of torturing conscience. And yet killing his mother's husband would be equivalent to committing the original sin himself, which would if anything be even more guilty. So of the two impossible alternatives he adopts the passive solution of letting the incest continue vicariously, but at the same time provoking destruction at the King's hand. Was ever a tragic figure so torn and tortured? (pp. 90–91)

Jones's account, frankly interpreting Hamlet as if he were the subject of an analytic case study but finding a great deal that is illuminating to say from that point of view, has had a lasting influence on the understanding of the play, no doubt even among critics who ostensibly disapprove of Jones's methods.

A later critical essay by Ella Freeman Sharpe (1950) — then considerably influenced by the work of Melanie Klein — begins from Jones's main insight into the unresolved Oedipus conflict, and also follows his method of considering the play in terms of a case study. But drawing on the work of Freud and Abraham on mourning and melancholia, she adds another dimension to the analysis. She identifies in Hamlet an initial state of mourning which becomes — with the catastrophes of his mother's speedy remarriage, the knowledge of his father's murder, and the loss of Ophelia — a state of melancholia. In contrast to Jones, Sharpe sees the tragedy of *Hamlet* as a tragedy not of procrastination but of impatience, the overtaking of the hero by blind impetuous action. In mourning, Sharpe says, 'the external world is robbed of interest'.

> 'This goodly frame, the earth, seems to me a sterile promontory.'

> 'Man delights not me: no, nor woman neither.' (II, 2)

In melancholia, the feeling of loss becomes an internal experience. Self-depreciation and self-reproach impoverish the mind.

> 'I could accuse me of such things that it were better my mother had not borne me;'

> 'What should such fellows as I do crawling between earth and heaven?' (III, 1)

The interest of this account from the point of view of the evolution of psychoanalytic ideas since Freud is in Sharpe's attempt to interpret the phantasies expressed within the play in pre-genital terms. She sees Hamlet tormented by a sadistic superego, and identifies a regression in his state of mind to the earliest level of oral preoccupation and phantasy. 'That the fundamental problem is the oral sadism attendant upon oral frustration is clear enough in the text of the play,' Sharpe says, quoting as follows:

> 'I should have fatted all the region kites with this slave's offal.' (II, 2)

> 'Now could I drink hot blood.' (III, 2)

> 'We fat all creatures, else to fat us.' (IV, 3)

> 'The ocean
> Eats not the flats with more impiteous haste
> Than young Laertes.' (IV, 5)

Though Sharpe's discussion is rather schematic in the way it imposes its psychoanalytic concepts on the text, it does nevertheless add considerably to Jones's account. This essay showed that Freud's theory of the Oedipus complex was by no means the only important source of psychoanalytic insights in regard to literature, and that the pre-genital phantasies explored by Abraham and Klein could also be illuminating: 'To read Freud and Abraham on the subject of mourning and melancholia alongside *Hamlet* is to be impressed again with the majesty of human achievement. Science and art here fit exactly; they are completely wedded.'

Rather different in method, and much more attentive to the form of Shakespeare's play, is Meg Harris Williams's paper 'The Undiscovered Country: the Shape of the Aesthetic Conflict in "Hamlet"' (in Meltzer and Harris Williams, 1988). Her principal concern is with the dramatization in *Hamlet* of the painful relationship between thought and emotional experience:

> *Hamlet* is probably Shakespeare's most enigmatic play. Founded on the metaphor of internal 'eruption', it explores the endeavour to find a container for the new and monstrous mystery which rears its beautiful and ugly head. Both the world of the play and the constitution of the hero are shaken by turmoil when it appears that the phenomenon of psychic growth is not a naturally-unfolding process but 'shakes our disposition' with 'thoughts beyond the reaches of our souls'; and the structure of the play correspondingly expands or rather cracks and undermines the classical self-contained model of the revenge tragedy which is its anti-type.

Hamlet, in this reading, represents as tragedy the ultimate failure of the capacity for imaginative thought. Hamlet uniquely struggles to grasp in his mind the destructive and corrupt forces which dominate the court and have brought both his family and the Denmark of the play virtually to disaster. Around him hypocrisy, trickery, spying and manipulation are the preferred modes of action, into which Hamlet himself is frequently drawn. Harris Williams sees in *Hamlet* a symbolization of a larger conflict between the intimate life of the imagination and a corrupt public world of institutional power. This contradiction between the values of emotional truth — belonging to the spheres of intimate relationship, art, and psychoanalytic practice — and the values of power and external appearances — belonging to the public realm of institutions — sometimes appears as a formal dichotomy in Donald Meltzer's work.

What is most valuable, however, in Harris Williams's very full and sugges-tive essay is her break with the limitations of psychoanalytic case analysis as applied to literature. She is able to view the play, not its principal character, as the primary containing vehicle for the experiences it explores. She is highly attentive to its changes in mood and atmosphere — in particular to the moments at which Hamlet's struggle with thinking is lost and frenetic action, with its inevitably disastrous outcome, takes its place. (This idea, in its most basic form, was also central to Sharpe's cruder reading of the play.) Harris Williams sees the play as a quest for understanding and self-understanding to a large degree conducted against the form and action of the plot:

> Through the casual, clumsy and meaningless chapter of deaths which concludes this tale of 'accidental judgement, casual slaughters', Shakespeare stresses the antagonism of the plot to the emotional drama. But in the midst of the unrevelatory action, Hamlet and Horatio once again, and for the last time, emerge to take the centre of the stage ... Hamlet has already said 'I am dead' twice, when – on seeing Horatio with the poisoned cup – he completely sheds his attitude of fatalistic acceptance of events. Suddenly filled with energy, he rises up to snatch it away:

> > 'As th'art a man
> > Give me the cup. Let go, By Heaven I'll ha't.
> > O God, Horatio, what a wounded name
> > Things standing thus unknown, shall I leave behind me.
> > If thou didst ever hold me in thy heart,
> > Absent thee from felicity awhile,
> > And in this harsh world draw thy breath in pain
> > To tell my story.'

Throughout, Hamlet has been struggling to write his story, to find an aesthetic correlative to image the idea of a new prince. At each potential point of revelation he has, through lack of resonance from the other protagonists, fallen impulsively into collusion with an anti-aesthetic mode – such as play-acting, pursuing directions through indirections, or trying to riddle out the heart of the mystery as if it were a secrecy. But though the struggle may not have availed, he has no intention of allowing it to sink into oblivion. He is content to allow 'the election of the state' to a simplistic figure like Fortinbras; but the inner 'story' which has been taking place in the latent structure of the play has yet another revolution to undergo, another species of labour before it may be born into a form which speaks to a further generation.

The main argument of this paper is that the 'aesthetic' is to be understood as the process by which symbolic form is given to experience, as a primary basis of mental life. It is highly relevant, therefore, to see how current psychoanalytic thinking, related to a work such as *Hamlet*, is now able to view the play as itself a dramatization and accomplishment of that process. Earlier Freudian readings were able to grasp the unconscious emotions which could be seen as the material to which the play tried to give form, but had less to say about the process of symbolization itself. Bion's work has made possible a recognition of the psychic forces working against understanding and truth, and the possibility of recognizing these forces as the subjects of tragedy.

Kant's *Critique of Judgement*

The classical psychoanalytic approach to aesthetics outlined by Freud and the Kleinians proposed an implicitly realist view of art, within its particular view of reality. That is to say, works of art were seen as representations or expressions of a specific set of 'truths' of experience, just as social realists often saw art as the representation of a truthful world-view based on the experience of social classes. The 'realist' idea that the purpose of art and literature is to represent truths of human experience, albeit by methods quite distinct from those of generalizing scientific discourse, is an influential and important one, and is not necessarily tied to the legitimation of particular world-views such as those of Marxism or psychoanalysis. Aristotle's theory that works of art represent universal truths, but do so through particular instances, has the power to explain the effectiveness of at least those genres of art which aim at representation. The development of the realist novel, or the increasing mastery of space represented in the development of European painting during and after the Renaissance, or the greater attention paid by art from the seventeenth century onwards — and especially in the modern period — to 'interior' psychological depth, reflect different aspirations to represent newly discovered aspects of reality.

In recent years, as I have suggested in previous chapters, the standards and conventions of 'science' have come to seem somewhat less relevant and significant to many psychoanalysts working in the Kleinian tradition. The discourses of the sciences themselves — even the natural sciences — have come to seem (and perhaps also to be) less uniform, and a more latitudinarian and pluralist view of the methods and procedures of science has been advanced by philosophers. Some have argued that sciences construct rather than merely reflect or represent their objects of study, selecting certain aspects of reality from an infinity of possible perspectives. The human sciences, according to idealist or hermeneutic theories, study cultures which can be understood only within their own terms — that is to say, in a process more akin to the translation or interpretation of a text than the description of an external world independent of the observer. Evident differences of perspective among human scientists, and a greater plurality of contending perspectives more generally, have made it more difficult to have confidence in the idea of a set of fixed universal truths which are there waiting to be discovered.

'Post-modern' philosophers such as Lyotard, Rorty or Vattimo[11] have attacked the whole idea of a fixed corpus of truths about human society or history, from which moral or political judgements could be drawn. They have argued instead for the necessity or virtue of choice, contingency, subjectivity and difference, in contrast to singular prescriptions for the good life or 'grand narratives' supposedly explaining the expected arrival of the good society. I argued in Chapter 6 above that 'late Kleinian' or 'post-Kleinian' psychoanalysis has been tacitly influenced by this contemporary cultural climate, moving in the direction of greater regard for subjectivity, contingency and difference (and away from the idea of scientific explanation, moral judgement, and an implicit teleology of development). But it has by no means burnt the bridges which join it to the earlier assumptions and aspirations of classical psychoanalysis (in regard both to scientific explanation and to the improvement of human lives). For the most part, I suggest, the continuities with the Kleinian tradition are more important than the breaks within it. 'Late Kleinian' is thus probably a more apposite term for this climate of work than 'post-Kleinian'.

In the sphere of aesthetic theory, this move by late Kleinian psychoanalysis away from the 'vertices' of science and ethics has important implications. It undermines the latently 'realist' assumption of classic psychoanalytic views of art and literature — that is to say, the assumption that there is a certain range of truths to be found 'beneath the surface of the work' if one excavates deeply enough, or attends to it with enough sensitivity. The focus of recent psychoanalytic work on the development of the thinking apparatus — on the relation of thought and its objects, whatever these objects may happen to be — suggests to me the need substantially to modify a 'realist' model of art, and to set out to explain the aesthetic qualities in a different way.

One needs to differentiate the functions and processes of science and art, rather than assimilate them to one another through an overarching and unifying system of understanding, conceived as a science. The classic philosophical text in which the aesthetic is differentiated from the two other major axes of human understanding, science and ethics, is Kant's *Critique of Judgement*, Part One of which is concerned with Aesthetic Judgement. The *Critique of Pure Reason* and the *Critique of Practical Reason* dealt respectively with the other two major spheres of rationality posited by Kant. Late Kleinian writing on the origins of mental functioning help to illuminate in psychological terms what Kant described in his philosophical argument as the nature of aesthetic judgement. Kant's account, in a complementary way, enables us to place the aesthetic as one of three distinct moments or aspects of mental life, parallel to the cognitive and the ethical. (Parallels between Bion's approach to mental function and Kant's ideas in *The Critique of Judgement* have also been noted in a valuable article by Meira Likierman [1989].[12])

In his *Critique of Judgement*, Kant sets out a classification of kinds of understanding. He distinguishes cognitive judgments (of nature effected through the faculty of understanding, and of law effected through reason) from aesthetic judgements, or judgements of taste. Cognitive judgements seek knowledge of concepts, and to subsume instances gained from experience under distinct concepts. These spheres correspond to what we think of as scientific knowledge (which for Kant was always an imperfect approximation to a pure conceptual realm) and moral understanding, which Kant thought consisted of or aimed at a rational knowledge of moral law. These kinds of cognitive judgement seek to formulate knowledge or understanding of an objective world external to human experience.

Aesthetic judgements, by contrast, do not aim at knowledge of objects or concepts, but state or express a relation between human subjects and the objects of their experience. Aesthetic judgements state how objects of experience are perceived by individuals, in the actual process of apprehension or cognition. They assert not that objects form instances of some general concept, or are causally related to other objects considered as instances of a general concept (the procedure of science) but that they are pleasing or unpleasing to the observer in the light of this or that property which they possess, and to which the observer forms some subjective response.

Aesthetic judgements are formed, Kant asserts, through the exercise – or, as he several times terms it, the 'play' – of the cognitive faculties. The judgements of the beautiful and the sublime (the two aspects of aesthetic judgement, corresponding to apprehension of forms which are respectively pleasing or awesome and terrible) arise from the recognition of order and form in nature of experience. The sense of the beautiful or the sublime expresses a harmony of the faculties achieved in its perceptions of objects. It is concerned, we might say with the process, not the results or purposes, of cognition or thinking.

Kant's formulations of this are rarely easy to follow, being embedded in the system of terms through which he constructs his monumental analysis of the categories of understanding:

> But I have already stated that an aesthetic judgement is quite unique, and affords absolutely no (not even a confused) knowledge of the Object. It is only through a logical judgement that we get knowledge. The aesthetic judgement, on the other hand, refers the representation, by which an Object is given, solely to the Subject, and brings to our notice no quality of the object, but only the final form in the determination of the powers of representation engaged upon it. The judgement is called aesthetic for the very reason that its determining ground cannot be a concept, but is rather the feeling (or the internal sense) of the concert in the play of the mental powers as a thing only capable of being felt.[13]

Kant insists that 'the judgement of taste, with its attendant consciousness of detachment from all interest, must involve a claim to validity for all men, and must do so apart from universality attached to Objects, i.e. there must be coupled with it a claim to subjective universality.'[14] It would, says Kant,

> be ridiculous if any one who plumed himself on his taste were to think of saying: 'This object (the building we see, the dress that person has on, the concert we hear, the poem submitted to our criticism) is beautiful *for me*. For if it merely pleases *him*, he must not call it *beautiful*. Many things may for him possess charm and agreeableness — no one cares about that; but when he puts a thing on a pedestal and calls it beautiful, he demands the same delight from others. He judges not merely for himself, but for all men, and then speaks of beauty as if it were the property of things.[15]

Underlying this assertion of the universality of aesthetic judgement is the idea of a common human nature. Judgements of the beautiful make implicit reference to the way any human being would feel, in response to a given experience, on the basis of feelings and cognitive faculties shared with others. Whilst denying a cognitive or moral basis of aesthetic judgements, Kant is nevertheless able to presuppose a different kind of universality, that of the human cognitive faculties and their action. The aesthetic sense arises from 'pleasure in the harmony of the cognitive faculties' or, as he also terms it, 'the free play of imagination and understanding'. It is the experience of mental work itself, the perception of form and order in experience, in which aesthetic sensations consist.

Although Kant describes differentiated spheres of mental functioning, the larger design of his philosophy presupposes that the universe, and mankind within it, is subject to a rational design, of which men and women have imperfect knowledge. The harmony and order perceived subjectively through aesthetic judgement are thus emblematic or exemplary in some way of the larger design of existence which is set out in Kant's philosophy:

> The spontaneity in the play of the cognitive faculties whose harmonious accord contains the ground of this pleasure, makes the concept in question, in its consequences, a suitable mediating link connecting the realm of the concept of nature with that of the concept of freedom, as this accord at the same time promotes the sensibility of the mind for moral feeling.[16]

Kant's deep confidence in this state of unity-in-difference is sustained by an ultimate faith in the idea of a universe created and sustained by God, though his philosophical argument is made as far as possible to stand independently of this.

The Place of the Aesthetic Sense

Kant's argument rightly establishes the irreducibility of aesthetic experience. The aesthetic is not merely another way of arriving at knowledge or moral truth. It follows, therefore, that it would be committing a category mistake to judge works of art in terms of how well they approximate to scientific understandings already won, or to how far they advance moral or political purposes already subscribed to. Psychoanalytic criticism has rarely been explicitly prescriptive or judgemental in these ways, though it has tended to approach works in search of correspondences with its own prior descriptive and explanatory models. (Its relatively modest objective has been to show that the psychoanalytic paradigm can do some real work in thinking about the world of art, claiming kinship rather than superiority in the task of human understanding.) Marxist criticism, more closely tied to political movements and goals, has more often found itself in a position to make and enforce prescriptive judgements on the arts, both applying judgemental standards of 'realism' to works, and assessing the political benefit or harm they are deemed likely to do.

While insisting on the specificity of the aesthetic sense, Kant's theory does not trivialize or marginalize art into a merely self-sufficient or self-regarding activity, as could be implied by the analogy with the gourmet's attitude to life which the term 'taste' might nowadays suggest. Kant's differentiated view of art is not a version of 'art for art's sake', as his placing of the aesthetic as part of a unified three-dimensional system of understanding makes clear. The idea of aesthetic judgement as an achieved harmony of the faculties, of the 'free play of the imagination and understanding', locates the aesthetic sense as an essential aspect of the working and development of the mind. The order of the universe and the external world of objects takes shape for the individual only through thought or mental function. Its harmony or form of individuals, in their subjective life (and this is naturally, Kant tells us, a shared, social experience, which it is also pleasurable to communicate to others) is distinct from its objective existence as the ordered form of nature. It is 'making sense' of the world in the minds of individuals which is expressed in the beautiful and the sublime. The sublime is that whose power or fearfulness strains and threatens our sense of the possible and the imaginable, but whose resolution in art then strengthens our confidence in the power of understanding.

Kant comes much nearer in his description of aesthetic judgement than in his austere and rationalistic moral philosophy to recognizing the diversity and richness of human sensory and emotional experiences. Where he is concerned with shared, public judgements of the beautiful and all its cognate terms for qualities of objects and persons, rather than with the judgements of moral obligation, he is able to acknowledge a diversity of values and preferences, each corresponding to some aspect of human feeling and mind. Some at least of Kant's repressive puritanism seems to be lifted in his discussion of aesthetic faculties.

Kant's idea of the distinctiveness of the aesthetic is consistent with a more diverse specification of human need and purpose than is apparent in his moral theory. This specification of need should include the idea of the aesthetic as a process of 'making sense' or 'giving form' to experience, seen as a unique and essential process in each life. Not merely 'pleasures' or 'wants' as given desires for objects or things, but the possibility of forming an individual sense of the world, and of developing relations to objects which allow of judgements of beauty or value, are thus among the building blocks of human nature. Necessary to this process are relationships in which learning can take place, symbolic resources, and emotional and cognitive space. Psychoanalytic research has identified particular preconditions for this development in early life, and also in the experience of relationships and institutional settings in later life which may be more or less favourable to emotional and mental development.

223

What is Specific to a Psychoanalytic Aesthetics?

Recent developments in psychoanalysis, and Kant's aesthetic theories, thus converge in the idea that the primary function of works of art is to give containing form to subjective experience, both for individuals and for the communities of which they are members. It follows that the potential themes or subject matters of art are as various as the different areas of human experience. The experience of disharmony and chaos, and the rendering of harmony and form through art, can occur in the registers of perception, of emotion, of morality, or of politics alike. The threats to cognitive order embodied in upheavals of the life worlds of social classes, in the anomic bombardment of the metropolis, or in the emotional transitions of adolescence or old age, are each the subjects of the 'mental work' of the artist as someone who seeks to give form and harmony to the perception of these states. There is thus no single privileged subject of the arts — not even the primary states of feeling privileged by psychoanalysis — to be determined from some ulterior theoretical vantage point outside them.

Artists and writers, as specialists in the means of expression, will be concerned not only with the 'problems' posed to mental life by their external experience, and by their own inner world ('problems' which to some degree they share with their audiences). They will also be especially sensitive to inadequacy and inauthenticity in the forms of expression available to them. Works of art, as Clifford Geertz[17] has pointed out, may be preoccupied with the inner or the outer worlds, with personal or public meanings. They may also take as their primary preoccupation the validity of expressive languages, either as entire genres or conventions, or as issues of vocabulary and syntax within a genre. Since works of art are concerned with the relationship between symbolic forms and other phenomena of experience, both the referents and the formal languages of art (the 'content' and the 'form', as they used clumsily to be called) are almost bound to be issues for any artist. The debates surrounding 'modern' and 'traditional' architecture today, which raise issues regarding both the inner consistency of any work and its vocabulary and its relation to generic architectural traditions, are instances of the importance of these problems of language and convention for modern artists.

Whether works of art are primarily concerned with 'public' or 'private' worlds, and how solid or subject to transformation and upheaval are the available forms of expression, is itself a subject for historical and sociological explanation. In rapidly expanding cultural markets, both an increasing plurality of experience and a greater anarchy of forms seem unavoidable.[18] As social barriers of class, race and gender are broken down, so more and more 'voices' gain access to means of communication. Communication becomes cheaper and more rapid, but at the same time powerful homogenizing market forces seek to reduce this diversity to packaged and profitable order, sometimes inhibiting the emergence of authentic traditions and means of expression. It is not difficult for 'post-modernists' and relativists to seem to have a point when they assert that in this proliferating supermarket there is no longer any single standard of rationality, or any overriding goal for human society.

Attention to the problematic nature of forms of communication, and their complex relations with their ostensible objects, both 'inner' and 'outer', are important themes in recent psychoanalytic writing, as I have suggested above. The difficulties of achieving a truthful relation to experience, and of finding an authentic form of communication through which this can be shared with others, is often a major theme of a personal psychoanalysis. Bion's 'vertex' of knowledge, as a now-problematic and threatened faculty of experience, problematizes 'meaning' and rationality as precarious states of mind more than did earlier psychoanalytic writing, whose main preoccupation was with specific instinctual sources of distortion of thought.

The idea that understanding is always relative to the experience of a particular individual, and is always mediated through a specific perceptual and affective apparatus, though apparently very unspecific to psychoanalysis, is in fact one of its most important discoveries and insights. There is no path to well-being, whether material or political, which does not lead through the space being made available for men and women to make sense in their own personal terms of the realities of their world. This idea takes the form in psychoanalysis of the privileging of the intimate, in the different intense relationships of mother and baby, of the creative sexual couple, the analyst and analysand, or, by analogous extension, the artist and his or her inner world. In Kant's philosophy, this idea is formulated as the aesthetic sense, as the individual's pleasure in the apprehension of beauty understood as an active perception of form. In Habermas's writing, this possibility is given the more rationalistic form of 'non-distorted communication' and shared participation in rational discourse. The habitual privileging by artists of the practical and immediate tasks of 'making' or writing over imposed doctrines or rules gives a similar force to authentic and personal meanings, which have to be struggled for in experience, over merely external forces and categories.

It follows both from Kant's view, and from the psychoanalytic perspective derived from Bion, that the aesthetic sense needs to be accorded a value and autonomy in and for itself. Works of art, and cultural forms more generally, can clearly be regarded from other than aesthetic perspectives — that is, as ends in themselves. They can alternatively, and at times illuminatingly, be regarded also as carriers of truth about nature or human nature, as realist theories argue or imply. Or, from another point of view, sometimes linked with the realist perspective, as bearers of moral or social values, as both F.R. Leavis and Marxist criticism, in their different ways, have asserted. Terry Eagleton (1990), in this latter tradition, has recently argued, in a full and admirable account of the development of aesthetic theory, for a view of the aesthetic as primarily the embodiment of ideologies, both of dominant classes and of those who resist them, serving to naturalize or denaturalize a system of social relations. In recent years — thanks not least to the work of Raymond Williams — this perspective has become steadily more subtle, requiring the acknowledgement of the specific properties of the aesthetic in order properly to understand how its social effects are achieved.

Whilst developments within the Marxist tradition which have attempted to give due weight to the specificity of symbolic forms have been important and valuable correctives to an earlier reductionism, my argument is a more radical one. It is that none of these three distinct spheres of the explanatory or scientific, the ethical, or the aesthetic, is reducible to any other, even if they are conceptually and causally connected as frames of discourse within any historical formation. Even though there are historical unities to systems of thought, with their explanatory, ethical, and aesthetic dimensions, the functions of each of these different modes of thinking within a formation remain distinct, and indispensable.

Ethical decisions and responsibilities are relevant and necessary for all human actors, in any context, even if they will always be formulated in terms specific to their time and place. The denial of the relevance of 'ethical' judgements as ideological not merely in their particular but in their general form was an error made by Marxists at a particular time of catastrophic proportions, as Lukes (1985) has pointed out. The same recognition must be given to the autonomy of 'aesthetic' judgement, which equally describes an essential moment of human experience, that in which individuals, and groups in a communicative relation to one another, make sense of their world in relation to their own experiences, desires, and values. The point of the autonomy of art is not that art should be for 'art's sake' (as if it would be as valuable if it were located on the moon) but for the sake of what it indispensably does for human experience. Just as each generation's experience constitutes an *ethical* value in itself (which is not to say that this may not have to be weighed against the needs of its successors), so there is an irreducible aesthetic imperative here too: that of 'making sense' and 'finding meaning' in the life of each generation, and indeed each individual.

Some fear a hypertrophy of the 'aesthetic', the diminution of experiences of suffering or injustice through their rendering as subjects of art. However, the contention by Kant and Habermas that in modern society thought has become differentiated in three distinct spheres is an argument for acknowledging the necessity of all of them and their complex relationship, not for a choice of the aesthetic over all other ways of thinking. Reduction of the explanatory or the ethical *to* the aesthetic is as little justified or warranted on this view as the reduction *of* the aesthetic. The perils of aestheticism are also somewhat less when its proper object is recognized to be not beauty or the ideal as such, but meaning, understanding and order achieved in relation to the largest possible part of our experience. Seen in this way, these three moments or dimensions of mental life are indispensably linked to one another as materials and forms of understanding, whilst each retains its distinct value and function.

Current psychoanalytic understanding, drawing on the work of Bion, can thus make possible a broader recognition of the central place of art and aesthetic experience in mental life. In this respect it provides a new foundation for contemporary cultural theory, as Kleinian ideas did — or should have done — for modern ethical theory. But of course, writers about art from a psychoanalytic perspective will continue to attend to the particular dimensions of meaning to which their paradigm gives a privileged access, especially the dimensions of unconscious emotion. Works of art can represent, in the most intense and vivid ways, states of mind which are also the objects of investigation — studies and theoretical writings — of psychoanalysis. Such correspondences of subject matter and preoccupation between art and psychoanalysis will obviously remain of keen interest to analysts. Psychoanalytic interest in the phenomena of mental conflict, and latterly in the destructive forces of the mind, also give rise to a particular area of aesthetic value. Works which are able to engage with deeper levels of disorder and confusion, and to achieve some resolution of these states in artistic or formal terms, are likely to seem more substantial and important achievements than those with a lesser internal range or depth. But such judgements of relative value or importance are also made by audiences, and explain the degree and lasting nature of admiration for great works.

But there has nevertheless been a significant shift of psychoanalytic attention. A moment of recognition, the metaphor produced in a patient's material which allows a particular feeling to be caught hold of and made real for the first time, the complex relations to emotional truth to be found in patients' communications, are now of more importance to the psychoanalytic approach to art than the theoretical or developmental models of the mind which earlier dominated psychoanalytic approaches to aesthetics. Even though such models retain their importance in psychoanalytic theory (and in its approach to works of art), much more important than hitherto are the particulars of mental experience. Theories and concepts cannot be approached or utilized except as they are instantiated in the immediate phenomena of experience and language. The reduction of the flow of inner experience to external forces and imposed categories, which is opposed by psychoanalysis in other spheres as a matter of principle, also applies to its own practices, and enforces its own respect for the specificity of works of art.

These developments in psychoanalytic practice should make possible a new subtlety and scope in psychoanalytic writing about art and literature. In particular, this is likely to be influenced by the example of clinical writing. When this is able to escape from the straitjacket of technical language, it is able to achieve a remarkable and beautiful intensity, metaphorical richness and delicacy in registering moments of transformation in the dialogue between two persons.

The first chapter in this book argued that fundamental building blocks for a social theory of human nature were set out by the first phase of Kleinian psychoanalysis. The argument of this chapter is that 'late Kleinian' psychoanalysis makes an equal contribution to the understanding of the importance of the aesthetic (or, more broadly, cultural) possibilities and needs in human lives. Each phase of psychoanalytic work has of course been concerned primarily with clinical analytic practice, devoted to achieving development in individuals in treatment, not to wider social issues. But the current phase of Kleinian analytic thinking does have its wider social implications. The chief of these is its elaboration of the importance of the process of understanding, and its emotional preconditions, as a basis of authentic experience. This not only has relevance for values in regard to individual lives, but also indicates an agenda of social action.

Notes

1. For an account of the development of Kleinian ideas by Bion see D. Meltzer, *The Kleinian Development*, Clunie, 1978. Two recent collections of articles edited by Elizabeth Spillius, *Melanie Klein Today* (Routledge, 1988), include many key articles in this tradition. For Bion's work, see *Learning from Experience* (1962), *Attention and Interpretation* (1970), both republished in *Seven Servants* by Maresfield Reprints, 1984; and the outstanding papers collected as *Second Thoughts*, Heinemann, 1967.

2. Summarized, for example, in his reply to other authors' comments on his work, 'Questions and Counterquestions', in Richard J. Bernstein, ed., *Habermas and Modernity*, Polity, 1985.

3. 'The Importance of Symbol Formation in the Development of the Ego' (1930), 'A Contribution to the Psychogenesis of Manic-Depressive States' (1935), 'Mourning and its Relation to Manic-Depressive States' (1940), and 'Notes on Some Schizoid Mechanisms' (1946) are key sources for these ideas. These essays are all reprinted, with a useful introduction, in *The Selected Melanie Klein*, ed. Juliet Mitchell, Penguin, 1986.

4. See especially 'Notes on Symbol Formation' and 'A Psychoanalytical Approach to Aesthetics', in Hanna Segal, *The Work of Hanna Segal*. Free Association Books/Maresfield Library, 1986; and *Dream, Phantasy and Art*, Tavistock, 1991.

5. Published as 'Delusion and Artistic Creativity', in *The Work of Hanna Segal*.

6. There is a section on literary interpretations in Ella Freeman Sharpe's *Collected Papers on Psychoanalysis*, Hogarth, 1950.

7. Adrian Stokes's collected writings have been published as *The Critical Writings of Adrian Stokes*, vols 1–3, Thames & Hudson, 1978. There is also a shorter collection, *The Image in Form: Selected Writings of Adrian Stokes*, ed. Richard Wollheim, Penguin, 1972.

8. The major statement of Merleau-Ponty's position is in *The Phenomenology of Perception*, Routledge & Kegan Paul, 1962, and there are also several collections of essays available which present his phenomenological perspective in its many fruitful applications to psychology, culture, and politics. Stuart Hampshire's *Thought and Action*, Chatto & Windus, 1959, presented a critique of empiricist theories of perception which had some parallels with Merleau-Ponty's.

9. I am indebted to Margaret Rustin for this clinical fragment.

10. S. Freud, *Jokes and their Relation to the Unconscious* (1905b), *Standard Edition*, vol. 8, Hogarth, 1960. A useful development of this argument, especially in regard to the interpretation of the social meanings of jokes, is to be found in Mary Douglas's paper on jokes in her *Implicit Meanings: Essays in Anthropology*, Routledge & Kegan Paul, 1978.

11. Jean-François Lyotard, *The Postmodern Condition: A Report on Knowledge*, Manchester University Press, 1986; Richard Rorty, *Philosophy and the Mirror of Nature*, Basil Blackwell, 1980; Gianni Vattimo, *The End of Modernity*, Polity Press, 1988. Introductions to these debates may be found in Andreas Huyssen, 'Mapping the Postmodern', *New German Critique*, no. 33, Fall 1984, and in other articles in this issue; and in H. Foster, ed., *Postmodern Culture*, Pluto, 1985.

12. Meira Likjerman, 'The Clinical Significance of Aesthetic Experience', *International Review of Psycho-Analysis*, vol. 16, part 2, 1989. This article, which appeared whilst a final version of the present chapter was being written, makes a critique of earlier psychoanalytic positions with much of which I agree, but its substantive view of the origins of the aesthetic sense differs from that presented here.

13. Kant, *The Critique of Judgement*, Oxford University Press, 1952, p. 71, lines 10 *et seq.*

14. Ibid., p. 51, lines 212–16.

15. Ibid., p. 52, lines 8 *et seq.*

16. Ibid., p. 39, lines 8–14.

17. Clifford Geertz, 'Blurred Genres: The Refiguration of Social Thought', in *Local Knowledge: Further Essays in Interpretive Anthropology*, Basic Books, 1983. I have discussed the application of this argument to debates in architecture in M.J. Rustin, 'Postmodernism and Anti-modernism in Contemporary British Architecture', *Assemblage: a Critical Journal of Architecture and Design Culture*, no. 8, MIT, February 1989. An earlier version of this appeared as 'English Conservatism and the Aesthetics of Architecture', *Radical Philosophy* 40, Summer 1985.

18. I discuss the implications of this new plurality of cultural 'voices' in 'What is Cultural Studies: The Virtues of Educational Pluralism', *Anglicista*, vol. XXVII, no. 3, 1984, Istituto Universitario Orientale, Naples.

9

Thinking in *Romeo and Juliet**

Melanie Klein's work opened up in psychoanalysis the issue of the development of the capacity to think, which she linked with the emergence of the emotional capacity to accept and hold in mind mother as a whole person, continuous in time and body, and able to be remembered in her absence. Whereas the emphasis in Freud's thought had been on the negative connotations of child-hood curiosity, particularly as an intrusion into parental sexual life, Klein was struck by its creative possibilities. The precondition of thought in human infants, said Klein, was the achievement of a certain state of human relatedness. Bion took this understanding a good deal further through his work with extremely disordered psychotic patients, which led him to examine the mental states of patients who were not able to think in connected and coherent ways at all.

Bion had the insight that in the earliest stages of mother–infant relations, 'thinking' was done *for* the infant by the mother. Thinking he defined as the transmutation of sensations and feelings – pain, distress, desire, hunger, longing – into mental or symbolic forms. His view (which has some similarities to Winnicott's ideas on 'primary maternal preoccupation') was that mothers took in the troubled feelings of their babies, modulated them through under-standing and thought, and thus gradually made it possible for their infants to experience their feelings in a more tolerable or manageable form. So when the parents of newborns (or other bystanders) ask themselves, as they do, why is he,

*This chapter was first presented as a paper at a seminar at the Institute for Advanced Studies, Princeton, on St Valentine's Day, 1985. Thanks are due especially to Clifford Geertz.

she or — as one sometimes says of infants at first — 'it' crying, this is a sign that parental *work* — think-work — is going on: thinking about and *for* the child. This is more than a matter of the alleviation of the infant's physical discomforts. Klein and Bion noted that parents have to be able to tolerate their infants' mental pain and distress — an exhausting experience — if the child's capacities for feeling and thought are to develop.

Bion went on to postulate that a 'need for truth' — an epistemophilic impulse — was an innate human drive, equal in status to the libidinal drives described by Freud and to the needs for relationship (with its necessarily positive and negative aspects) which are presupposed in the Kleinian tradition. In his own analytic work, he attempted to distinguish between the 'non-thinking' ways of dealing with feelings, and thought itself. The 'non-thinking' modes include discharging feelings through physical tension and gesture, expressing them through somatic symptoms including physical illness, in unthinking actions, and in the more complicated confusions between language as the bearer of meanings and language as the literal carrier of feelings and sentiments — words as missiles, as we sometimes use them. (Perhaps swearing particularly has this words-as-objects quality.) He also went on to think about attacks on meaning and truth, in lies and the like. Fundamental in this paradigm is the idea that emotional realities are the fundamental material of human communication. Bion, however, contrasted in his theory of groups those communications and collective actions which are dominated by unconscious emotions, and those in which disturbing anxieties are sufficiently contained to allow rational thinking to take place. This is the contrast he describes between the different activities of the 'basic assumption' and the 'work' group. However, the aspects of communication which most interested him as a psychoanalyst were those which had unconscious experience as their primary basis.

This concern with the internal and external preconditions of thought seems to me to be a significant theoretical departure for psychoanalysis. The idea that what distinguishes well-functioning individuals (and groups, we might add) is the capacity to 'contain' impulse in the form of thought, and the attention to the institutions and symbolic forms that might be satisfactory containers for such thought, may bring psychoanalysis into a fruitful relationship with some other contemporary social scientific approaches to culture. Bion's work defines a clear and necessary boundary between the pre-symbolic world of animal behaviour (however social it may be) and the necessarily *cultural* world of human beings. How far families, or schools, or the broader social climate, facilitate the capacity for thought among their members (this being understood as an everyday capacity and not one which depends on formal education) also becomes an important criterion of social value. Whereas a Durkheimian sociology would draw our attention to the morally anomic and structureless features of modern social life, an approach influenced by Bion's ideas might be more concerned with the presence or absence of the symbolic containers which make mental process possible.

In earlier chapters in this book I have described the distinctive concern of late Kleinian psychoanalysis, as shaped by the influence of Bion's work, with mental function. This work has significantly broadened the scope of analytic understanding. It has brought within its field of analytic view the capacity to think, or the relation of the mind to truth and meaning, as distinct dimensions of psychic development. Not only the content of mental process — suffused, as Freud and Klein said, by powerful libidinal and destructive emotions — but its form, indeed the existence or non-existence of the capacity for thought in individuals, has become the object of psychoanalytic inquiry in recent writing. Joyce McDougall's work (1986, 1989) provides a most lucid demonstration of the explanatory power of this perspective in understanding psychosomatic patients, in whom physical symptoms sometimes do serve to give form and expression to psychic forces not able to be represented or processed in the mind. This approach has also proved fruitful in understanding the functioning of some social institutions. Isabel Menzies Lyth's (1988) work on nursing care, and on the institutional care of young children, has revealed the defence mechanisms set up by professionals within caring systems to avoid thinking about the mental pain to which they are exposed, and the dysfunctions for both staff and clients of such forms of institutional denial.

I have also suggested that this late Kleinian perspective has important implications for thinking about art, literature, and other forms of symbolic expression. This new emphasis on mental process and symbolization (and its numerous distortions and negative forms) can enable psychoanalytic approaches to culture to avoid a particular kind of partiality or reductionism. This tendency arose because psychoanalytic interpreters were preoccupied with what they identified (correctly) as a distinctive set of latent meanings in artworks, disclosed by their own analytic perspective, but lacked a sufficiently sensitive vocabulary for describing the *forms* of these works, and the functions fulfilled by artistic forms themselves. The technical deficiency of psychoanalytic criticism in this area, however, was due as much to inadequate conceptualization of the process of thought within the field of psychoanalysis as to lack of literary training *per se*. Now that post-Kleinian analysts, following the example of Bion, have started to give serious attention to the 'containing' functions of thought, it may become more possible to conceptualize in analytic terms more formal aspects of literary and other art-works. (These issues have been explored more fully above in Chapter 8.)

I have defended the value of good writing for children as providing a 'symbolic space' in which aspects of readers' experience can be explored and made available for reflection, albeit most beneficially perhaps in metaphorical and poetic forms (Rustin, 1985b). *Narratives of Love and Loss* (Rustin and Rustin, 1987) provided a number of detailed case studies of classic modern stories written for children, from this point of view. The significance of language and play in the emotional lives of children is explored within the narrative of some of these stories.

I also suggest that one criterion of the adequacy of a society for the develop-ment of those who live in it lies in the 'cultural' or 'symbolic space' it provides for members at different stages of their lives. The Klein–Bion theory of neces-sary 'containment' in infancy as a precondition of development is one appli-cation of this idea, but it can also be extended to other phases and aspects of life. The development of a more plural culture in recent years, and the partial enfranchisement in it of new voices (those with different class origins, women, ethnic minorities, gays, the young) is a positive one, in so far as it provides access to symbolic resources and capacities for those previously denied them. Whilst everyone can see how obvious this is when totalitarian systems collapse in the face of overwhelming popular pressure, the complications and conflicts of pluralism are often less acceptable at home.

In this chapter, I attempt to develop an application of these 'late Kleinian' ideas to a classic work of 'high culture', namely Shakespeare's *Romeo and Juliet.*[1] In a selective approach to this play, I seek to show how 'thinking' (that is, the capacity or incapacity to reflect on the forces unleashed by overwhelming emotions) is a central issue, perhaps *the* central issue. In *Romeo and Juliet* Shakespeare explores what happens when 'modern' emotions (in this case of romantic sexual love) are experienced and seek expression in a familial and social context which is largely unprepared for them. The tragedy shows almost all its participants being carried away by feelings they cannot think about — about which, indeed, they choose *not* to think, preferring precipitate action instead. Or, faced with the possibility of confronting and acting upon the truth, other participants choose the apparently safer path of deception and lies. Since the thunderstorms of adolescence (and the envies, jealousies and struggles for control which they evoke in older adults) remain disturbing in our own society,

Romeo and Juliet remains almost as evocative as it ever was, since Shakespeare understood and gave shape to this particular moment of the life cycle at the point when it was first possible to experience it in its modern form. It is not a tragedy of evil or bad intentions: nearly everyone — parents, children, Friar, Nurse — means well; this is one reason why the play remains one of the best-liked and most-often-performed in the canon. Those on the stage seem to have feelings little different from those which members of the audience are liable to experience in the corresponding adolescent or adult roles, when faced with the impact of similar emotions, events, and social pressures.

Romeo and Juliet explores the historical conjuncture of two opposed conditions. On the one hand, the emergence of individuals with identities to some extent separate from those prescribed for them by family and social roles, and capable of intense and personal choices of love-objects. On the other hand, the persistence of a social code and structure of patriarchy in which fathers controlled the lives and especially the marriage choices of their children, particularly of their daughters. The play emerges at a historical transition point, in which both the emergent romantic individualist conception of sexual love of modern times and the authoritarian structures of patriarchal authority could be seen to exercise great power over the lives of representative dramatic figures.[2] Both these structures are represented in *Romeo and Juliet* as fragile and unstable; hence the tragic outcome of the play. Patriarchical authority, at the level of both state and family, is weak, because of the feud of the two families and the uncertain authority of the Duke of Verona. The individual passions and desires of the son and daughter of the two leading families are shown as having some meaning and weight for their respective parents, but uncertainly so. Ultimately, family interest and authority are going to count for more, especially when these are both placed under severe external pressure.

The account of the play which follows attempts to show how these conflicting forces are represented. The primary interest of the account is not, as with earlier kinds of psychoanalytic writing, in the 'diagnosis' of the characters' inner states of mind, but rather in the way the action is shaped by emotional forces which are only fitfully and incompletely brought to consciousness. The title of this chapter arises from the Bion-influenced concern of current Kleinian psychoanalysis with thinking, but its contention is that *Romeo and Juliet* dramatizes a failure of thinking, of a still resonant kind.

Romeo and Juliet

What first strikes one in thinking about this play is how rushed and hectic it is. The action takes place within five days, and our attention is often drawn to what day, or time of the day or night, it is. On the first day, a Saturday, Romeo is in love with Rosaline, and his sadness and oppressed spirits are worrying his friends and his parents. 'What sadness lengthens Romeo's hours?' Benvolio asks him. But in the evening he is taken off to a party at the Capulets' house, and there he sees Juliet and falls instantly in love with her. The balcony scene takes place later that night. On the second day he secretly marries her, with the help of the Nurse and the Friar. But later, in the afternoon, there is an incident in which Tybalt kills Mercutio and is in turn killed minutes later (as it is shown on the stage) by Romeo. Romeo is then banished by the Prince, and after his night with Juliet he flees to nearby Mantua. On the third day (Monday) Juliet's father Capulet tells her that she must marry Paris, a kinsman of the Prince, only three days later, on Thursday. But when, on the next day (Tuesday), she pretends to consent to this, after visiting the Friar supposedly to obtain absolution for her earlier disobedience to her father, Capulet brings the wedding forward one day, to 'tomorrow', despite Lady Capulet's doubts. On Tuesday night, on the eve of her obligatory wedding (she is of course already secretly married to Romeo), she takes a potion intended to simulate her death, the plan being that Romeo will come and help her to escape when she awakes in the family tomb. Just to conclude the story, on Thursday morning in Mantua Romeo receives the false news that Juliet is dead. His response is swift action:

> ROMEO: … get me ink and paper,
> And hire post-horses, I will hence tonight. (V, i)[3]

When he goes to buy poison for his own death, he finds that the apothecary's shop is shut for a holiday, as shops often are when you need them in a hurry, and he has to knock him up. In the graveyard, on his way to die with Juliet, he meets Paris, her suitor, and 'is provoked', as he says, to kill him. He has failed to take in, on the journey, what his man has told him of Paris:

> ROMEO: What said my man, when my betossèd soul
> Did not attend him as we rode? I think
> He told me Paris should have married Juliet.

He also fails to take in the evidence before him that Juliet might after all be
alive:

ROMEO: … beauty's ensign yet
               Is crimson in thy lips and in thy cheeks,
               And death's pale flag is not advancèd there.   (V, iii)

He kills himself:

ROMEO: O true apothecary:
               Thy drugs are quick. Thus with a kiss I die.

Juliet wakes to find Romeo dead, and she is also impelled to act without delay:

JULIET: Yea, noise? Then I'll be brief. O happy dagger!
               This is thy sheath; there rust, and let me die.   (V, iii)

This headlong pace is not merely a consequence of dramatic convenience
and compactness. The words of the play repeatedly draw our attention to the
undue haste of what is happening. When Romeo asks the Friar in Act II:

ROMEO: … but this I pray,
               That thou consent to marry us today.

the Friar replies:

FRIAR: Holy St Francis! What a change is here?
               Is Rosaline, that thou did love so dear,
               So soon forsaken?

Their dialogue concludes with Romeo exhorting:

ROMEO: O let us hence! I stand on sudden haste.

The Friar replies:

FRIAR: Wisely and slow. They stumble that run fast.   (II, iii)

Later in Act III the audience is made aware that Capulet's decision to insist on Juliet's marriage to Paris two days after Tybalt, his nephew, is killed is precipitate. Capulet tells his wife:

CAPULET: Wife, go you to her ere you go to bed;
Acquaint her here of my son Paris' love,
And bid her (mark you me?) on Wednesday next —
But soft! What day is this?

PARIS: Monday, my lord.

CAPULET: Monday! Ha! ha! Well, Wednesday is too soon,
A' Thursday let it be — a' Thursday tell her,
She shall be married to this noble Earl:
Will you be ready? Do you like this haste?
We'll keep no great ado — a friend or two;
For hark you, Tybalt being slain so late,
It may be thought we held him carelessly,
Being our kinsman, if we revel much. (III, iv)

Another dimension of this is that the normal boundaries of day and night are continually upset in the play. Romeo's father is worried about him:

MONTAGUE: Away from light steals home my heavy son,
And private in his chamber pens himself,
Shuts up his windows, locks fair daylight out,
And makes himself an artificial night. (I, i)

Capulet later decides not to go to bed at all on the eve of his daughter's intended wedding:

CAPULET: I'll not to bed tonight; let me alone:
I'll play the housewife for this once ... (IV, ii)

and he spends the night hurrying the servants along in the kitchen. Then he has another burst of impatience when morning breaks:

CAPULET: ... hie, make haste,
Make haste! The bridegroom, he is come already;
Make haste I say.

When they wake up after their night together, Romeo and Juliet dispute over whether or not it is morning, and time for Romeo to flee:

JULIET: Wilt thou be gone? It is not yet near day:
It was the nightingale, and not the lark,
That pierced the fearful hollow of mine ear ...

and Romeo replies:

ROMEO: It was the lark, the herald of the morn;
No nightingale ...   (III, v)

Very different experiences of the passage of time are represented in the play, by no means wholly corresponding with the conventionally opposed perspectives of youth and age. The sense of time remembered and anticipated by the Friar and the Nurse is contrasted with Romeo and Juliet's desperate immediacy of sensation and desire. The Friar's measured reflections on the coming of the day and the natural cycle of nature in Act II, as he collects flowers and herbs:

FRIAR: The grey-eyed morn smiles on the frowning night,
Check'ring the Eastern clouds with streaks of light:

and

The earth that's Nature's mother is her tomb,
What is her burying grave, that is her womb:

is interrupted by Romeo's unexpected arrival so early in the morning. The Friar notes the mental disorder which this signifies:

FRIAR: Benedicite!
What early tongue so sweet saluteth me?
Young son, it argues a distempered head
So soon to bid good morrow to thy bed: (II, iii)

In another scene the Nurse fondly remembers Juliet's childhood:

NURSE: 'Tis since the earthquake now eleven years,
I never shall forget it and she was weaned,

> Of all the days of the year, upon that day:
> For I had then laid wormwood on my dug,
> Sitting in the sun under the dove-house wall.
> My Lord and you were then at Mantua.

But Lady Capulet wants to get on with immediate business:

LADY CAPULET: Enough of this. I pray thee hold thy peace.

The Nurse insists on completing her train of thought:

NURSE: Peace, I have done. God mark thee to his grace,
Thou wast the prettiest babe that 'ere I nursed.
And I might live to see thee married once,
I have my wish.

But Lady Capulet gets to her urgent point:

LADY CAPULET: Marry, that 'marry' is the very theme
I came to talk of. Tell me, daughter Juliet,
How stands your disposition to be married?   (I, iii)

Later, for the Friar, Romeo's banishment promises the eventual prospect of his happy return to Juliet and his reconciliation with the Prince. But the idea of separation from Juliet has, on the contrary, left Romeo:

FRIAR: There on the ground, with his own tears made drunk.   (III, iii)

Romeo and Juliet can imagine each other as stars looking down from heaven:

ROMEO: … her eyes in heaven
Would through the airy region stream so bright,
That birds would sing, and think it were not night: (II, ii)

but cannot bear even hours of separation. Troubled in a different way is their parents' sense of time. Their main experience of it is that there is little of it left to them. Their anxieties about this — and especially the Capulets' — have a major influence on the action.

Not only is time disordered in the play, but its customary properties are disrupted. The undue haste of Juliet's proposed wedding to Paris, so soon after Tybalt's death, is commented on. Paris understands that:

PARIS: These times of woe afford no time to woo.   (III, iv)

Juliet protests that she will not marry him:

JULIET: Now by Saint Peter's Church, and Peter too,
               He shall not make me there a joyful bride!
               I wonder at this haste, that I must wed
               Ere he that should be husband comes to woo.   (III, v)

And the Friar observes to Paris:

FRIAR: On Thursday, sir? The time is very short.

The action of *Romeo and Juliet* depends on many sudden and impetuous changes of mind. Romeo falls out of love with one woman and into love with another, in the course of an evening — almost in a moment. Capulet is at the beginning considerate of his daughter's feelings regarding the choice of her future husband:

CAPULET: But woo her, gentle Paris, get her heart,
                My will to her consent, is but a part.
                And she agreed, within her scope of choice
                Lies my consent, and fair according voice.   (I, ii)

But later he peremptorily tells her to marry when and whom she is told to marry:

CAPULET: ... mistress minion you?
                Thank me no thankings, nor proud me no prouds,
                But fettle your fine joints 'gainst Thursday next
                To go with Paris to Saint Peter's Church:
                Or I will drag thee on a hurdle thither.   (III, v)

In the Mantuan street Romeo at first refuses to fight Tybalt, feeling himself now to be kin to him following his secret marriage to Juliet. Mercutio, not understanding this, fights on his behalf, and Romeo's intervention leads to his death. 'Why the devil came you between us? I was hurt under your arm,' protests the dying Mercutio, and Romeo replies feebly, 'I thought all for the best' (III, i). Moments later, Romeo feels that he must avenge Mercutio, and his own reputation; he fights Tybalt and kills him.

The Friar, who has advised Romeo against marrying hastily, in fact then conducts his marriage to Juliet. The Nurse, who has abetted Romeo and Juliet's marriage and its consummation, then advises Juliet to forget about Romeo and to marry Paris as her father orders:

> NURSE: Then since the case now stands as so it doth,
> I think it best you married with the County,
> O he's a lovely gentleman!
> Romeo's a dishclout to him: (III, v)

Romeo, told of Juliet's death, decides at once to return to Verona, against his servant's caution:

> BALTHASAR: I do beseech you sir, have patience:
> Your looks are pale and wild, and do import
> Some misadventure. (V, i)

The misadventure that follows is that Romeo buys poison to join Juliet in her grave.

What are the explanations for this precipitate and, as it turns out, catastrophic rush of events? We have already noted the disruption of time in the play, and I want to suggest that this is both cause and symptom of the disruption or pre-emption of thought. Space as well as time are at issue. The Chorus tells us that Romeo, 'Being held a foe, [he] may not have access / To breathe such vows as lovers use to swear' (Prologue, II).

Romeo risks death to visit Juliet:

> JULIET: The orchard walls are high and hard to climb,
> And the place death, considering who thou art,
> If any of my kinsmen find thee here. (II, ii)

Their courtship and its consummation take place at a masked party where Romeo should not be, outside her window, in the Friar's cell, and in Romeo's illicit presence in her bedroom on the night of their secret wedding. There is no place where they are able to be peacefully together, which can symbolically and actually contain their intense feelings. Night thus becomes the only 'place' where they can be and do what is forbidden to them by day.

One central aspect of all this confusion is clearly the nature of sexual passion itself, as it is depicted in the play. Love is represented as a madness, and Romeo's state of mind is the subject of worried comment by his mother and father, by his friends Mercutio and Benvolio, by the Friar, and later by his servant. Both Romeo and Juliet threaten to stab themselves if the Friar will not find a way for them to remain together after Romeo's banishment, and of preventing Juliet's forced marriage to Paris. Romeo describes himself as driven out of his mind towards the end — by grief, and guilt for the deaths he had caused. In the grave-yard, he tells Paris to:

> ROMEO: ... live, and hereafter say,
> A madman's mercy bid thee run away.   (V, iii)

But I want to stress not so much the feelings of the lovers themselves as the absence in the play of any sufficient symbolic or social containment for them. Juliet says:

> JULIET: ... Romeo is banished:
> There is no end, no limit, measure, bound,
> In that word's death; no words can that woe sound.   (III, ii)

It is the understanding of why these feelings are too overwhelming for words or thought that most concerns me. In some of his later comedies Shakespeare shows that such sexual feelings, given a more hopeful imaginary setting, can have a more benign outcome. The dreams described by Mercutio in his Queen Mab speech become the forest of *A Midsummer Night's Dream*, in which the enchantments of love end happily. So our attention should be focused, in thinking about *Romeo and Juliet*, on the setting of these passions, as much as on the passions themselves.

One situation bearing on this in the action of the play is the weight of political power on everyone taking part. This is by no means attributable only to the quarrel of the two feuding families, the Montagues and Capulets. A third looming presence over the action is the interest of the Prince, and the fear of his power. The play may reflect a moment — still significant at the time when Shakespeare was writing — in which the English monarchy's authority over its most powerful aristocratic families, and its effective monopoly of the means of violence, is only just being consolidated, and we can see the play as a transposition of the experience of this situation into the fictional world of Verona and Mantua.

We initially see the effects of this impulsion to obey in the first scene. The servants of Capulet and Montague are cautiously going through the motions of quarrelling as their loyalties seem to require, while stopping short of actual violence, when Benvolio and Tybalt, kinsmen respectively of Montague and Capulet, come into sight and the servants decide that they had better make their fight more authentic. The pacific Benvolio's reaction is to tell them to:

> BENVOLIO: Part, fools!
> Put up your swords. You know not what you do.

But the servants had correctly anticipated Tybalt's attitude, and he immediately draws his sword on Benvolio.

We must understand that the Prince's threats to both houses after he has restored order are taken seriously:

> PRINCE: On pain of torture, from those bloody hands,
> Throw your mistempered weapons to the ground ...

and,

> If ever you disturb our streets again,
> Your lives shall pay the forfeit of the peace.   (I, i)

So when Mercutio, the Prince's kinsman, is killed by Tybalt, a Capulet, and Romeo is awarded only the comparatively lenient sentence of banishment, old Capulet is made fearful. The Prince takes reprisals against both houses for the death of his kinsman:

> PRINCE: But I'll amerce you with so strong a fine
> That you shall all repent the loss of mine.   (III, i)

But it is a Capulet, not a Montague, who has killed the Prince's kinsman, and Capulet is seeking to restore his family's good grace with the Prince by bringing about Juliet's marriage to Paris, who is also the Prince's kinsman. Earlier, Capulet had put Paris off:

244

CAPULET: My child is yet a stranger to the world,
                She hath not seen the change of fourteen years;
                Let two more summers wither in their pride
                Ere we may think her ripe to be a bride.   (I, ii)

But in the new political circumstances, there can be no delay. The precarious authority of the Prince, who later blames himself for 'winking at your discords', is itself a cause of uncertainty. The climate of weak and disputed authority is reflected also in Tybalt's challenge to his uncle's authority at the party over the presence of Romeo and his friends, and even in Romeo's distance from his father. More important is the way violence keeps erupting, as the Prince says:

PRINCE: Three civil brawls, bred of an airy word,
              By thee, old Capulet and Montague,
              Have thrice disturbed the quiet of our streets ...   (I, i)

Though there is a clear awareness of who *ought* to obey whom, and the Prince shows the capacity to exercise his due powers, in practice authority everywhere seems to be precarious and unstable.

Such considerations of fear and policy are also the background to the Friar's and Nurse's respective changes of mind. The Friar's reason for supporting Romeo and Juliet's marriage is political. He says to Romeo:

FRIAR: But come young waverer, come go with me,
           In one respect I'll thy assistant be:
           For this alliance may so happy prove,
           To turn your households' rancour to pure love.   (II, iii)

Later, when he has already married Romeo and Juliet and yet is called on to conduct the marriage of Juliet and Paris, he is in a dangerous position, and the desperate expedient of counterfeiting Juliet's death is a possible means of escape for him as well as for her. Juliet suspects as much:

JULIET: What if it be a poison which the Friar
           Subtly hath ministered to have me dead,
           Lest in this marriage he should be dishonoured
           Because he married me before to Romeo?
           I fear it is; and yet methinks it should not,
           For he hath still been tried a holy man.   (IV, iii)

We see the Friar genuinely concerned for the young people, and able to give them good advice, but also feeling compelled for political reasons to undertake risky actions — first the marriage of Romeo and Juliet, then the expedient of faking Juliet's death. He is able to maintain his friar's appearance of holiness and propriety even while concealing the truth. He reproves the Capulets for their intemperate grief at the loss of Juliet:

FRIAR: Peace ho, for shame! Confusion's cure lives not
      In these confusions. Heaven and yourself
      Had part in this fair maid — now heaven hath all,
      And all the better is it for the maid: (IV, v)

while knowing that she is neither dead nor a maid. His panic-stricken flight from the graveyard finally contributes to Juliet's death.

The Nurse's about-face is also to be understood as a realistic adjustment to the dangers facing both her (as the abetter of Juliet's marriage) and Juliet herself. It is particularly disastrous for the young people that the understanding on which they depend from their older friends is betrayed under these various pressures. Juliet says as much after the Nurse has advised her to forget Romeo, and she begins to think of her own death:

JULIET: ... Go counsellor,
      Thou and my bosom henceforth shall be twain.
      I'll to the Friar to know his remedy;
      If all else fail, myself have power to die.   (III, v)

In this climate of authoritarian relationships and obligations, fears are rapidly converted into swift action. Norbert Elias's argument, in *The Civilizing Process*, that the development of thoughtfulness and complexity of affections in individuals historically depended on the removal of the threat of violence from everyday life is powerfully realized in this play, where the threat and fact of violence are very much present. The rapid conversion of fear into action overwhelms the space where reflection might otherwise take place. While sometimes this is commented on, as in the Friar's reproaches to Romeo, mostly it is dramatized in action. We learn of Capulet's fear and anxiety not because he tells us about it but through his fierce temper, rapid changes of mind, and manic excitement.

Another anxiety of Shakespeare's time which weighs heavily on all the participants in the action is the fear of death. We learn early on that the

Capulets and Montagues are old ('A crutch, a crutch! Why call you for a sword?' cries Lady Capulet) and that theirs is an old quarrel. Romeo and Juliet are their parents' only surviving children:

> CAPULET: Earth had swallow'd all my hopes but she;
> She is the hopeful Lady of my earth.   (I, ii)

Their anxiety is for their succession, both as natural parents and in regard to the fortunes of their houses, and this is stirred up by the deaths of Tybalt and Mercutio. In the end, Montague reports his wife's death from grief at Romeo's exile moments before he hears that Romeo has preceded him into the grave.

The graveyard and its spectres, after the deaths of Mercutio and Tybalt and the reported death of Juliet, are powerful images for both Romeo and Juliet, and Juliet terrifies herself at the thought of waking from her sleep there:

> JULIET: O if I wake, shall I not be distraught,
> Environèd with all these hideous fears,
> And madly play with my forefathers' joints.
> And pluck the mangled Tybalt from his shroud ...   (IV, iii)

These images generate terror, especially because of an inability properly to mourn the dead. Lady Capulet is full of feelings of revenge rather than grief for Tybalt, and Capulet and she are enraged by Juliet's apparently excessive sorrow. The plan to marry Juliet to Paris within three days seems in part motivated by the wish to displace one feeling with another:

> LADY CAPULET: Well, well, thou hast a careful father, child;
> One who, to put thee from thy heaviness,
> Hath sorted out a sudden day of joy,
> That thou expect'st not, nor I looked not for.   (III, v)

Capulet seems to be in manic flight from mourning in his nocturnal preparations for the wedding day. Romeo and Juliet give no thought to the dead Mercutio and Tybalt during their night together, but we learn later that Juliet has her dead cousin much in mind, and Romeo, also oppressed by his guilt for the earlier deaths, rushes to join her in her supposed grave. An inability to mourn individuals in this play coexists with a state of terror and guilt for their deaths, and obsession with their physical realities.

Also at issue in the play is the capacity for understanding other strong feelings, and especially the passionate states of mind of Romeo and Juliet. They depend on the Friar and the Nurse for sympathy and understanding more than they do on their parents. Juliet is very young (not yet fourteen), and there is an implication that both she and Romeo live in a world of feelings which their parents do not at all share. But the Friar and Nurse are both weak in relation to these noble families, and it is hard for them to remain consistent and loyal either in word or deed in relation to the young people. Romeo and Juliet are also both adept at making the old feel deficient in feeling. Juliet says of her nurse, while she is waiting impatiently for her to return from Romeo:

JULIET: ... yet she is not come.
                Had she affections and warm youthful blood,
                She would be as swift in motion as a ball;
                My words would bandy her to my sweet love,
                And his to me:
                But old folks, many feign as they were dead —
                Unwieldy, slow, heavy, and pale as lead.   (II, v)

Romeo takes a similar tone with the Friar, who is trying to advise him:

FRIAR: Let me dispute with thee of thy estate.

Romeo replies:

ROMEO: Thou canst not speak of that thou dost not feel.
                Wert thou as young as I, Juliet thy love,
                An hour but married, Tybalt murderèd
                Doting like me, and like me banishèd,
                Then mightst thou speak, then mightst thou tear thy hair,
                And fall upon the ground, as I do now,
                Taking the full measure of an unmade grave.   (III, iii)

In other words, you can't *understand*. The distance of the parental relationships and the manipulability of their substitutes — both by the lovers and by more powerful external forces — is what leaves Romeo and Juliet so isolated and thus vulnerable to their own overwhelming feelings.

There is also a dimension of symbolic or cultural space whose destruction is dramatized in the play, and which helps to explain both its intense lyricism and its fateful consequences. This seems to be the meaning of the balcony scene where Romeo overhears Juliet's soliloquy about him. While this might seem like a romantic wish come magically true, Juliet is troubled by the impropriety:

JULIET: Thou knowest the mask of night is on my face,
                      Else would a maiden blush bepaint my cheek,
                      For that which thou hast heard me speak tonight.
                      Fain would I dwell on form, fain, fain deny
                      What I have spoke: but farewell compliment!

She goes on:

                      I should have been more strange, I must confess,
                      But that thou overheard'st ere I was ware,
                      My true love passion ...   (II, ii)

There is reference here to the convention that such revelations of feeling should take place more slowly, so that trust can be established and a woman not give herself too easily. Or to put it more generally, as the Friar does, that lovers should not become committed to each other too quickly. Once their love has been openly declared, immediate marriage and its consummation seem to be required:

FRAIR: Come, come with me, and we will make short work;
                      For by your leave, you shall not stay alone
                      Till Holy Church incorporate two in one.   (II, vi)

There seems to be in particular the idea that sexual desire, once experienced and acknowledged as such, is uncontrollable.

Improper self-disclosure is the topic of another exchange — between Juliet and Paris at the Friar's cell. Paris asks her:

PARIS: Come you to make confession to this father?
JULIET: To answer that, I should confess to you.
PARIS: Do not deny to him that you love me.
JULIET: I will confess to you that I love him.
PARIS: So will ye, I am sure, that you love me.
JULIET: If I do so, it will be of more price,
                      Being spoke behind your back, than to your face. (IV, i)

Juliet here asserts the proper boundaries between one kind of conversation and another, reminding us of how privacy has earlier been breached in the balcony scene. The failure to mourn Tybalt and the confusion of the time of his funeral with Juliet's wedding is a further invasion of ceremony which is enacted and commented on in the play. The disruption of due form is another aspect of the destructive isolation of Romeo and Juliet.

Finally, I would like to draw attention to the ways in which thinking is an explicit topic of *Romeo and Juliet*, and how its absence or perversion is pointed to as a chief source of harm. This is the topic of the Friar's reproachful speech to Romeo, when he denounces his 'unreasonable fury' and points to wit, or reason, as the essential attribute of a man:

> FRIAR: Thy wit, that ornament, to shape and love,
> Misshapen in the conduct of them both,
> Like powder in a skilless soldier's flask,
> Is set afire with thine own ignorance,
> And thou dismember'd with thine own defence. (III, iii)

Juliet's main appeal to her father is to listen to her:

> JULIET: Good father, I beseech you on my knees,
> Hear me with patience, but to speak a word.

She is told angrily:

> CAPULET: Speak not, reply not, do not answer me.

The Nurse intervenes:

> NURSE: May not one speak?

and is told:

> CAPULET: Peace, you mumbling fool!
> Utter your gravity over a gossip's bowl,
> For here we need it not.

Lady Capulet adds her own refusal:

LADY CAPULET: Talk not to me, for I'll not speak a word. (III, v)

There are still more violent attacks by Lady Capulet on truth, after the death of Tybalt:

LADY CAPULET: He is a kinsman to the Montague,
Affection makes him false, he speaks not true:
Some twenty of them fought in this black strife,
And all those twenty could but kill one life. (III, i)

Misinformation is the immediate cause of Romeo and Juliet's tragedy, when Romeo receives the false news about her pretended death which was intended for everyone but him. Thus the recourse to deception initiated as a desperate expedient by the Friar with Juliet ends in disaster.

In contrast is the Prince, whose principal strength is his commitment to the truth. On his arrival after each of the two occasions of killing, he insists in measured tones on finding out what has really occurred before indulging in emotion:

PRINCE: Seal up the mouth of outrage for a while,
Till we can clear these ambiguities,
And know their spring, their head, their true descent.
And then will I be general of your woes,
And lead you even to death. Meantime forbear,
And let mischance be slave to patience. (V, iii)

He recognizes his own share of blame, too. ('All are punished.')

My argument is that the flight from thinking into desperate action in *Romeo and Juliet* is a central aspect of the failure of the society it depicts to contain the feelings of the young hero and heroine in any sufficient form. The feud of the two families, which the Chorus describes as the main source of tragedy, seems in fact to be only one element in a larger story. We can see a certain kind of familial relationship, and a general climate of violence, in conflict with the youthful romanticism of the hero and heroine. Romeo and Juliet convert little of their experience into conscious thought, and differ from Shakespeare's later tragic heroes in their lack of acquired self-knowledge.

Romeo and Juliet find mental pain unbearable, whether it arises from separation or guilt. They seek escape from it in marriage, sexual embrace, physical action, drugs, and death, reactions to anxiety typical of adolescence.

Romeo kills twice in a state of deep distress and confusion and, if we count Mercutio, is responsible for three deaths. This image of the young being unable to bear the feelings inside them is perhaps the most potent and resonant of the play, now many times repeated and elaborated in the history of what we call youth culture. Their tragedy reveals the incompatibilities between an idealized world of feelings — which must already have been a powerful presence in Shakespeare's world, and for his audience — and the sometimes unyielding and brutal qualities of actual Elizabethan life. This has also been transformed into a lasting image of misunderstanding between the generations.

In some of his later comedies Shakespeare explores similar situations — of conflict between youthful passions and patriarchal authority — in other ways, and he imagines other possible outcomes of it. The Forest of Arden, in *As You Like It*, the forest in *A Midsummer Night's Dream*, and the enchanted island in *The Tempest*, provide more benign and magical environments in which love can be pursued, not as the naked and instantaneous merger of two bodies and souls but as more sustained encounters and conversations. These later plays create a symbolic space — a literal place and time, more benign parents (Duke Senior and Prospero) and roles of make-believe (Orlando wooing Rosalind in her disguise as Ganymede) through which real persons can become known to each other. A symbolic containment is thus created by Shakespeare through which audiences, then and now, can imagine more hopeful outcomes of sexual feeling.

It should be evident that the method of analysis which I have used here is not based primarily on the psychoanalysis of character, but more on a response to the emotional states aroused in the reader by the action of the play as a whole. It is what the characters do and say in the here and now of the action, under the pressures which this play very vividly evokes, which conveys the play's meanings to us. This method is consistent with the emphasis within Kleinian and Bionian psychoanalysis on thinking about present feelings within the analytic relationhip, as the main experience with which analysts and patients can work, rather than on the bringing to consciousness of past biographical events or states of mind.

I hope I have succeeded in showing that the concept of thinking, as a human capacity which depends on a certain kind of benign social environment, and on relationships of parental affection, is illuminating in understanding *The Tragedy of Romeo and Juliet*.

Notes

1. Another paper on *Romeo and Juliet* which explores its implications from a Klein–Bion point of view was given by Beta Copley at the first 'Psychoanalysis and the Public Sphere' Conference. organized by *Free Associations* and the Sociology Department, Polytechnic of East London, in October 1986. This paper, called 'A Plague on All Our Houses', is concerned with the play's implications for the understanding of the psychodynamics of adolescence.

2. The consequences of patriarchal and authoritarian family structures for emotional life and a sense of individual identity are explored in Lawrence Stone (1979). A different view of this transition to 'modern' family forms is taken by Linda Pollock (1983).

3. All quotations are taken from *The New Cambridge Shakespeare*, ed. G. Blakemore Evans, Cambridge University Press, 1984.

Bibliography

Abercrombie, N., Hill, S. and Turner, B. (1986) *Sovereign Individuals of Capitalism*. Allen & Unwin.

Alford, C.F. (1989) *Melanie Klein and Critical Social Theory*. Yale University Press.

Anderson, B. (1983) *Imagined Communities: Reflections on the Origin and Spread of Nationalism*. Verso.

Anderson, P. (1968) 'Components of the National Culture'. *New Left Review*, 50, July–August.

Banks, O. (1981) *Faces of Feminism: A Study of Feminism as a Social Movement*. Martin Robertson.

Barnes, B. (1977) *Interests and the Growth of Knowledge*. Routledge & Kegan Paul.

—— (1982) *T.S. Kuhn and Social Science*. New York: Columbia University Press.

Bateson, G. (1972) *Steps Towards an Ecology of Mind*. Paladin.

Becker, H. (1970) *Sociological Work*. New Brunswick: Aldine.

Benvenuto, B. and Kennedy, R. (1986) *The Work of Jacques Lacan: an Introduction*. Free Association Books.

Berger, P. (1966) *Invitation to Sociology*. Harmondsworth: Penguin.

Berman, M. (1983) *All that is Solid Melts into Air*. Verso.

Bernstein, B. (1975) *Class, Codes and Control, Vol. 3*. Routledge & Kegan Paul.

Bettelheim, B. (1978) *The Uses of Enchantment*. Harmondsworth: Penguin.

Bhaskar, R. (1978) *A Realist Theory of Science*. Brighton: Harvester.

—— (1979) *The Possibility of Naturalism*. Brighton: Harvester.

Bick, E. (1964) 'Notes on Infant Observation in Psychoanalytic Training'. *International Journal of Psycho-Analysis*. (*Int. J. Psycho-Anal.*) 45: 558–66.

—— (1968) 'The Experience of the Skin in Early Object-Relations'. *Int. J. of Psycho-Anal.* 49: 484–6.

Bion, W.R. (1977) *Seven Servants* (containing *Elements of Psychoanalysis*; *Learning from Experience*; *Transformations*; and *Attention and Interpretation*). New York: Jason

Aronson (republished Maresfield Reprints, London, 1984).

Bion, W.R. (1978) *Second Thoughts.* Heinemann.

—— (1981) *Experiences in Groups.* Tavistock.

Boston, M. (1975) 'Recent Research in Developmental Psychology'. *Journal of Child Psychotherapy (J. Child Psychother.),* vol. 4, no. 1.

—— and Szur, R. (1983) *Psychotherapy with Severely Deprived Children.* Routledge & Kegan Paul.

Bott, E. (1971) *Family and Social Network.* Tavistock.

Bowlby, J. (1969, 1973, 1980) *Attachment, Separation and Loss,* 3 vols. Harmondsworth: Penguin.

Bradbury, M. (1971) *The Social Context of Modern English Literature.* Oxford: Basil Blackwell.

Brown, G. and Harris, T. (1978) *The Social Origins of Depression: A Study of Psychiatric Disorder in Women.* Tavistock.

Centre for Contemporary Cultural Studies (1982) *The Empire Strikes Back.* Hutchinson.

Chodorow, N. (1978) *The Reproduction of Mothering.* Berkeley: University of California Press.

—— (1989) *Feminism and Psychoanalytical Theory.* Polity.

Clarke, J. (1979) 'Social Democratic Delinquents and Fabian Families', in Fitzgerald, M. et al., eds, *Permissiveness and Control.* Macmillan.

Cohen, G.A. (1980) *Karl Marx's Theory of History.* Oxford University Press.

Cohen, P. (1987) *Racism and Popular Culture: a Cultural Studies Approach.* London University Institute of Education.

—— *The Perversions of Inheritance: Studies in the Making of Multi-Racial Britain* (forthcoming).

Craib, I. (1989) *Psychoanalysis and Social Theory.* Brighton: Harvester Wheatsheaf.

Davidson, D. (1982) 'Paradoxes of Irrationality', in Wollheim, R. and Hopkins, J. eds, *Philosophical Essays on Freud.* Cambridge University Press.

Deleuze, G. and Guattari, F. (1983) *Anti-Oedipus* (translated by R. Hurley, M. Seem and H.R. Lane). New York: Viking.

Denzin, N. (1970) *The Research Act in Sociology.* Hawthorne, NY: Aldine.

Dews, P. (1987) *Logics of Disintegration.* Verso.

Dicks, H.V. (1970) *Fifty Years of the Tavistock Clinic.* Routledge & Kegan Paul.

Dinnerstein, D. (1976) *The Mermaid and the Minotaur: The Rocking of the Cradle and the Ruling of the World.* New York: Souvenir Press.

Douglas, M. (1978) *Implicit Meanings: Essays in Anthropology.* Routledge & Kegan Paul.

Durkheim, E. (1976) *The Elementary Forms of the Religious Life.* Allen & Unwin.

Dyne, D. (1985) 'Questions of "training" — a Contribution from a Peripatetic Cousin'. *Free Associations* 3: 92–147.

Eagleton, T. (1990) *The Ideology of the Aesthetic.* Oxford: Basil Blackwell.

Etzioni, A. (1961) *A Comparative Analysis of Complex Organizations.* New York: Free Press.

Evans-Pritchard, E.E. (1976) *Witchcraft, Oracles and Magic among the Azande* (abridged edn). Oxford University Press.

Fanon, F. (1963) *The Wretched of the Earth.* New York: Grove Press.

Forrester, J. (1990) *The Seductions of Psychoanalysis: Freud, Lacan and Derrida.* Cambridge University Press.

Foster, H., ed. (1985) *Postmodern Culture.* Pluto.

Freud, S. (1900) *The Interpretation of Dreams. Standard Edition* vol. 5. Hogarth (1953).

—— (1905a) *Three Essays on Sexuality. Standard Edition* vol. 7. Hogarth (1953).

—— (1905b) *Jokes and their Relation to the Unconscious. Standard Edition* vol. 8. Hogarth (1960).

Frosh, S. (1987) *The Politics of Psychoanalysis.* Macmillan.

—— (1989) *Psychoanalysis and Psychology.* Macmillan.

Fuller, P. (1980) *Art and Psychoanalysis.* Writers & Readers.

Gay, P. (1988) *Freud: A Life for Our Time.* Macmillan.

Geertz, C. (1983a) 'Blurred Genres: the Refiguration of Social Thought', in *Local Knowledge: Further Essays in Interpretive Anthropology.* New York: Basic Books.

—— (1983b) 'From the Native's Point of View: on the Nature of Anthropological Understanding', in *Local Knowledge: Further Essays in Interpretive Anthropology.* New York: Basic Books.

Gellner, E. (1964) *Thought and Change.* Weidenfeld & Nicolson.

—— (1973) *Cause and Meaning in the Social Sciences.* Routledge.

—— (1985) *The Psychoanalytic Movement.* Paladin.

—— (1988) *Plough, Sword and Book: The Structure of Human History.* Collins Harvill.

Gilligan, C. (1982) *In a Different Voice.* Cambridge, MA: Harvard University Press.

Gilroy, P. (1987) *There Ain't No Black in the Union Jack.* Hutchinson.

Gough, I. (1979) *The Political Economy of the Welfare State.* Macmillan.

Greenberg, J. and Mitchell, J.A. (1983) *Object Relations in Psychoanalytic Theory.* Cambridge, MA: Harvard University Press.

Greene, G. (1980) 'Beatrix Potter', in Egoff, S. *et al.,* eds, *Only Connect: Readings on Children's Literature.* Oxford University Press.

Grosskurth, P. (1985) *Melanie Klein.* Hodder & Stoughton.

Grunbaum, A. (1984) *The Foundations of Psychoanalysis.* Berkeley, CA: University of California Press.

Guntrip, H. (1961) *Personality Structure and Human Interaction.* Hogarth.

Habermas, J. (1972) *Knowledge and Human Interests.* Heinemann.

—— (1976) *Legitimation Crisis.* Heinemann.

—— (1985) 'Questions and Counterquestions', in Bernstein, Richard J., ed., *Habermas and Modernity.* Polity.

Hacker, A. (1987) 'American Apartheid', in *New York Review of Books,* vol. 34, no. 19, December.

Hall, S. and Jefferson, T., eds (1976) *Resistance through Rituals.* Hutchinson.

—— *et al.* (1978) *Policing the Crisis.* Macmillan.

Hampshire, S. (1959) *Thought and Action.* Chatto & Windus.

Harré, R. (1972) *Philosophies of Science: An Introductory Survey.* Oxford University Press.

—— (1983) *Introduction to the Logic of the Sciences.* Macmillan.

Harvey, D. (1987) 'Flexible Accumulation through Urbanization: Reflections on Post-Modernism in the American City'. *Antipode,* vol. 19, no. 3.

—— (1989) *The Condition of Postmodernity.* Blackwell.

Heimann, P. (1950) 'On Counter-Transference', *Int. J. Psycho-Anal.* 31: 81–4.

Henry, G. (1974) 'Doubly Deprived'. *J. Child Psychother.,* vol. 3, no. 4: 15–28.

Hinshelwood, R.D. (1987) *What Happens in Groups.* Free Association Books.

—— (1986) 'Eclecticism: the Impossible Project – a Response to Deryck Dyne'. *Free Associations* 5: 23–7.

—— (1989) *A Dictionary of Kleinian Thought.* Free Association Books.

Hoban, R. (1976) *The Mouse and his Child.* Harmondsworth: Penguin.

Holbrook, D. (1961) *English for Maturity.* Cambridge University Press.

—— (1964) *English for the Rejected.* Cambridge University Press.

—— (1972) *The Masks of Hate.* Pergamon.

Hollis, M. and Lukes, S., eds (1982) *Rationality and Relativism.* Oxford University Press.

Huyssen, A. (1984) 'Mapping the Postmodern'. *New German Critique* 33, Fall.

Jameson, F. (1984) 'Postmodernism, or the Cultural Logic of Late Capitalism'. *New Left Review* 146, July–August.

Jaques, E. (1977) 'Social Systems as a Defence against Persecutory and Depressive Anxieties' in Klein, M. *et al.,* eds (1977) *New Directions in Psychoanalysis.* Maresfield Reprints.

Jay, M. (1972) *The Dialectical Imagination.* Sphere.

Johnson, T.J. (1972) *Professions and Power.* Macmillan.

Jones, E. (1949) *Hamlet and Oedipus.* Gollancz.

Joseph, B. (1990) *Psychic Equilibrium and Psychic Change.* Institute of Psycho-Analysis/Tavistock.

Kant, I. (1952) *The Critique of Judgement* (trans. J.C. Meredity). Oxford University Press.

Klein, M. (1923) 'The Role of the School in the Libidinal Development of the Child', in Klein, M. (1975a).

—— (1930) 'The Importance of Symbol Formation in the Development of the Ego', in Klein, M. (1975a).

—— (1931) 'A Contribution to the Theory of Intellectual Development', in Klein, M. (1975a).

—— (1946) 'Notes on Some Schizoid Mechanisms', in Klein, M. (1986).

—— (1961) *Narrative of a Child Analysis.* Hogarth.

—— (1963) *Our Adult World and its Roots in Infancy.* Hogarth.

—— (1975a) *Love, Guilt and Reparation and Other Works, 1921–1945.* Hogarth.

—— (1975b) *Envy and Gratitude and Other Works, 1946–1963.* Hogarth.

—— (1975c) *The Psycho-Analysis of Children.* Hogarth.

—— Heimann, P. and Money-Kyrle, R., eds (1977) *New Directions in Psychoanalysis.* (new edn) Karnac.

—— (1986) *The Selected Melanie Klein* (ed. Juliet Mitchell). Harmondsworth: Penguin.

Kohon, G., ed. (1987) *The British School of Psychoanalysis: The Independent Tradition.* Free Association Books.

Kohut, H. (1971) *The Analysis of the Self: A Systematic Approach to the Treatment of Narcissistic Personality Disorder.* New York: International Universities Press.

—— (1977) *The Restoration of the Self.* New York: International Universities Press.

Kuhn, T.S. (1970) *The Structure of Scientific Revolutions.* Chicago: University of Chicago Press.

Kuper, L. (1974) *Race, Class and Power.* Duckworth.

Lacan, J. (1968a) 'The Mirror-Stage as Formative of the Function of the I'. *New Left Review* 51, September–October.

—— (1968b) *The Language of the Self* (trans. and with commentary by Anthony Wilden). New York: Delta.

—— (1977) *Ecrits – a Selection*, trans. A. Sheridan. Tavistock.

Lakatos, I. (1970) 'Falsification and the Methodology of Scientific Research Programmes', in Lakatos and Musgrave, A., eds, *Criticism and the Growth of Knowledge.* Cambridge University Press.

Laplanche, J. and Pontalis, J.B. (1973) *The Language of Psychoanalysis.* Institute of Psycho-Analysis/Karnac.

Lasch, C. (1977) *Haven in a Heartless World.* Basic Books.

—— (1979) *The Culture of Narcissism.* New York: Norton.

—— (1981) 'The Freudian Left and Cultural Revolution'. *New Left Review* 129, September–October.

—— (1985) *The Minimal Self: Psychic Survival in Troubled Times.* New York: Norton.

Lash, S. and Urry, J. (1987) *The End of Organized Capitalism.* Polity.

Leavis, F.R. (1973) *D.H. Lawrence: Novelist.* Harmondsworth: Penguin.

Lemaire, A. (1970) *Jacques Lacan.* Routledge & Kegan Paul.

Likierman, M. (1989) 'The Clinical Significance of Aesthetic Experience'. *International Review of Psycho-Analysis*, vol. 16, part 2.

Lodge, D. (1977) *The Modes of Modern Writing: Metaphor, Metonymy, and the Typology of Modern Literature.* Edward Arnold.

Lukes, S. (1985) *Marxism and Morality.* Oxford University Press.

Lyotard, J.-F. (1968) *The Postmodern Condition: A Report on Knowledge.* Manchester University Press.

McDougall, J. (1986) *Theatres of the Mind: Illusion and Truth on the Psychoanalytic Stage.* Free Association Books.

—— (1989) *Theatres of the Body.* Free Association Books.

Malcolm, J. (1981) *Psychoanalysis: The Impossible Profession.* New York: Alfred Knopf.

Mannoni, O. (1956) *Prospero and Caliban*. Methuen.

Marcuse, H. (1956) *Eros and Civilization*. Routledge & Kegan Paul.

Marshall, T.H. (1963) *Sociology at the Crossroads and Other Essays*. Heinemann.

Mayer, A.J. (1990) *Why Did the Heavens Not Darken? The 'Final Solution' in History*. Verso.

Meltzer, D. (1968) 'Terror, Persecution and Dread'. *Int. J. Psycho-Anal.* 49: 396–400, republished in Meltzer, D. (1973).

—— (1973) *Sexual States of Mind*. Perthshire: Clunie.

—— (1978) *The Kleinian Development*. Perthshire: Clunie.

—— (1984) *Dream Life*. Perthshire: Clunie.

—— (1986) *Studies in Extended Metapsychology: Clinical Applications of Bion's Ideas*. Perthshire: Clunie.

—— and Williams, M.H. (1988) *The Apprehension of Beauty*. Perthshire: Clunie.

—— Hoxter, S., Weddell, D. and Salzberger-Wittenberg, I. (1975) *Explorations in Autism*. Perthshire: Clunie.

Menzies Lyth, I. (1960) 'A Case-Study in the Functioning of Social Systems as a Defence Against Anxiety: a Report on a Study of the Nursing Service of a General Hospital', *Human Relations* 13 (1960): 95–121.

—— (1983) *The Psychological Welfare of Children Making Long Stays in Hospital*. Tavistock Institute of Human Relations Occasional Papers No. 3.

—— (1988) *Containing Anxieties in Institutions: Selected Essays, Vol. 1*. Free Association Books.

—— (1989) *The Dynamics of the Social: Selected Essays, Vol. 2*. Free Association Books.

Merleau-Ponty, M. (1962) *The Phenomenology of Perception*. Routledge & Kegan Paul.

Miliband, R. (1978) 'A State of De-subordination'. *British Journal of Sociology*, vol. 29, no. 4.

Mill, J.S. (1975) *The Subjection of Women*. Oxford University Press.

Miller, L., Rustin, M.E., Rustin, M.J. and Shuttleworth, J., eds (1989) *Closely Observed Infants*. Duckworth.

Milner, M. (1957) *On Not Being Able To Paint* (2nd edn). Heinemann.

Mitchell, J. (1975) *Psychoanalysis and Feminism*. Harmondsworth: Penguin.

—— and Rose, J. (1982) (eds & trans.) *Feminine Sexuality: Jacques Lacan and the Ecole freudienne*. Macmillan.

Morris, W. (1934) *William Morris: Selected Writings*, ed. G.D.H. Cole. Nonesuch Library.

Mulhern, F. (1981) *The Moment of Scrutiny*. Verso.

Mulkay, M. (1972) *The Social Process of Innovation*. Macmillan.

—— (1979) *Science and the Sociology of Knowledge*. Allen & Unwin.

—— and Knorr Cetina, C., eds (1983) *Science Observed: Perspectives on the Social Structure of Science*. Sage.

Murdoch, I. (1953) *Sartre*. Fontana, 1967.

Murray, C. (1989) 'Winnicott and the Development Psychology of Infancy', *British Journal of Psychotherapy*, vol. 5, no. 3.

Murray, L. (1988) 'Effects of Post-natal Depression on Infant Development: Direct Studies of Early Mother–Infant Interactions', in Kumar, L. and Brockington, I.F., eds, *Motherhood and Mental Illness*. Wright.

Nairn, T. (1981) *The Break-up of Britain*. Verso.

Oakley, A. (1970) *Becoming a Mother*. Martin Robertson.

—— (1980) *Women Confined*. Martin Robertson.

Offe, C. (1984) *Contradictions of the Welfare State*. Hutchinson.

Packman, J. (1981) *The Child's Generation: Child Care Policy in Britain*. (2nd edn). Blackwell/Martin Robertson.

Parkes, C. Murray (1975) *Bereavement: Studies of Grief in Adult Life*. Harmondsworth: Penguin.

Parkin, F. (1979) *Marxism and Class Theory: a Bourgeois Critique*. Tavistock.

Parry, N., Rustin, M. and Satyamurti, C., eds (1978) *Social Work, Welfare and the State*. Edward Arnold.

Pincus, L. (1981a) *The Challenge of a Long Life*. Faber.

—— (1981b) *Death in the Family: the Importance of Mourning*. Faber.

Pollock, L. (1983) *Forgotten Children: Parent–Child Relations from 1500 to 1900*. Cambridge University Press.

Pontalis, J.-B. (1981) *Frontiers in Psychoanalysis: From the Dream to Psychic Pain*. Hogarth.

Popper, K.R. (1963) *Conjectures and Refutations*. Routledge & Kegan Paul.

—— (1974) 'Replies to My Critics', in Schilp, P.A., ed., *The Philosophy of Karl Popper, Book 2*. La Salle, IL: Open Court.

Reich, W. (1950) *Character Analysis*. Vision Press.

Rex, J. (1986) *Race and Ethnicity*. Open University Press.

Richards, B., ed. (1985) *Capitalism and Infancy*. Free Association Books.

—— (1989a) *Images of Freud*. Dent.

—— ed. (1989b) *Crises of the Self*. Free Association Books.

Ricoeur, P. (1970) *Freud and Philosophy*. New Haven, CT: Yale University Press.

—— (1974) *The Conflict of Interpretations (Part 2)*. Evanston, IL: Northwestern University Press.

Rieff, P. (1959) *Freud: The Mind of the Moralist*. Gollancz.

Rorty, R. (1980) *Philosophy and the Mirror of Nature*. Oxford: Basil Blackwell.

Rose, J. (1984) *The Case of Peter Pan, or the Impossibility of Children's Fiction*. Macmillan.

—— (1986) *Sexuality in the Field of Vision*. Verso.

Rosenfeld, H. (1964) 'On the Psychopathology of Narcissism'. *Int. J. Psycho-Anal.* 45: 332–7, republished in Rosenfeld, H. (1965).

—— (1965) *Psychotic States*. Hogarth.

—— (1971) 'A Clinical Approach to the Psychoanalytic Theory of the Life and Death Instincts: an Investigation into the Aggressive Aspects of Narcissism'. *Int. J. Psycho-Anal.* 52: 169–78.

—— (1987) *Impasse and Interpretation*. Institute of Psycho-Analysis/Tavistock.

Rustin, M.J. (1979) 'Social Work and the Family', in Parry, N., Rustin, M.J. and Satyamurti, C., eds, *Social Work, Welfare and the State*. Edward Arnold.

—— (1981) 'Integrated Codes and Professional Education'. *SIP Papers*, no. 10.

—— (1984) 'What is Cultural Studies: The Virtues of Educational Pluralism', *Annali Anglicista*, vol. XXVII, no. 3. Istituto Universitario Orientale, Naples.

—— (1985a) *For a Pluralist Socialism*. Verso.

—— (1985b) 'A Defence of Children's Fiction: Another Reading of *Peter Pan*'. *Free Associations* 2.

—— (1987) 'Place and Time in Socialist Theory'. *Radical Philosophy* 47.

—— (1988a) 'Absolute Voluntarism: Critique of a Post-Marxist Concept of Hegemony'. *New Germany Critique* 42.

—— (1988b) 'Shifting Paradigms in Psychoanalytic Thought'. *History Workshop Journal* 26.

—— (1989) 'Postmodernism and Anti-modernism in Contemporary British Architecture'. *Assemblage: a Critical Journal of Architecture and Design Culture*, no. 8, MIT.

—— (1991) 'Different Conceptions of Citizenship', in McLennan, D. and Sayers, S., eds, *Socialism and Democracy*. Macmillan.

Rustin, M.E. and Rustin, M.J. (1987) *Narratives of Love and Loss: Studies in Modern Children's Fiction*. Verso.

—— (1985) 'Relational Preconditions of Socialism', in Richards, B. (1985).

Rutter, M. (1972) *Maternal Deprivation Reassessed*. Harmondsworth: Penguin.

Sacks, O. (1976) *Awakenings*. Penguin.

—— (1986) *The Man Who Mistook His Wife for a Hat*. Picador.

Salzberger-Wittenberg, I. (1977) *Psychoanalytic Insight and Relationships: a Kleinian Approach*. Academic Press.

—— Henry, G. and Osborne, E. (1981) *The Emotional Experience of Learning and Teaching*. Faber.

Sandler, A.M. (1982) 'The Selection and Function of the Training Analyst in Europe'. *Int. Rev. Psycho-Anal.* 9: 386–98.

Sartre, J.-P. (1948) *Anti-Semite and Jew*. New York: Schocken.

Schorske, C. (1980) *Fin-de-Siècle Vienna*. New York: Knopf.

Seabrook, J. (1973) *City Close-up*. Penguin.

Searle, J.R. (1969) *Speech Acts*. Cambridge University Press.

Segal, H. (1975) *Introduction to the Work of Melanie Klein*. Heinemann.

—— (1983) 'Some Clinical Implications of Melanie Klein's Work'. *Int. J. Psycho-Anal.* 64: 269–76.

—— (1986) 'A Psychoanalytical Approach to Aesthetics', in Segal, H. (1986).

—— (1986) *The Work of Hanna Segal: a Kleinian Approach to Clinical Practice*. Free Association Books.

—— (1987) 'Silence is the Real Crime'. *International Review of Psychoanalysis* (Issue on Warfare and Nuclear Arms), vol. 14, part 1.

—— (1991) *Dream, Phantasy and Art.* Tavistock.

Sharpe, Ella Freeman (1950) 'The Impatience of Hamlet', in *Collected Papers in Psychoanalysis.* Hogarth.

Shuttleworth, A. (1966) *Two Working Papers in Cultural Studies.* Birmingham: Centre for Contemporary Cultural Studies.

Shuttleworth, J. (1989) 'Psychoanalytical Theory and Infant Development' (Chapter 2 of Miller, L. *et al., Closely Observed Infants*). Duckworth.

Simmel, G. (1950) *The Sociology of Georg Simmel.* ed. K. Wolff. New York: Free Press.

Spillius, E. Bott, ed. (1988) *Melanie Klein Today, Vols. 1 & 2.* Institute of Psycho-Analysis/ Routledge.

Steiner, J. (1985) 'Turning a Blind Psychotic States Eye: the Cover-Up for Oedipus'. *Int. Rev. Psycho-Anal.,* vol. 12, part 2.

Steiner, R. (1985) 'Some Thoughts about Tradition and Change Arising from an Examination of the British Psycho-Analytical Society's Controversial Discussions (1943—44)'. *Int. Rev. Psycho-Anal.,* vol. 11, part 1.

Stern, D.N. (1985) *The Interpersonal World of the Infant: A View from Psychoanalysis and Developmental Psychology.* New York: Basic Books.

Stokes, A. (1972) *The Image in Form.* (ed. Richard Wollheim). Harmondsworth: Penguin.

—— (1978) *Critical Writings Vols 1–3.* Thames & Hudson.

Stone, L. (1979) *The Family, Sex and Marriage in England 1500–1800.* Harper.

Strachey, J. (1934) 'On the Nature of Therapeutic Action of Psychoanalysis'. *Int. J. Psycho-Anal.* 15: 127–59.

Tawney, R.H. (1965) *Equality.* Allen & Unwin.

—— (1982) *The Acquisitive Society.* Brighton: Harvester.

Taylor, C. (1979) *Hegel.* Cambridge University Press.

—— (1985) *Philosophy and the Human Sciences, Vols. 1 & 2.* Cambridge University Press.

Timpanaro, S. (1975) *On Materialism.* Verso.

—— (1976) *The Freudian Slip.* Verso.

Titmuss, R. (1970) *The Gift Relationship.* Allen & Unwin.

Tizard, B. and Phoenix, A. (1989) 'Black Identity and Trans-Racial Adoption'. *New Community,* vol. 15, April.

Trilling, L. (1951) 'Freud and Literature', in Trilling, L., *The Critical Imagination.*

Turkle, S. (1978) *Psychoanalytic Politics: Freud's French Revolution.* New York: Basic Books.

Turner, R.H. (1969) 'The Theme of Contemporary Social Movements'. *British Journal of Sociology* XX: 390–405.

Tustin, F. (1972) *Autism and Childhood Psychosis.* Hogarth.

—— (1981) *Autistic States in Children.* Routledge & Kegan Paul.

—— (1986) *Autistic Barriers in Neurotic Patients.* Karnac.

Urwin, C. (1986) 'Development Psychology and Psychoanalysis: Splitting the Difference', in Richards, M. and Light, P., eds, *Children of Social Worlds.* Polity.

Van den Berghe, P.L. (1978) *Race and Racism: a Comparative Perspective.* (2nd edn) John Wiley.

Vattimo, G. (1988) *The End of Modernity.* Polity.

Walzer, M. (1983) *Spheres of Justice: A Defence of Pluralism and Equality.* Martin Robertson.

Will, D. (1980) 'Psychoanalysis as a Human Science'. *British Journal of Medical Psychology* 53: 201–11.

—— (1984) 'The Progeny of Positivism: the Maudsley School and Anti-Psychiatry'. *British Journal of Psychotherapy* 1: 50–67.

—— (1986) 'Psychoanalysis and the New Philosophy of Science'. *Int. Rev. Psycho-Anal.* 13: 163–73.

Williams, B. (1962) 'The Idea of Equality', in Laslett, P. and Runciman, W.G., eds, *Philosophy, Politics, and Society, Second Series.* Oxford: Basil Blackwell.

Williams, M.H. (1982) *Inspiration in Milton and Keats.* Macmillan.

—— (1987) *A Strange Way of Killing: the Poetic Structure of Wuthering Heights.* Perthshire: Clunie.

—— (1988) (See Meltzer, D. and Williams, M.H.)

Williams, R. (1958) *Culture and Society.* Harmondsworth: Penguin.

—— (1980) *Problems in Materialism and Culture.* Verso.

Wilson, E. (1977) *Women and the Welfare State.* Tavistock.

Wilson, W.J. (1975) *The Declining Significance of Race.* Chicago University Press.

—— (1987) *The Truly Disadvantaged.* Chicago University Press.

Winnicott, D.W. (1958) 'Transitional Objects and Transitional Phenomena', in *Through Paediatrics to Psychoanalysis.*

—— (1967) 'The Mirror-role of Mother and Family in Child Development', in Lomas, P., ed., *The Predicament of the Family: a Psychoanalytical Symposium.* Hogarth. Republished in Winnicott (1971).

—— (1971) *Playing and Reality.* Tavistock.

—— (1975) *Through Paediatrics to Psychoanalysis.* Hogarth.

Wollheim, R. (1971) *Freud.* Fontana.

—— (1984) *The Thread of Life.* Cambridge University Press.

—— (1987) *Painting as an Art.* Thames & Hudson.

Zorza, R. and V. (1981) *The Way to Die: Living to the End.* Sphere.

Index

Abercrombie, N. 167–8
   Sovereign Individuals of Capitalism 168
Abraham, Karl 214, 216
'absent object' 189
Adorno, Theodor 169
aesthetic judgements, universality of 221
aesthetic sense 169
   autonomy of 226
   in children 211–12
   containment and 207
   psychoanalysis and 199–228
   specificity of 222–3
aestheticism, perils of 227
aesthetics
   psychoanalytic approaches to 202–6, 224–8
   see also art
Alford, C.F. 5 n1
alpha function (Bion) 124, 206, 208
Althusser, Louis 15, 16, 180
analytic descent 105
Anderson, Benedict 83 n2
anti-racist strategies 71–9
   see also racism
Aristotle 218
art
   active response to 213
   Freud on 202–6, 212
   'late Kleinian' psychoanalysis and 156–7, 206–13
   and separation and loss 212
   see also aesthetics
attachment theory 147
autism 154

Banks, Olive 112
Barnes, Barry 119, 131, 142
'basic assumption group' 91–2

Bateson, Gregory 40 n17
beauty, sense of 201–2, 208
Becker, H. 143 n4
Bell, Daniel 146
Benvenuto, Bice 141, 197 n2
Berlin, Isaiah 44
Bernstein, Basil 94
Bernstein, Richard 229 n2
beta function (Bion) 124, 206
Bettelheim, Bruno 84 n23
Bhaskar, Roy 2, 126, 127, 136, 140
Bick, Esther 125, 130, 191
biological basis of human experience 34
Bion, Wilfred 2, 3, 5 n1, 39 nn, 48, 63–77 *passim*, 83
   nn, 84 nn, 91–2, 111, 121, 124–5, 128, 132, 141,
   152–70 *passim*, 173 n6, 188, 195, 200–33 *passim*
   Learning From Experience 124
   Second Thoughts 152, 190
borderline states 160
Boston, Mary 111, 135
   Psychotherapy with Severely Deprived Children 46,
   64
Bowlby, John 21, 24, 44, 55, 135, 147
Bradbury, Malcolm 89
British Institute of Psycho-Analysis 157, 162
British Psycho-Analytical Society 99–100, 151, 167
   Middle Group 149
   publication programme 106
   Scientific Bulletin 106
British School 27–30, 134

cannibalism 67
'catastrophic change' 155
causes, meanings functioning as 127
Centre for Contemporary Cultural Studies 72, 84
   n28

Printed in the United States
by Baker & Taylor Publisher Services